Praise for *Addicted in Film*

"This book is a must-have if you or anyone you know has been touched by addictive problems. It's filled with enlightening stories about powerful films that could become a turning point for people."

—**DR. TOM HORVATH,**
CO-FOUNDER, SMART RECOVERY,
AUTHOR OF *SEX, DRUGS, GAMBLING & CHOCOLATE*

Here is an excellent, moving book on addiction recovery to read and share. Ted Perkins uses stories in movies about addictions as a vehicle to understand the complexities, heartbreak, and horror of addictions while leading us to real hope of radical transformation. His own life story is a dramatic example of recovery and its redemptive power.

—**MICHAEL WERNER,**
PRESIDENT OF THE AMERICAN HUMANIST
ASSOCIATION (RETIRED)

Perkins has produced a literary work that is a wonderful mélange of intriguing movie plots, personal vignettes, and a fun collection of Inside Hollywood revelations. It is an engrossing read and an encyclopedic review of alcohol and substance abuse issues that are important to discuss. I will be binge-watching most of these films!

—**JOE GERSTEIN, MD, FACP,**
HARVARD MEDICAL SCHOOL FACULTY (RETIRED),
CO-FOUNDER OF SMART RECOVERY

Ted Perkins is a person for whom films have deep personal meanings. Ted also (obviously) has deep feelings about addiction. In his marvelous book, he combines these meaningful parts of *his* life for the benefit of those who seek meaning in their *own* lives, whether addicted themselves or not.

—**STANTON PEELE, PH.D**
BESTSELLING AUTHOR OF
A SCIENTIFIC LIFE ON THE EDGE
AND *LOVE & ADDICTION*

Perkins has pulled off a feat that many thousands of us in the addiction treatment industry believe was a long time coming. He has very skillfully discerned which films about addiction and recovery have important things to say, and what valuable lessons can be learned. I have wished for this kind of analysis of addiction oriented films for years. Clever, insightful, and accessible to anyone in or out of recovery. No exaggeration; a book like this will inevitably end up saving lives!

—**DAN HOSTETLER,**
EXECUTIVE DIRECTOR,
ABOVE & BEYOND RECOVERY CENTER

Addicted in Film

Movies We Love About the Habits We Hate

Ted Perkins

Addicted in Film
Copyright © 2022 Ted Perkins

All rights reserved. No part of this book may be reproduced by any means without the written permission of the author, except for short passages used in critical reviews.

ISBN: 979-8-9871036-0-9

221015 Trade

To Brian, Nacho and Paula

ACKNOWLEDGMENTS

As Goethe said, "The moment one definitely commits oneself, then providence moves too. All sorts of things occur to help one that would never otherwise have occurred.... Unforeseen incidents, meetings, and material assistance, which no man could have dreamed would have come his way."

In the spirit of this, I'd like to thank some wonderful people: Ron Lott who encouraged me to take the first step; Charles True for providing me with the background of where other thinkers on the matter had gone before; Mark Ruth for supporting my work at SMART Recovery; Leya Booth who is an amazing editor; Steven Booth who is an amazing book designer; Jessica Keet a very methodical proofreader; Erin Vokes who designed our cover; Stacey McKeever for reading everything I send her; Dr. Tom Horvath for recognizing the book's potential to help people in their recovery; Michael Werner for much-needed advice and inspiration; Jeffry Muhleman for being a great BS detector; and lastly to my daughter Quinn who—by joking with me that nobody would ever buy my silly book—lit a fire under my ass to show her that anything is possible.

TABLE OF CONTENTS

ACKNOWLEDGMENTS　　vi

INTRODUCTION　　1

PART I: MACRO-ADDICTIONS
Trainwrecks: Drug & Alcohol Abuse
On the Big (and Small) Screen
9

| CHAPTER 1 | Alcohol Abuse's Cinematic Universe Origin Story | 11 |
| | *The Lost Weekend* | *11* |

| CHAPTER 2 | Death as a Life Choice | 21 |
| | *Leaving Las Vegas* | *21* |

| CHAPTER 3 | The Great Danish Alcohol Experiment | 31 |
| | *Another Round* | *31* |

CHAPTER 4	Be Very Cautious With Cautionary Tales	39
	Reefer Madness	*39*
	Trainspotting	*50*
	Requiem for a Dream	*57*

CHAPTER 5	God It's Tough Being a Supermodel	67
	Gia	*67*

CHAPTER 6	Mammas Don't Let Your Babies Grow Up to be Country Music Stars	77
	Crazy Heart	*77*
	A Star is Born	*87*

CHAPTER 7	Evil Incarnate: Purdue Pharma & OxyContin®	97
	Dopesick	*97*

CHAPTER 8	Parenthood is the Scariest 'Hood of All	107
	Four Good Days	*107*
	Beautiful Boy	*122*

CHAPTER 9	Addiction as a Ménage à Trois	133
	Days of Wine and Roses	*133*
	When a Man Loves a Woman	*149*

PART II: MICRO-ADDICTIONS
Hopefully Not Deadly; Frequently Problematic: Other Addictions That Cause Chaos
159

CHAPTER 10	The Good, The Bad, & The Downright Yucky of Sex Addiction	160
	A Dirty Shame	*171*
	Boy Erased	*177*
	Shame	*184*

CHAPTER 11	Gambling Addiction & Luck Cosmologies	190
	The Gambler	*199*
	Uncut Gems	*206*
CHAPTER 12	Do I Look Too Fat in This Eating Disorder?	213
	Fatso	*213*
CHAPTER 13	Almost Nailed It! Addiction to Perfection	233
	Black Swan	*233*
	Whiplash	*249*
CHAPTER 14	Cigarettes are Funny & Chocolate is Satanic	257
	Cold Turkey	*257*
	Chocolat	*265*

PART III: RECOVERY
They Tried To Make Me Go To Rehab: Fantasy vs. Reality In and Out of Treatment
269

CHAPTER 15	Seriously, I Can Stop Any Time I Want	271
	Clean and Sober	*271*
CHAPTER 16	Nailed Rehab; Now What?	283
	Recovery Boys	*283*
CHAPTER 17	Rehab as a Luxury Staycation	295
	28 Days	*295*

CHAPTER 18   Star-Studded Sexual Sobriety   305
             Thanks for Sharing   *305*

PART IV
Final Thoughts
323

INDEX   327

Addicted in Film

INTRODUCTION

When I was in high school I saw a segment on the evening news about some man with a terminal disease; and instead of just laying around waiting to die, he brought an old movie projector into his hospital room and watched Marx Brothers comedies and cartoons all day long. And it worked. He experienced a miraculous recovery, seeming to confirm the old aphorism that "Laughter is the best medicine."

Cut to 30 years later and I was locked in some psych ward on a 5150 hold after a week-long bender. I harbored no illusions about laughing myself to successful recovery. I knew there was quite a bit of work to do, including therapists, mutual support meetings and self-study. But I wondered if watching movies about addiction and recovery might also help.

After all, I had been involved with movies most of my professional life—first as a film studio executive at Warner Bros and Universal, then later as an independent film distributor, working screenwriter, film producer, and TV writer. Massive amounts of social drinking was a big part of the job. Booze was my erstwhile aide-de-camp for decades of First-Class travel to over 50 countries; lavish parties on $100 million yachts; partying with Bruce Willis, Charlize Theron, Mick Jagger, Bono; red-carpet premieres at the Cannes Film Festival and dates with movie stars. I figured if films had helped get me into my current predicament, maybe they could also help get me out.

Now, I know what some of you may be thinking. Addiction is a very serious problem that demands very serious solutions. I couldn't agree more. This book isn't an attempt to say that watching films is any substitute for professional intervention. But professionals will also tell you that the more you can learn about the actual topic of addiction, the better your chances of successfully recovering from it. To learn about addiction is really to learn about yourself, what drives you, what triggers you, and why you choose to act in certain ways and not others.

Addiction is also part of a vast intellectual landscape that includes everything from neuroscience, psychology, and philosophy to ethics, morality, and spiritualism. All of these disciplines have different ways of understanding and explaining addiction. In other words, they're telling us different *stories* about it. And because of their scope and popular appeal, movies are one of the best ways to tell these stories.

Recovery from addiction is another powerful part of the story, told from countless viewpoints, and approached from different recovery pathways. In many ways beating addiction is like an epic adventure or tear-jerking drama, a heroic quest for greatness and redemption. For some people recovery is the single most important achievement of their lives. For others it's a struggle that ends tragically, and in vain. But that's okay, because we can all learn from these setbacks and move forward.

Movies about addiction and recovery can educate us, inspire us, entertain us, and console us. We could read a hundred well-researched books on the topic and never have the kind of "aha moment" we might experience watching a great film. Movies touch us emotionally in ways books and research papers on addiction simply can't. How we *feel* about recovery is often a better predictor of success than what we actually do about it.

Unfortunately, Hollywood doesn't produce a lot of movies about this topic. They're considered "hard sells" to a public more interested in escapist comedies, scary horror movies, and CGI action extravaganzas. Executives literally roll their eyes every time a drug or alcohol abuse project comes across their desks. Except in rare circumstances, they're always non-starters. I should know; I was one of the executives who passed on **Trainspotting**. *Doh!*

But you can't really blame the studio brass for trying to save their necks. Movies are very risky consumer products that cost hundreds of millions of dollars to develop, produce, and market. These costs must be recouped across large multinational distribution channels. And these channels place a premium on uniformity, mass customer satisfaction, and repeat business in the form of endless sequels. It's the reason why in movies today everybody seems to be wearing a cape.

The first barrier to making films about addiction and recovery is casting. Studios usually only greenlight a movie if there is A-List talent attached. But few stars are willing to take a risk playing someone with an addiction. It tarnishes their brand—especially if they hope to work for Disney or present at the Nickelodeon Awards ever again. In music and television there seems to be more acceptance of celebrities with addiction issues, but movie stars are held to a much higher standard because they're Hollywood royalty, role models with aspirational standards to uphold.

There are brave outliers of course, like when Bradley Cooper drank his way to country music oblivion in **A Star is Born**, or when

Sandra Bullock fell out of a tree to score some Vicodin in **28 Days**. Some actors and actresses took huge gambles with their careers and it paid off handsomely, like when Nicolas Cage won the 1995 Academy Award for Best Actor in **Leaving Las Vegas**, or when Angelina Jolie went supernova after her (mostly naked) performance in **Gia**. We'll be going behind the scenes of these and many more movies shortly to see what they can teach us about successful—and not-so-successful recovery.

Another challenge is the marketing of a film, which is usually more important than the film itself. One of my greatest mentors once told me, "There is no such thing as a crappy movie, just crappy marketing." Any deep-pocketed studio can spend its way out of a bomb because everybody watches TV spots and sees movie posters, while relatively few people actually read film reviews. At Universal we spent $150 million on an international marketing campaign to convince everyone to see **Waterworld**. All of us got nice Christmas bonuses that year.

But that was a "tent-pole" movie. When it comes to marketing films about addiction and recovery, no amount of clever advertising can overcome the fact that these movies are about…well…addiction and recovery. The word itself—addiction—comes with a ton of baggage, most of it bad. People have divergent views about whether alcoholism is a disease, or whether telling someone they're an "addict" might actually make things worse. I'm not sure the term "in recovery" is helpful either. At least if you have a disease you get cured. But "in recovery" smacks of perpetuity. Some scientists argue addiction is a treatable brain disorder; others say it boils down to personal choice and the only way to change people is to punish them. Even the insistence on "abstinence-only" is being called into question in some treatment programs. It doesn't surprise me that Hollywood would prefer not to dip its toe into these muddy waters.

But luckily there are exceptions to every Hollywood rule. As screenwriting legend William Goldman famously said, "Nobody knows anything." On occasion some brave Hollywood producers and directors have taken a huge risk and made an honest film about a difficult subject. Some of these movies became instant classics, several won Academy Awards, and many just went straight-to-video. Regardless, all of them were important and thought-provoking in their own ways, and welcome additions to our ongoing conversations about a problem we'd all really like to solve.

The idea for this book came to me a few years ago after I had achieved long-term sobriety with the help of therapists, family, mutual support meetings and my Apple TV. Armed with an iTunes account, I used it to watch 100 movies about addiction and recovery over the course of 100 days. I found big and little nuggets of inspiration in all of them, but chose to write about 27 of them. I intentionally left out films that romanticize or glorify alcohol or substance abuse. I chose films that not only helped me in my own recovery, but ones I also felt had important things to say about other types of addictions and recovery in general. Each reader will likely have different take-aways from each chapter, and those who have gone down the addiction rabbit hole may see their own recovery experiences reflected to some degree in some or all of these films.

In PART I we look at films about drug and alcohol abuse, or what I call "macro-addictions." The really serious stuff. People with macro-addictions will go through terrible withdrawal symptoms or may even die if they suddenly quit. Prolonged use leads to some of the results we're all familiar with: careers destroyed, families torn apart, financial losses, jail time, and sometimes even death. The films we'll discuss include abuse of alcohol, cocaine, heroin, meth, and OxyContin®. Some of the films have wonderfully uplifting happy endings; others end in total trainwrecks.

In PART II we'll explore films about what I call "micro-addictions," which are maladaptive behaviors that are generally non-lethal, not illegal, don't lead to terrible physical withdrawal symptoms, but have the potential to wreak substantial havoc. These include gambling addiction, sex addiction, eating disorders, problematic amounts of exercise, and addiction to perfection. We'll also discuss social addictions to coffee, cigarettes, and chocolate. The severities and adverse consequences of these addictions vary quite a bit, but the underlying physiological and psychological issues are the same as those in macro-addictions, and the desire to return to healthy indulgence levels or quit outright is the same.

Lastly, in PART III we'll look at the best films about the brave struggles to conquer these addictive behaviors in treatment and mutual support settings. Rehab's not for everyone; I never went and I've been sober for years. But there's no doubt it's a crucial starting point in many people's overall recovery journey. As we'll see, rehab is a frustrating, often painful, but sometimes hilarious experience. The countless meetings can make even the most unflappable among us suddenly go postal. And the hardest part isn't just the weeks of inpatient care—it's the struggle to stay sober and build a new life afterwards.

I did my best to choose films whose themes run parallel to issues I think are worth discussing in the addiction and recovery universe, and consistent with what I've experienced in real life. But I'm not a medical professional or clinician; my thoughts are those of a guy who loves movies, writes and produces movies, and used them as part of his successful overall recovery plan. And that plan included therapists and mutual support meetings. If you feel backed into a corner and really need help, don't just watch a movie. Go get help first, then figure out the movie part.

There are several important films I couldn't fit into this volume, including **Flight**, **Less Than Zero**, **Permanent Midnight**, and **Cherry**, to name just a few among many others. And there are also several fine Made-for-TV movies I unfortunately also had to leave out. But I will add chapters about some of these films in subsequent editions of the book and in my monthly blog.

Also, I'm not big on labels, so I've tried to avoid stigmatizing terms like "alcoholic" and "addict" as much as possible. But often it's a hell of a lot easier writing sentences using general terms like these than it is writing the more PC terms like *"person with alcohol use disorder"* or *"individual with maladaptive behavior"* every other sentence.

Lastly, I know addiction and recovery is no laughing matter. People really need help. It's one of the reasons I became a SMART Recovery Facilitator, host weekly mutual support meetings, volunteer as a sobriety mentor, and produce YouTube videos about recovery. Along the way I've learned that rampant positivity and a good sense of humor can go a really long way in successful recovery. They certainly did in mine. We may not always be able to change our circumstances, but we can completely remake our attitudes and beliefs about them. That may include laughing at them too.

Who knows. Maybe this is what cured the guy who watched all those Marx Brothers films. Or maybe not. Doesn't matter. As my hero Mark Twain once said: Comedy = Tragedy + Time. If you're one of these people like me who has some time to fill, sit back, make some popcorn, crack open a tasty non-alcoholic beverage of your choice, and keep kicking ass in your recovery as we talk about some great movies.

PART I: MACRO-ADDICTIONS
Trainwrecks:
Drug & Alcohol Abuse
On the Big (and Small) Screen

CHAPTER 1
Alcohol Abuse's Cinematic Universe Origin Story
The Lost Weekend

No discussion of drug/alcohol addiction and recovery-related films would be complete unless we start with the film that opened the whole national conversation about alcohol use disorder to begin with: The 1945 classic *The Lost Weekend*, directed by Hollywood legend Billy Wilder. It was the first Hollywood studio film to dramatize the issue of alcohol use disorder, or "alcoholism" as they called it back in the day (the term itself was coined 100 years before that by a Swedish physician).

When I first got sober, I must have rented and watched this film at least six times before I bit the bullet and actually bought a copy of it. It now sits at the top of my AppleTV Purchased Movies queue—a constant reminder of a life I never plan to return to. I even insisted that some of my family members watch the film with me, so they could better understand the bizarre mindset I was operating under while I was drinking heavily.

A little bit of movie trivia: Preview audiences thought the film was such a downer that Paramount Pictures wondered whether or not to even release it. They also received mountains of mail from alcohol companies claiming it would destroy their liquor sales. Billy Wilder even claimed that one company offered Paramount a $5 million bribe to shelve the film forever. Lucky for us they didn't acquiesce, because **The Lost Weekend** is a really powerful and important film (about addiction or otherwise) that ended up winning four Academy Awards, including Best Picture. It's the only Best Picture Oscar winner to also win the Cannes Film Festival Grand Prix du Festival International Film prize.

When it comes to stories about alcohol abuse, this film has it all: self-loathing, anxiety, depression, regrets, triggers, bargaining, enabling, codependency, rock-bottoms, 5150 psychiatric holds, suicidal ideation, and the brave—albeit often misguided—efforts of family and friends to try to help as best they can. Very few subsequent films have ever come close to fitting so many important key aspects of alcoholism into 100 minutes of screen time.

But most of all, the film features the amazing actor Ray Milland as Don Birnam. Milland is one of those brave actors I alluded to in the Introduction who had the courage to risk their Hollywood careers for parts they cared about. Everybody—including his agent, manager, and even the studio bosses, warned him this movie would kill his career. Every other A-List actor had passed on the project. But Milland took a flier and was rewarded with an Academy Award for Best Actor.

In the film, Milland plays a struggling writer dealing with regrets, low self-esteem, and writer's block who medicates himself with alcohol. The film never establishes whether Don drinks because his writing career has failed, or his writing career has failed because he drinks. It's the kind of chicken-and-egg conundrum we'll encounter several times in many other addiction and recovery-related films. In the original book upon which the film is based, written by trailblazing author Charles Jackson, Don wasn't fighting writer's block; he was guilt-tripping over a homosexual affair. No surprise Paramount Studios shut that whole part down. Imagine how much further along the fight for LGBTQ civil rights could have been if only Paramount had not lost its nerve. Jackson would go on to develop a longer exploration of the emotional stresses caused by closeted homosexuality in his subsequent novel ***The Fall of Valor***. Similarly, his publishers lost their nerve and didn't promote this novel strongly enough, and Jackson's career began to trend downward thereafter.

In the movie, Don has a girlfriend named Helen, played by the amazing actress and Ronald Reagan's future first wife Jane Wyman. Even though the focus of the story is on Don, Helen is actually a very important character with a lot to tell us about the influence friends and family can have on a person struggling with addiction. She falls in love with Don even though he treats her disrespectfully and pushes her away for most of the movie. Helen stays with Don because she thinks she can "fix" him. Problem is, by never establishing boundaries, in a way she may be enabling him.

This goes double for Don's brother, Wick Birnam, played by Phillip Terry. Wick covers all of Don's living expenses, a classic enabling strategy common to siblings in this situation. Wick even goes so far as to lie to Helen about his brother's problem to protect him. But like Helen, his love and sense of loyalty to his brother is only further enabling Don's problem to continue. In later chapters we will discuss many of the challenges family members of friends of individuals with addictions face.

What made this movie so controversial when it was released in 1945 was the stark, raw depiction of Don's weekend bender. After finding a spot of cash his brother hid for the cleaning lady on a Friday afternoon, he goes to his local bar to self-medicate. Cue the now cliché "friendly-but-concerned-bartender" trope played out in the form of Nat, featuring wonderful character actor Howard Da Silva. Da Silva has the dubious distinction of being 1 of the 324 actors whose blacklisting during the McCarthy era almost ruined his career.

Nat tries his best to tap dance around Don's alcohol problem by offering tidbits of advice and encouragement for Don to take it easy on the booze. He even gets increasingly agitated at the great waste of talent unfolding in front of him. Yes, on the one hand bartenders don't have much credibility when it comes to asking their patrons to drink less, after all it's their job. But in these scenes, Wilder touches on a subtle but interesting dynamic that sometimes develops between addicts and their suppliers. In later stages of addiction, individuals often have burned through all their friends and family and become socially isolated. Bartenders and drug pushers are sometimes the only "friends" addicts can interact with or even talk to. Something akin to Stockholm syndrome develops between them where users come to love and trust the very people whose job it is to supply them with the substances that are destroying their lives.

The bar scene is also an incredible rendition of the night-and-day effect alcohol can actually have on people, where you would think alcohol was the greatest thing in the world (and many people agree it is). After just one drink, Don's entire demeanor instantly changes from anxious and insular to friendly and gregarious. Every word that comes out of his mouth is more interesting than the last. His imagination expands. Whatever writer's block he may have had quickly seems to dissipate. He even quotes Shakespeare, not once but twice. We've all seen people change after a few drinks, but with this scene Wilder seems to have wanted to make a point about how alcohol can instantly transport some people into a dangerous alternate reality.

With a few bucks left after his bar bash, Don goes to a local liquor store to stock up for the weekend. He buys two bottles, drinks one, and hides the other. The next day he can't remember where he hid the other bottle, so he then spends the rest of the weekend engaging in ever more desperate ways to find money to buy more alcohol: lying, borrowing, shoplifting, pickpocketing, begging, even a weird form of prostitution—where Don feigns love for a local barmaid so that she'll spot him some cash.

Worst of all, but perhaps also ironic because he's a writer, Don lugs his typewriter around to various pawn shops but can't seem to find one that's open because it's Yom Kippur. He finally does, and with his typewriter gone, so too is the last thing that could possibly turn his life around: writing. This irony is especially cruel because alcohol can slowly rob creative people of the talents and skills they need to feel emotionally fulfilled in life, and then they have to drink even more to fill that void. I know this from personal experience.

Don eventually ends up in the detox ward of a local mental hospital. Welcome to scared-straight—1940s style—where the whole scene plays out like a mashup of the **Twilight Zone** and **One Flew Over the Cuckoo's Nest**, punctuated by a male-nurse-from-hell character played by actor Frank Faylen and catatonic detainees mumbling gibberish to themselves, men clearing away imaginary spider webs from their faces, and a poor guy in advanced stages of withdrawal who goes totally postal because he thinks he's being eaten alive by cockroaches. Granted, the detox psych ward scene is a bit over the top, even by today's standards, but people really experience these kinds of hallucinations in real life. A friend told me a story about his buddy who saw lobsters all over his walls and almost jumped off his 20-story balcony.

As excessive as the scene is, it does give the nurse a platform to tell Don—and by extension the audience—some important facts about alcohol abuse without being too preachy, like how prevalent it actually is, and how it doesn't discriminate by age or occupation. This was probably the first time that audiences had taken an honest look at a health problem people never talked about in polite company. The end result was a much-needed non-preachy Public Service Announcement that is a real wake-up call about addiction in general, not just to alcohol.

Don eventually manages to escape from the psych ward. And then it's home to his dark apartment where he suffers a terrible bout of DTs. And this is where the story takes a rather bleak turn. Remember, this is the 1940s and treatment options for addiction were still underdeveloped. In most cases they were worse than the problem they were intended to fix. Alcoholics were either headed to the funny farm, a prison cell, or a casket. The idea of mutual support meetings and mental health treatment was still in its infancy. For too many people like Don, at the time suicide seemed like the only way out. Sadly, this still holds true for many people even today, and is why addiction is second only to depression as the top risk factor for suicide.

But luckily for Don, Helen hasn't given up on him. Any sane woman who had been as mistreated as she has would have left a long time ago, but Helen has chosen to stick it out. Lucky for him, because when she sees Don has a gun, she grabs it and tries to talk him off the ledge. She's unsuccessful at first, and the tension gets ratcheted up further. But she persists until Don sees whatever light there is left at the end of whatever tunnel he can find. He drops the gun.

But here's the thing: To talk him back from the ledge Helen is forced to strike a Faustian bargain of sorts. We will see this dynamic play out in several other movies discussed in this book. It's the seemingly unavoidable solution that the loved ones of alcohol-dependent people must settle for. In Helen's words: "I'd rather you drink than be dead." Allowing and even helping Don to continue drinking is Helen's only way forward. The problem is, by never drawing a line in the sand around Don's behavior, she's still letting him die—albeit more slowly. In a sense, Don's addiction is blackmailing Helen into allowing it to survive and continue to flourish all the way to the end.

So yes, crisis averted—but not problem solved: Will Don keep drinking?

Well, it's here, at the emotional climax of the film, that Helen goes from being an enabler to an addiction and recovery all-star. She convinces Don that "he is good." It's the "other Don" who's bad. Yes, it seems that people like Don can be of two minds. It's a pathology first popularized in fiction with Robert Louis Stevenson's gothic novella **Strange Case of Dr. Jekyll and Mr. Hyde**. And it's a facet of the addiction story that we will see over and over again in other films.

In **The Lost Weekend**, it's also the most psychologically profound theme of the movie because it highlights the dissociation many addicts try to maintain between their best intentions and their worst impulses in order to justify their destructive behavior. In this case, Helen convinces Don to collapse the false dichotomy between the "good Don" and the "bad Don." And the moment he does, he stops playing the victim card and assumes sole personal responsibility for his bad choices in life. And just as importantly, he assumes ownership over where he will now take his life without alcohol.

And that's where the real work starts. Quitting is easy. Filling all that extra time with meaningful pursuits requires a new boost of confidence that many people don't have (or have had stripped away by their drug of choice). They also need the support of people around them to make sure they don't falter, feel guilty, and resort to old habits to self-medicate over that guilt. Luckily in Don's case, he seems to have those things. He will heal "naturally" without meetings or shrinks[1]. Which is what happens in real life anyway. Most people kick the habit without ever stepping foot in an AA meeting or therapist's office.

To fill the time and infuse his life with new meaning, Don also returns to the pursuit that used to give his life purpose before alcohol ripped it away: writing. He decides to write a book about his problems

---

1 Or perhaps if they had made a sequel, we would have found Don in an AA meeting.

with alcohol. Not only is this a hopeful end to a harrowing journey, but it's a wonderful instance of art imitating life—inasmuch as Don writing about his lost weekend is exactly what novelist Charles Jackson did when he wrote the book upon which the film is based.

It's amazing how director and Hollywood legend Billy Wilder, working off a script he co-wrote with Charles Brackett, can fit so many aspects of addiction and recovery into a two-hour film. Wilder, of course, is a master when it comes to the cinematic examination of our darkest impulses laid bare—vanity, jealousy, and murder—in other great films, like **Sunset Boulevard** and **Double Indemnity**.

Technical props must go to Oscar-winning composer Miklós Rózsa for the haunting music score that so perfectly captures the feelings of anxiety and desperation Don experiences as he struggles to find his next drink. And John F. Seitz's black and white cinematography, with his use of framing and shadows, does an exemplary job of building tension and distress.

Back to Charles Jackson for a moment. His life was both triumphant and tragic. He wrote **The Lost Weekend** to chronicle his experience after he had quit drinking several years earlier. When his book and the film became unlikely successes, Jackson leveraged this fame into a string of appearances at Alcoholics Anonymous meetings around the country. I highly recommend that you listen to his famous 1959 AA speech available on YouTube.[2]

In the decade after the novel was published, Jackson suffered from writer's block and his finances became problematic. He and his wife and children became estranged as a result. It was later revealed that he was a closet bisexual, and the pressure to keep this secret over decades no doubt added to the stress that saw him relapse in 1968—a few months before killing himself with a barbiturate overdose that same year.

---

[2] https://www.youtube.com/watch?v=QoiP5xsJzvs

The Lost Weekend can seem like anti-booze messaging overkill to modern audiences so accustomed to the realities of addiction, and so inured to its terrible effects. Believe me, there are many movies that address the problem with a much more even hand. But for those who are interested in the key takeaways about addiction, repeated viewings reveal a goldmine of inspiring quotes, metaphors, and allegories that can inspire anyone to stay the course in their recovery. It certainly worked for me. I watch the film every couple of months and always find something of value for my recovery.

CHAPTER 2
Death as a Life Choice
Leaving Las Vegas

Director/Writer/Jazz Musician and creative polymath Mike Figgis' 1995 indie movie classic **Leaving Las Vegas** is a bitter pill to swallow for some, and an endless source of fascination for others. The slow and inevitable descent of its main character, Ben Sanderson (Nicolas Cage), into alcohol-fueled oblivion is like a four-car pileup on the Hollywood Freeway. Everybody says they're too grossed-out to look at it, but in the end they just can't tear themselves away.

Showing graphic, over-the-top alcohol abuse was a huge part of the film's appeal among general audiences, but a source of consternation for many people in the recovery universe. Cage's constant binge drinking and overlapping rock bottoms were like the film equivalent version of a "drunk-a-log"—those AA meeting speeches by invited guests or shares by participants who go into excruciating detail about their disastrous drinking habits. Many outside (and some even inside) AA frown on the practice because it can tend to "glamorize" past bad behavior.[3] Others have so little confidence in their own support programs that they think references to drinking or images of alcohol will cause all of their participants to instantly relapse.

Still other people, especially clinicians and treatment facility professionals, thought it was irresponsible to make a movie where the main character simply refuses to get help and has no intention to ever quit drinking. If the aim of the film was to issue a strong caution about the dangers of alcohol abuse, they argued, then Cage's character should end up in rehab at the end. In other words, they wanted a nice Hollywood ending. But that's not the ending the world got. The ending of the film was the whole point of it.

This was apparently a concern also shared by all the U.S. studios who had refused to finance and distribute the film when the opportunity was offered to them in late 1994/early 1995. I was having lunch with some friends in Cannes in May of 1995, and **Leaving Las Vegas** had a lot of "buzz" around it. For those who don't know, the Cannes Film Festival is also a large supermarket where independent films are bought and sold by smaller distributors—including the company Lumiére Pictures, which financed the film. When a studio refuses to finance your film, this is where it ends up.

Over lunch, a colleague related a story about how Lila Cazès—the producer of the film, had met with some studio muckety-muck who offered to finance the film on condition that Figgis tone down the graphic binge drinking and change the ending to where Nicolas Cage goes to rehab, gets all better, and marries Elizabeth Shue when he gets out. Since this story came to us anecdotally, I can't confirm its

---

3 Some AA "drunk-a-logs" are retold for 20+ years. People in meetings also sometimes feel they have to spice up their stories to one-up others. It can sometimes devolve into theater.

complete accuracy, but apparently when Cazès heard this ultimatum she burst out laughing and abruptly left the meeting. She would savor her comeuppance ten months later on Oscar night. The film was nominated in four categories at the 1995 Academy Awards, with Cage taking home the Best Actor trophy.

Ben Sanderson (played exquisitely by Cage) is a Hollywood production executive whose drinking has spiraled out of control. I suspect Cage must have been the obvious choice to play the role. He seems so unmoored both on camera and off that each one of his drunken outbursts in the film is cringe-worthy but brand-consistent. Lately, his on-and-off-screen weirdness has evolved into his trademark; he now appears in films as himself playing a parody version of himself. And he gets paid tons of money to do this, mind you. I want his job.

Before Leaving Las Vegas, writer/director Mike Figgis had a love-hate relationship with Hollywood. He made a bit of a splash with his 1988 feature debut **Stormy Monday**, and then cashed in a Hollywood A-Lister paycheck two years later with the must-see **Internal Affairs** starring Richard Gere. But he always remained a studio outsider, a kind of anti-film film guy. He always looked disheveled at industry parties, his hair crazy and unkempt. It was rumored that he loved the fact that **Leaving Las Vegas** had no studio involvement or money. He seems most comfortable shooting low-budget films instead of Hollywood-style extravaganzas.

And it's the low-budget feel of the film that really turned it into a classic. Figgis chose to shoot in Super-16mm, which gives the story a grainy, almost dirty feeling—consistent with the subject matter. With a vastly scaled-down production crew and much smaller camera package, Cage had more latitude to do "his thing" and push the boundaries of method acting. There was a rumor in Hollywood that Cage was always in character during production, three sheets to the wind in the proud tradition of W.C. Fields. After he was nominated for an Oscar, some even argued that he should be disqualified because he was drunk—the thespian equivalent of being banned for taking performance-enhancing drugs. None of this was true. Cage was completely sober during production but did binge drink in Ireland for two weeks prior to production to get his liver in shape.

Figgis leverages the First Act of the film to show the broad spectrum of shifting character attributes alcohol generates in its victims. Depending on his intake levels, Ben is alternatively charming, obnoxious, serene, angry, hopeful, and pathetic. Figgis really put Cage through his paces early on. Some of the most amazing acting of the whole film takes place in the first ten minutes. Most notable is when he crashes a dinner some agents and managers are having at a Beverly Hills restaurant.

Cage channels over-the-top Hollywood producer bravado one minute, then grovels for an agent friend—played by comedian Richard Lewis—to loan him money the next. Probably because I've been part of the Hollywood meat-grinder myself, I found this scene particularly difficult to watch. The film industry has a very strict hierarchical structure where everybody is so busy clawing their way to the top that they seldom care about those on their way down. Lewis does a wonderful job playing a guy who wants to help Ben but seems terrified that his career might be harmed if people even see them together.

Drink fund secured, Ben ventures to a dive bar, sees a pretty girl, and slams down the requisite number of vodka tonics required to instantly transform into The Most Interesting Man in the World. But the girl, played by Italian actress Valeria Golino (of **Rain Man** and **Hot Shots! Part One & Deux** fame), takes one whiff of his breath and clocks out. An abrupt alcohol-induced mood swing follows, and Ben is reduced to begging Golino to go home with him because he's, well, really lonely. It's a sad but wonderful scene where we see alcohol as a truth serum. If only he could tell the truth to himself.

The next day Ben is fired from his job, secures a severance check, and decides to drive to Las Vegas and spend it all on his favorite pastime.

But before he does, he burns all his bridges. Literally. He gathers all his possessions (minus a few items of clothing, his car, and a liquor supply), tosses them into a pile, and lights a match. As crazy as this sounds, I and many of my Hollywood colleagues continually fantasize about this exact same scenario. The business is very unforgiving at times, and the stress of not getting that production deal or selling that script drives us to fantasize about "burning it all down." At certain drunken rag-fests, my colleagues and I would even go so far as to list the studio executives and producers we would assassinate on our way out of town.

On one level Ben torching his belongings is great eye candy that propels the story into Act 2. But there are also deeper themes at play. It's no coincidence that many individuals in advanced stages of addiction are homeless. In many ways, this is a choice. To fully dedicate themselves to their drug of choice, people need to get rid of all the *things* that stand in the way: homes, cars, husbands and wives, children, furniture, jobs, foreseeable futures, etc. In fact, getting rid of everything is a kind of ritual cleansing experience. Get rid of the shit you own before your shit owns you. If you want to see this paradigm played out in a film I recommend watching **Everything Must Go** starring Will Ferrell.

Ben's divestiture of *things* continues at a Las Vegas pawn shop. The "pawn shop scene" is somewhat of an addiction-movie trope, first used in the film **The Lost Weekend** when Don Birnam hocks his typewriter to finance his drinking habit. The tragic irony there—since he's a writer by trade—is that Don's typewriter is the one thing that could save him. But as we see time and time again, an addicted individual's drug of choice strips value from anything that stands in its way. Cut to half a century later, and the exact same dynamic plays out with Ben in Las Vegas. Only in his case, Ben has bypassed salvation entirely and lost all interest in *time* itself. Which is why he hocks his Rolex Daytona watch—a timepiece—for pennies on the dollar without batting an eyelash. Let's face it, alcohol is the ultimate time machine anyway.

Ben eventually crosses paths with the second most important character in the film besides ethanol. Played by the underrated Elizabeth Shue (nominated for an Oscar for her outstanding performance), Sera is a local prostitute that Ben almost runs down at a crosswalk. Wanting for company, he asks her to come to his seedy motel. After Sera begins to ply her trade, Ben stops her. It's not about sex for him; it's about human companionship. Sera desperately wants the same thing, and after they see each other a second time, Sera gets Ben to come live with her.

Now, if this were a typical Hollywood movie, we could reasonably expect a happy ending based on this set-up. The studio executive who asked producer Lila Cazès to change the ending would get their wish: Inspired by his female muse, and because love conquers all, Ben would go to rehab, realize how wonderful life is, make amends to everyone, and emerge Phoenix-like from treatment all shiny and new. Sera would quit prostitution, get a master's in social work, and both she and Ben would live happily ever after in the suburbs.

Luckily that didn't happen. Obviously this is not a typical Hollywood movie. It's not typical anything. It becomes clear why Ben has lost interest in time. It's because he has lost all interest in existence too. He tells Sera he's come to Vegas with the intention of drinking himself to death. Furthermore, as a condition of him living with her, she must agree to never ask him to stop. So Sera strikes the same sad Faustian bargain millions of concerned family members and friends of addicted individuals have struck with loved ones since time immemorial[4]: enable them to keep using under their care instead of letting them die without it.

We can't fault Sera for standing idly by while Ben kills himself in slow motion. She's a scared, lonely young woman whose self-esteem

---

4 ...and a topic we will return to again and again in this book.

has been stripped away by every trick she was forced to turn for her abusive Eastern European pimp, Yuri—played by former Merchant-Ivory heartthrob Julian Sands. And she's in no position to judge Ben either, lest the mirror get turned on her. For the limited time he has left on earth (about four weeks in Ben's estimation), Sera's need to overcome her loneliness trumps any instinctual desire to try to save the man she's come to love.

And yet, Figgis does dangle a few red herrings that hint at a possible Hollywood ending. In one scene, Sera asks Ben why he's killing himself. Ben answers, "I don't remember; I just know I want to." It stands to reason that if he really can't remember the why, perhaps he could be convinced of the many why nots. Maybe his suicide plans are just the ramblings of a drunk, or a desperate cry for help. Later in the film, Ben enthusiastically tells Sera, "You're some kind of antidote that mixes with the liquor and keeps me in balance." Perhaps with Sera's help an extreme like suicide can be avoided, balance restored.

But Ben's continued downward spiral in Act 2 renders this unlikely. So Sera tosses up a Hail Mary and tells Ben, "I want you to see a doctor." Ben threatens to move out. So once again, Sera agrees to stand aside in exchange for the few remaining hours of company they have left. Until, that is, Ben brings home a prostitute. Then Sera kicks him out. And with that, the die is cast. No Hollywood ending. Ben will commit slow suicide.

Now that we know the story will end in death, it is a good time to discuss what can be learned from this. Nobody likes to talk about suicide, but it should be talked about—especially as it relates to addiction and recovery. As was stated before, addiction is second only to depression as the top risk factor for suicide. The so-called "Question of Suicide" has been firmly rooted in philosophy for millennia. And inasmuch as one of philosophy's goals is to examine how best to live, it can also challenge us to question whether to keep living at all.

Enter French philosopher Albert Camus. To him, suicide was the only real question in philosophy. In his 1942 essay ***The Myth of***

Sisyphus, Camus introduces us to the philosophy of "The Absurd"—the total disconnect between an individual's natural impulse to find meaning in life and the universe's stubborn silence on the matter.

Which is not to say that people can't find meaning in life. A few years after Camus' essay was published, Holocaust survivor Viktor Frankl's seminal 1946 book **Man's Search for Meaning** argued quite successfully that meaning can be found in every moment of life, even the shittiest ones. It's up to us to find that meaning, leverage it into hope, and keep darkness at bay. We need to spend more time creating meaning, not searching for it.

All of which brings us back to Ben. He's lost his wife, his son, his job, his self-respect. His life appears to have lost all meaning. The question may be asked: Did his life cease to have meaning because his drinking stripped it all away, or did he start drinking because he realized his life had no meaning to begin with?

Ask anyone who has recovered successfully, and they'll tell you the answer to that question: It doesn't matter. Individuals suffering from addiction are expert mental gymnasts. They will come up with any justification, philosophical or otherwise, to continue using their drug of choice unimpeded. The *"I'm suffering from post-modern existential ennui which is causing me to question the true meaning of life"* claim is as flimsy and banal an excuse as *"I really like getting wasted."*

At the end of the day, no amount of rock-bottoms on one end of the recovery spectrum or recovery success on the other will derail some addicted individuals' best-laid plans. And this includes John O'Brien, the author of the novel upon which **Leaving Las Vegas** is based. He struggled with alcohol for decades, perhaps because he had convinced himself that he was a failed novelist, just like Don Birnam in **The Lost Weekend**. Or a Hollywood reject, like Ben Sanderson.

And yet O'Brien managed to sell the film rights to his book, a film that was fully financed and about to be produced with major Hollywood stars and an award-winning director. O'Brien the writer had found real success. The kind of success that could help vanquish his inner demons, overcome his addiction to alcohol, and turn his whole life around. But a mere two weeks before production began on the film, O'Brien committed suicide. His father called the novel "one long suicide note." We may never truly know why O'Brien did it. It was rumored O'Brien had become convinced that writer-director Mike Figgis would give the story a sanitized Hollywood ending, which he clearly did not.

Perhaps most tragic of all? The timing. If O'Brien had lived just one more year, he would have seen his story light up the Academy Awards. He would have seen Nicolas Cage share the Best Actor award with him in his Oscar acceptance speech. And yet, despite all these ifs, the truth was—and O'Brien's sister said it best—his addiction would have claimed his life regardless: "Not that a little cash or fame would have changed anything…"

Which leaves us with a brutal truth about addiction and recovery. Addiction can and often does win in the end. Successful recovery is never guaranteed. Suicide—slow or otherwise—is the end result for many. Too many. So for us as a society to honestly acknowledge this fact may be an important step in helping overcome these avoidable tragedies in the future.

So thank you, **Leaving Las Vegas**, and congratulations Lila Cazès. Your two-hour-long Academy Award winning suicidal trainwreck of a movie may help people appreciate life all the more—whether they're in recovery or not.

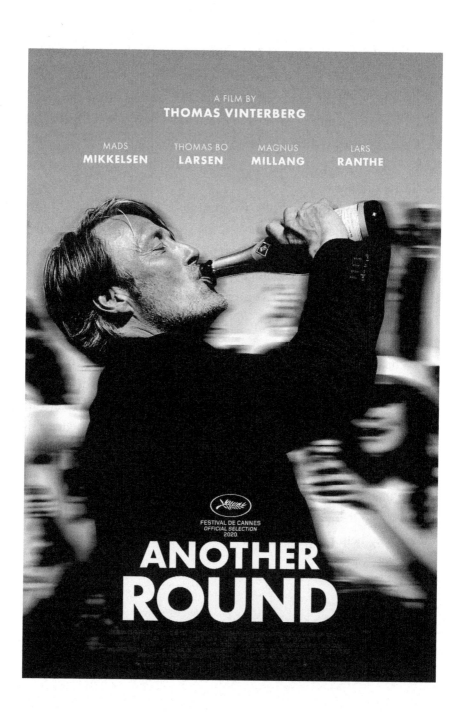

CHAPTER 3
The Great Danish Alcohol Experiment
Another Round

Up to now we have discussed addiction and recovery-related films produced in English. Now I'm pleased to add a "foreign language" entry in the form of *Another Round*, written and produced by Danish filmmaker Thomas Vinterberg. The film, whose (apt) original title is **Druk**, Danish for "binge drinking," is exceptional on several levels and won the Academy Award for Best Foreign Language Film in 2020.

For anyone familiar with Vinterberg's directorial career and commercial track record, the award was as ironic as it was improbable. For decades, along with fellow Dane Lars von Trier, Vinterberg opposed the Hollywood "system" with its gargantuan production budgets, sexy movie stars, and awesome special effects. Together in 1995 they created **Dogme 95**, a "movement" complete with a "manifesto" whose goal was a return to "traditional values" of story, acting, and theme in filmmaking. Basically that meant a hand-held camera, no sets, natural sound, no action, and no special effects of any type. In short, dogmatic. He and Mike Figgis are obviously artistic soulmates.

Vinterberg's first Dogme film, **Celebration**, was a modest critical and commercial success. But as time went on and more films came out, critics and the scant audience members who bothered to show up in theaters were left scratching their heads. None of the Dogme films made even one-tenth of what a Hollywood movie typically rakes in (even ones that bomb)—possibly because of such off-putting film titles as **Fuckland**, **Julien Donkey-Boy**, and **The Idiots**.

But in **Another Round**, Vinterberg seems to have put his beef with Hollywood aside and made the most accessible, commercial, and heartfelt film of his career. Besides the accolades and awards it received, there was a deeper validation in the film's success. Vinterberg had developed the script with the enthusiastic help of his 19-year-old daughter, Ida. She was slated to make her acting debut in the film, and it was to be shot at her high school featuring her real-life friends as costars. But four days into principal photography, Ida was killed in a car crash caused by a distracted driver.

Such a tragedy would have sunk most other directors, but in Vinterberg's case it seems to have accomplished the opposite. Every frame of the film seems to radiate an ineffable glow of love, support, and remembrance for Ida—especially the scenes that take place at her high school. There is an energy and relevance and honesty about this film that is unmistakable. And when it comes to films about alcohol specifically, **Another Round** is a Jedi Master-Level accomplishment, and possibly my all-time favorite film on the subject.

Before I discuss the film, some words of caution: If you're at all triggered by a luscious opening sequence featuring beautiful Danish teenagers drinking a lot of alcohol in a consequence-free environment where excess is a time-honored, fully-sanctioned tradition that not only enhances the quality of their lives but is a central rite-of-passage to a happy, successful, well-adjusted adulthood—then please fast forward past the first 3 minutes of the film.

Still with us? Cool. Because in the rest of the film that follows, Vinterberg tells an amazing story that succeeds in dramatizing the greatest mystery of drinking itself: Why does a substance that makes many people's lives so awesome end up harming others? How is it that some people's lives are enhanced by drinking, while others are destroyed?

To explore this question, Vinterberg and his writing colleague Tobias Lindholm take us into a typical Danish high school (Vinterberg's daughter's actual school) and introduces us to its history teacher Martin (played by ex-James Bond *Casino Royale* super-villain Mads Mikkelsen). Martin is in a serious funk. His marriage is on autopilot, his kids are indifferent to him, and his teaching is so uninspired that his students' parents call a PTA meeting to complain.

Martin joins his work colleagues Tommy, Nikolaj, and Peter for an alcohol-soaked dinner to lament their similarly bleak situations in life. Tommy is a bored PE teacher who dislikes children. Nikolaj is a psychology teacher who hasn't slept in years because his children always wet the bed. And Peter is the school's choir director whose ears bleed every time his students try to sing.

But it's nothing that eighteen rounds of drinks can't fix. The evening devolves into a drunken midnight soccer game, but without the soccer or the game. One choice nugget emerges, however. Nikolaj tells his friends about a little-known Danish doctor who touts a radical theory: Humans were born with a blood alcohol level that's TOO LOW. Maximum human productivity, potential, and happiness can only be achieved by maintaining a Blood Alcohol Content (BAC) of .05%. *All day long.*

Quick side note: I tested this theory at a BAC of .10% for a whole year. Note to self: Really bad idea.

So Martin and his friends decide to test the theory. To give the experiment a sheen of respectability, they agree to fully document what happens if they stay continually buzzed from 8am to 8pm every day.

Those of us in recovery know exactly what will happen. *Or do we?* This is where the film gets really interesting.

Turns out that at this particular Danish high school, day drinking doesn't just result in mirth—it's also a boon to your teaching career. Martin takes a few belts of vodka between first and second period, then crushes his history class lecture with an amusing "who-had-their-shit-more-together" competition among Churchill, Roosevelt, and Hitler. Spoiler alert: Hitler wins.

Meanwhile, Tommy drinks copious amounts of Cognac as he coaches little league soccer. Lo and behold, he develops an interest in the actual coaching part, and his team starts to win actual games.

And lastly, the school's choir director, Peter, channeling Hemingway's famous quip, "I drink to make other people more interesting," turns the lights off and tells all his students to hold hands during choir practice. Their singing suddenly becomes a lot more interesting. At least to Peter.

Having demonstrated that a solid all-day buzz makes teaching history a cinch, Martin extends the experiment into the evening hours to see if it can help his marriage. It does (for now). He and his wife Anika really click, and the family goes on a long-delayed camping trip. They have an actual conversation with their two teenage sons instead of watching them watch their iPads. Tomas and Anika make love—and actually love each other—for the first time in years.

And all thanks to a BAC of 0.05%! Everyone should try this! Not.

Now, if this were where the story ends, **Another Round** would be little more than a two-hour infomercial for Tuborg Beer, Denmark's finest. But it doesn't end here. To Vinterberg's credit, the second and third acts of the film are fully balanced, honest explorations of what anyone in recovery already understands all too well. As Hollywood legend and **The Lost Weekend** director Billy Wilder put it, "*One is too many, and a hundred's not enough…*"

Martin and his buddies are so delighted with the experiment's results that they decide to push the envelope. Why not up their daily dosage to sustain a BAC of 0.06%? Or maybe 0.1%? And, hell, if you're going to go to all the trouble, why not just go all the way to 0.2%?

Doesn't take a rocket scientist to predict what happens next. Bad stuff, basically: Martin slams into a wall and gives himself a bloody nose at a school staff meeting. He passes it off as history-teaching-related stress, which apparently is a thing. Nikolaj becomes the bed-wetter of the family. Tommy makes a drunken fool out of himself at a teacher's meeting. But this being socialist Denmark, he'll likely wind up on paid leave, attend free five-star rehab in the French Riviera, and get a raise.

It's the school choir director, Peter, who seems to suffer the fewest consequences from experimental day drinking. Moderation works so well for him, in fact, that he spreads the word to others. The film has a scene where Peter helps an anxious student ace his final exams thanks to a quick shot of vodka under the table. The scene is both interesting and disturbing on so many levels. Especially given that the student aces the test.

What is so appealing about the film is how Vinterberg uses each character to experience different consequences from drinking—from moderate to severe—just like people do in real life. Most can handle it. Some can't. Some really can't.

It would have been easy for Vinterberg to dwell on the ugly extremes of drinking behavior, but he does the opposite through the character of Tomas. His experience of alcohol use and misuse is the most fully explored and multi-dimensional of the four friends. At first a teetotaler, later an alcohol-curious novitiate, then a happy-go-lucky lush, and eventually an All-Pro who wakes up face plastered to the sidewalk, Tomas is the narrative embodiment of the downward trajectory many people with drinking issues ultimately experience over time.

Does Martin learn his "lesson" by the end? Perhaps not, because he and his wife separate. But was the separation because of Martin's drinking? Or did Martin's drinking end up expediting something that should have happened a long time ago? Does moderate alcohol use help people communicate their truth? Could moderate levels of alcohol allow people to have more empathy for one another? More love?

Or does moderate use inevitably lead to misuse? Why do some people lose their shit after one drop of alcohol, while others thrive socially, professionally, and emotionally with 3-4 drinks a day? Their *entire* lives. I'm talking to you, Europe!

Vinterberg doesn't answer these questions. He leaves them hanging in the air, savory nuggets for debate. Some people in recovery may find his non-committal approach frustrating; others may find it fascinating. At the end of the day, there really are no easy answers. Everybody learns a different lesson about alcohol that can only be gained through the (often painful) experience of using or abusing it. Clearly there are some benefits (at least at the beginning of one's drinking career), and obviously there are consequences (toward the end).

Spoiler alert: One of those consequences in the film is Tommy, who takes himself for a drunken boat ride but never returns. The scenes of his struggle with alcohol leading up to the tragedy, and Martin's best efforts to help his dear friend, are gut-wrenchingly honest. Tommy's funeral represents a somber moment of reckoning. Again, Vinterberg could have ended the film here and rendered the drinking experiment a blunt cautionary tale: *Do not try this at home. Actually, don't try this at all.*

But that would have been overly...*dogmatic*, right? In the last glorious five minutes of the film, Vinterberg gives us the opposite. The three remaining friends get together and toast their fallen comrade. That's right, a toast with alcohol where Martin asks the question: What would Tommy do? And the answer is quite clear. He'd order another bottle of Juvé y Camps and celebrate the limited time life has given him. Would he need alcohol to do that? Maybe. Is it any of our business? No.

Vinterberg then blends the story of the film with the real-life story of his daughter's death into a loving homage to the beauty, power, and unlimited potential of youth. Martin (having reconciled with his wife) leads his friends Peter and Nikolaj outside to crash the kind of high school graduation party most people only dream about. Makes you want to move to Denmark. There is dancing, revelry, mirth, friendship, joyous optimism, love, compassion, and every other positive emotion you can think of. And all of it well-oiled with alcohol.

Again, if this kind of stuff triggers you, unplug your TV right now. Still here? Great.

Vinterberg's final question in the most general sense seems to be this: Do people need alcohol to be happy?

Vinterberg can't answer that question. I can't answer that question. Only you, the reader, can answer that question. And luckily a wonderful, well-rounded, un-dogmatic movie like **Another Round** exists to help you do just that.

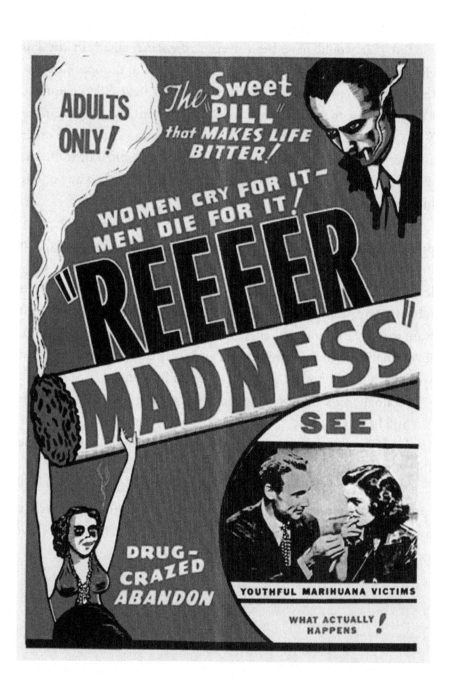

CHAPTER 4
Be Very Cautious With Cautionary Tales
Reefer Madness
Trainspotting
Requiem For a Dream

Any film or TV show about alcohol or drug macro-addictions is inherently cautionary. Were there ever a film produced that glamorized addiction and celebrated its countless personal and societal benefits free from all costs, it would belong in the realm of dystopian science fiction. But to categorize a film as "cautionary" in the absolute sense is not accurate; there are degrees of caution.

Some filmmakers, like those who made ***Reefer Madness***, had a clear goal in mind: Scare the living shit out of everyone by showing how marijuana would lead to the end of the world as we know it. Other filmmakers, like Danny Boyle in ***Trainspotting***, wanted to tell a great story, and that included an honest look at every aspect of heroin addiction. Yes, even the good parts. The audience could come to their own rather obvious conclusions that heroin addiction generally sucks, and that the bad clearly outweighs the good. And still other filmmakers, like Darren Aronofsky with ***Requiem for a Dream***, chose to tell a deeper story about addiction where the drug use itself was incidental to the study of an underlying human pathology. Just read between the lines (or frames, in this case) and you realize it's a pathology that affects all of us.

Reefer Madness was a "film" directed in 1936 by French polymath Louis J. Gasnier. I use the term "film" in quotes because it's actually a glorified high-budget public service announcement masquerading as a low-budget movie. The intent was very clearly cautionary (no surprise that it was entirely funded by a church group); it's the movie equivalent of a four-alarm fire, and so utterly terrible that it got Gasnier sentenced to life without parole in movie jail. It is not known whether Gasnier felt strongly one way or the other about the actual cautions in the film, or whether he was just trying to cash a paycheck. Regardless, the producers must all be turning in their graves. Their very earnest anti-marijuana screed ended up becoming a very funny pro-pot rallying cry and the butt of countless stoner jokes. The film was so kitsch that it was adapted into a hilarious comic book series and a musical. Talk about the Law of Unintended Consequences.

Theater owners preferred to sell popcorn than kill everyone's buzz, so ***Reefer Madness*** didn't catch on theatrically until Dwain Esper—a building contractor turned film empresario—snatched up the rights, recut the film, and released it in seedy, bad-side-of-town sticky-floor theaters starting in 1938. Esper's specialty was crass low budget exploitation films like ***Sex Maniac*** and ***How to Undress In Front of Your Husband***.

Think of him as a poor man's Ed Wood,[5] with an extra dash of smutty. He got the snazzy idea to market ***Reefer Madness*** as a

---

5 Speaking of Ed Wood, one of my early mentors was Martin Landau, who won the Oscar for his role in the film ***Ed Wood***. He helped guide development of my

sexploitation flick, with the anti-marijuana message thrown in as an afterthought. Audiences must have seen through the deceptive marketing because the only remotely salacious scenes in the film are when a stoned couple fumble to locate each other's lips, and a guy makes a lackluster attempt at date rape which is easily derailed by an uncooperative zipper.

After tagging out theatrically, the film was relegated to the dustbin of film history and stored away in a vault somewhere in Burbank, California. And there it would have remained, were it not for an ironic fluke of history. The producers of the original film had bungled their copyright registration so the film ended up in the public domain stored at the Library of Congress. A lawyer by the name of Keith Stroup ran across a 35mm copy and purchased it for $300, rights and all. And here's where the story gets interesting.

Stroup worked for the Consumer Product Safety Division alongside notables like Ralph Nader—and was looking for a way to help support his new venture, **NORML**, or the National Organization for the Reform of Marijuana Laws. He began to offer screenings of the film on college campuses as a way to poke fun at the absurdity of marijuana hyper-criminalization. Some of the stoned college kids who laughed at the film probably went on to become state legislators who decriminalized marijuana. So if you're on your comfy couch reading this book, happily buzzed on medical marijuana, you have Keith Stroup and **Reefer Madness** to thank.

But wait: There's more. A young enterprising gentleman named Robert Shaye attended one of Stroup's midnight screenings and noticed that the new copyright had been filed improperly. Public domain meant he could also exploit the film, so Shaye bought a

---

first screenplay **Where Truth Lies**, and was going to play the lead (which eventually went to Malcolm McDowell); however, his schedule would not allow it and we went with John Savage instead. Of note, Landau was also the first person in my Hollywood career to tell me I should cut down on my drinking.

print, copied it, released the film to his nascent college movie circuit, and made a ton of money for his new company, New Line Cinema. New Line would go on to produce some of the most memorable and financially successful films of all time. So if you're on your comfy couch binge-watching the **Lord of the Rings** Trilogy this weekend, and possibly stoned on medical marijuana whilst doing it, once again you have **Reefer Madness** to thank.

So why did **Reefer Madness** become such a cult hit? Well, for starters, the film is clearly horrible. Midnight movie and college circuits in the '70s were fed largely by anti-movie movies, like **Attack of the Killer Tomatoes** and (pick any) intentionally bad John Waters films. I have my own fond, albeit blurry, high school memories of driving from my tranquil Northern Virginia suburb down to Georgetown in DC to watch these midnight movie classics, including everyone's favorite: **The Rocky Horror Picture Show**. True to the Law of Unintended Consequences, **Reefer Madness** became yet another reason *to* get stoned, not to *not* get stoned—as the original producers intended. Think about it: It was the late '70s, the first head shops opened, we all subscribed to *High Times* magazine, pot was cool, nobody would actually go to jail for possession, right? I mean, unless they were black.

What made **Reefer Madness** so hilarious was just how alarmist it was. The film starts out with title cards warning the audience that what they are about to witness may "startle" them. *Promise?!* I mean, wasn't that the whole point of the movie? To caution parents and their kids about the impending marijuana apocalypse? More hilarity ensued with the use of old-timey words like "fretful" and "unspeakable scourge." My stoner friends and I read these titles out loud along with the rest of the audience as we all laughed our asses off.

Not that the producers hadn't warned us that laughter was a slippery slope. Our "sudden, violent, uncontrollable laughter" would be followed by "dangerous hallucinations" (*seriously?!*) and "monstrous extravagances" (*count me in!*). And it only got better…er…worse from there. Pot would cause us "the loss of power to resist physical emotions, finally leading to acts of shocking violence ending often in incurable insanity." Wow! It appears that the billions of people who've smoked reefer over the last 2,500 years—including me and most of my friends—didn't get that memo.[6]

Duly warned about the horrors we were about to witness, **Reefer Madness** proceeds to administer horrors of a different kind: completely senseless story structure, inane dialogue, a crazed honky-tonk piano player, a Gollumesque weirdo hot-boxing a joint, a fatal hit-and-run, attempted rape, accidental homicide, a botched cover-up, a melodramatic criminal trial, sordid testimony, a manslaughter conviction, ruined lives all around, and some of the worst white-person dancing ever committed to celluloid. By God, it was all hilarious. And like most things one does when they're wasted, entirely pointless.

However, at the time **Reefer Madness** was made, it wasn't pointless at all. It was a carefully crafted piece of political propaganda—the first shot across the bow in what would subsequently become the very un-funny, catastrophic, and ultimately unsuccessful War on Drugs. If I had known back in Georgetown what the film actually was as opposed to what we all naively thought it was, we would not have been laughing in the least. This is a great example of the famous definition of Comedy I mentioned in the Introduction, only in reverse: Comedy minus Time = Tragedy.

Before I tell you **Reefer Madness'** role in this tragedy, I should qualify the term War on Drugs. It became part of the national lexicon after President Richard Nixon, pissed off because he was losing an

---

6 Cannabis is one of the oldest cultivated plants in East Asia, grown for grain and fiber as well as for recreational, medical, and ritual purposes. Analysis indicates that cannabis plants were burned in wooden braziers during mortuary ceremonies at the Jirzankal Cemetery (ca. 500 BCE) in the eastern Pamirs region. This suggests cannabis was smoked as part of ritual and/or religious activities in Western China at least 2,500 years ago and that the cannabis plants produced high levels of psychoactive compounds.

actual war, decided in a televised speech in 1971 to declare a fake war against an overhyped enemy: drugs. A year earlier Congress had passed the Comprehensive Drug Abuse Prevention and Control Act of 1970, which laid out categories for drugs based on their medicinal use and potential for addiction.

But the War on Drugs as an overall concept goes back much further. After the U.S. Civil War and World War I, doctors noticed that wounded vets had become addicted to morphine. Addiction itself was not yet fully understood as a pathology and seemed like a medical oddity with limited consequences. Hence you could buy Coca-Cola that contained actual coke, laudanum (an opioid) was in everyone's medicine cabinets, morphine was added to every manner of "tonic," and heroin was sold over the counter in cough syrup (great for babies with colic!). Rates of addiction spiked, culminating with the Harrison Narcotics Tax Act of 1914 which outlawed opiates. Actual treatments for addiction were non-existent. "Addicts" were often sent to insane asylums, along with those other poor folks called "alcoholics."

Enter Harry Anslinger, America's first "Drug Czar." In the early '30s, after the U.S. had repealed Prohibition, his nascent Federal Bureau of Narcotics was the under-funded bastard stepchild of the U.S. Treasury—the agency responsible for going after the real Public Enemy Number One: organized crime. Anslinger knew that to play with the big kids, he'd have to create the ultimate bogeyman. And for him that bogeyman ended up being the "dope fiend." Gradually his operating budget increased.

But to really scale up, Anslinger knew he had to influence public opinion. And what better way than to use mass media to scare the living shit out of Middle America. To achieve this, he found a willing accomplice in the form of media magnate William Randolph Hearst. Hearst's newspapers specialized in publishing lurid headlines about hellish "Dope Dens"—places where unsuspecting white Americans would be peer-pressured by sinister forces into smoking "The Devil's

Weed." Which sinister forces? Why blacks, Asians, and Mexicans of course.

It was a win-win for Hearst. He sold tons of newspapers, and by vilifying marijuana, he vilified hemp—a cheaper substitute for paper pulp which was a threat to his extensive timber holdings. Some historians go a step further and claim that Andrew Mellon (the Secretary of the Treasury, Anslinger's boss, and his wife's uncle!) also wanted to destroy the hemp trade because it threatened his sizable investment in a new synthetic fiber called "nylon" developed by his zillionaire cronies at DuPont. All these players got their way in 1937 when the Marijuana Tax Act was passed, criminalizing marijuana.

Criminalizing pot addressed an imagined problem and distracted away from the real issue of alcohol addiction. No federal funds were allocated to solve that, much less even study it. Anslinger's War on Drugs was "supported by science," but only the science that fit his narrative. He completely disregarded the opinion of twenty-nine out of thirty pharmacists surveyed on the subject by the American Medical Association who agreed that pot was harmless and non-addictive. Anslinger also quickly learned how to lie with statistics and link violent crimes to marijuana use. Hearst was only too happy to sensationalize that narrative when he published a salacious account of a 1933 mass-murder where a troubled young man named Victor Licata chopped his family to death with an ax, purportedly under the influence of pot. There was also the insinuation that he had raped his sisters first. Hearst conveniently omitted the fact that Licata, and many members of his family, had been diagnosed with serious mental illnesses.

And so there we had it: "Dope Fiends" were morally weak reprobates whose weed-smoking made them hysterical, violent, psychotic ax murderers and rapists. Especially if you were black. Because let's face it, *this* was the real crux of the matter: race. Anslinger's "public service" campaigns were grounded in centuries-old fears of marauding gangs of stoned black guys with libidinous superpowers and the inability to feel pain, scouring the streets looking for white women to rape. Worst still, the blacks would force these white women to smoke pot themselves, turning them into nymphomaniac sex slaves. The very idea that a white woman might actually enjoy having sex with a better-endowed black man had been driving white men batshit crazy for generations. Isn't that what lynchings were all about?

If you think I'm going a little bit over the top here, I invite you to read Johann Hari's extraordinary book, **Chasing The Scream**. It details Anslinger's racist double standards, especially in how he treated singer Billie Holiday. My favorite must-read quote from Hari's book:

> *The arguments we hear today for the drug war are that we must protect teenagers from drugs, and prevent addiction in general. We assume, looking back, that these were the reasons this war was launched in the first place. But they were not. They crop up only occasionally, as asides. The main reason given for banning drugs—the reason obsessing the men who launched this war—was that the blacks, Mexicans, and Chinese were using these chemicals, forgetting their place, and menacing white people.*

Anslinger's popularization of the term "Dope Fiend" was just the start of his efforts to define reality. Everyone else on the reactionary right—from the churches on down—soon realized that stigmatizing terms could be leveraged as propaganda to stoke anti-drug hysteria. The media were only too happy to parrot the talking points because hysteria sold more newspapers and got higher Nielsen ratings. By the time President Nixon declared his "War on Drugs" in the '70s,[7] the

---

[7] "The Nixon campaign in 1968, and the Nixon White House after that, had two enemies: the antiwar left and black people. You understand what I'm saying? We knew we couldn't make it illegal to be either against the war or black, but by getting the public to associate the hippies with marijuana and blacks with heroin, and then criminalizing both heavily, we could disrupt those communities. We could arrest

terms "junkie" and "pot-head" had become common. When Reagan signed the Comprehensive Crime Control Act of 1984 that hyper-criminalized drug possession and imposed minimum sentencing guidelines, the term "crackhead" also came into vogue. Misogynists took it one step further with the term "crack whore."

As a result, addiction stigmas—specifically racially-tinged addiction stigmas—were normalized. And we've all been living with the consequences of this ever since: a failed War on Drugs that cost over a trillion dollars, destroyed countless lives (primarily black lives), and ravaged black communities. Can you imagine the staggering loss of human potential as state and federal funds that could have helped people recover from their addiction were instead spent on prison cells to punish them for it? Without any addiction counseling in prison, can you guess what the result was? When you calculate the effectiveness of a war on drugs by how many people you incarcerate versus how many you actually help kick the habit, you know how much of a public policy clusterfuck this all was.

Knowing what we know now, **Reefer Madness** is a sad example of how a false narrative can be used to further a group's political, financial, and personal goals. The film billed itself as a cautionary tale about the dangers of pot, and for some people maybe it was. Some may have sworn off the stuff after seeing the film. We'll never know. Regardless, because of Anslinger and these kinds of "cautionary" films (there were other B-movies made to scare people, by the way) a majority of Americans across three generations came to view addicted individuals through a lens dirtied by stigmatizing language and imagery.

Mass media were complicit in all of it. They told the story of addiction as a dumbed-down Good versus Evil morality tale. Luckily, thanks to books by Hari and many other great thinkers including

---

their leaders, raid their homes, break up their meetings, and vilify them night after night on the evening news. Did we know we were lying about the drugs? Of course we did." —John Ehrlichman

Maia Szalavitz, Anna Lembke, Gabor Maté, Stanton Peele, Marc Lewis, and Bruce Liese (to name but a few), society is finally coming to view addiction for what it actually is—a dense and complicated story told with a multitude of characters, interlaced storylines, and no guarantee of a happy ending.

So the next time you're sitting on your comfy couch, watching ***The Wire*** or ***Breaking Bad***, wondering why the richest country on the planet can't offer free universal health care but can afford housing the highest prison population on the planet, you have a "movie" like ***Reefer Madness*** to thank.

———

Addicted in Film

Trainspotting, directed by Scottish director Danny Boyle in 1996, holds an outsized profile in the addiction and recovery moviescape, and is always on Top-10 lists of must-sees on the subject. And this is interesting, given that the film is really more an exercise in style over substance. Anyone looking for a dense multi-character plot-heavy exploration of addiction won't find it in **Trainspotting's** brisk 93-minute run time. But oh what style! Boyle is one of those truly gifted visual storytellers who makes maximum use of everything in the filmmakers' toolkit: kinetic editing, perfect music cues, minimalist set design, hilarious blocking, and sublime breakout performances by first-time nobodies like Ewan McGregor, who would go on to become Obi-Wan Kenobi, of all people. **Trainspotting** has been voted the "Best Scottish Film of All Time" and holds a well-deserved spot in the British Film Institute's list of 100 Top British Films of the 20th Century. Boyle would eventually go on to win a Best Picture Oscar for **Slumdog Millionaire**.

I remember screening the film along with several other studio film acquisitions executives at the Cannes Film Festival. When the house lights finally came up and we were able to catch our breath, I knew two things: 1) I would need to pass on the film because my boss would never let me buy it in a million years, and 2) We all wanted to try heroin. Yes, the film made it seem *that* good. Who in their right mind wouldn't want to try a drug that felt 1,000 times better than the greatest sex they've ever had? Why waste 20 years sitting in silence on a mountaintop in Tibet when an ersatz experience of oneness with the universe could be had for only $20? One of my colleagues knew a guy who knew a guy who knew a guy from a local Gypsy drug cartel in Nice who could help us score the scag. We priced out different syringes at a local pharmacy. YouTube hadn't been invented yet, so we got a how-to-cook tutorial from a sketchy local pusher. A half-baked plan was set in motion. But then saner minds prevailed, we played the tape forward, and realized what a stupid idea this was.

The film was eventually acquired by Harvey Weinstein's Miramax Films. His U.S. release campaign for the film still ranks as one of the greatest accomplishments in film marketing of all time. Think of it: Weinstein actually managed to convince middle-Americans to pay money to see a low budget Scottish film about heroin addiction where 50% of the dialogue is totally unintelligible.[8] And this is because Weinstein recognized something Boyle already knew: A good cautionary film about heroin addiction should give equal time to both sides of the experience, good *and* bad. That was the film's central appeal. It was honest. Yes, heroin is horrible overall, but certain parts of it could be utterly amazing—or so some people tell us. Of course, I wouldn't know personally.

Critics were of course quick to charge Boyle with "glorifying" heroin use. And Boyle himself didn't necessarily disagree with them. He was by no means the first artist to dabble in "heroin chic." David Bowie, Iggy Pop, Lou Reed, and the supermodel Gia (more on her in the next chapter) had all channeled it and profited by it in their own ways. Boyle just took it to the next level. Iggy Pop posters are visible throughout **Trainspotting**, and Reed's classic **Perfect Day** is the central track of the film. But let's be clear: Showcasing heroin in movies doesn't imply glorifying it any more than showing guns in movies glorifies violence. Oh, wait…

Trainspotting is a rather simple story about a group of friends ("lads") in their early 20s trawling through life in late 20th century Edinburgh, Scotland. Mark—played by McGregor—is their defacto alpha and seems to be the only "normal" one of the lot. His buddy Simon (aka "Sick Boy") is a narcissistic James Bond fanatic, Spud is the Scottish equivalent of Urkel, Tommy is a hopelessly romantic sap, and Begbie is a violent psychopath. They have no plans to go to college,

---

8 The Scottish Brogue used by the actors in the film was so hard to understand that Weinstein dubbed some parts of the film, and eventually released a version with Queen's English subtitles.

and actively avoid getting actual jobs. No family trauma to speak of; no crushing poverty per se. Boyle doesn't depict Edinburgh as a bleak, economically depressed hell-hole like most other U.K. directors, so there's really no obvious reasons why Mark, Simon, and Spud would become heroin addicts. The lads just take heroin, as Mark reminds us, "for the pleasure of it all; otherwise we wouldn't do it."

Boredom is clearly a factor, but that alone seems like a feeble justification for jabbing your veins. No, there's something more elemental at work here, and Boyle taps into an underlying reason why millions of people use opiates to begin with: to mute the tedium of daily existence—chronic dissatisfaction with reality. Some might call it anomie, ennui, or misanthropy. Whatever the reasons, life appears meaningless, boring, and utterly pointless to Mark. Like many drug addicts, he makes a very rational choice to use as a way to avoid the experience of actually living. At this advanced stage of existential denialism, reasons are pointless. "Who needs reasons when you've got heroin?"

Mark's ambivalence is wonderfully depicted in a scene where the lads loiter at the bottom of a beautiful Scottish heath. The grass is perfectly green and walkable, the air fresh with possibilities. Tommy entreats them to go hiking with him, to explore, to wander, to learn, to experience everything it is to be alive, to be human, to be Scottish. But Mark just can't see the forest for the heath. He doesn't want to, either. It's easier for him and his friends to accept and wallow in their mediocrity. No catchy new-age power-of-positive-thinking or "law of attraction" bromides to the rescue here. They're wankers and they know it. The odds of happiness and success are impossibly stacked against them. Sean Connery is the only guy who ever made it out of Scotland alive. Make peace with reality. Then score some heroin and simply snuff it out.

Predictable behaviors ensue. The lads shoplift, steal, pawn tellies from local nursing homes, and wait around for their monthly dole checks to clear. Their "dope den" is an unfurnished apartment in the Scottish equivalent of The Projects where their pusher, played by the amazing Peter Mullan, doles out heroin like it was haute cuisine. The den even doubles as a day care facility for a cute toddler and his addict mother. This arrangement ends badly when the toddler is found dead, apparently from Sudden Infant Death Syndrome. It's a terrifying scene that would signal a rock bottom for any normal person. But heroin addicts aren't normal people, and Mark's reaction to the tragedy is as simple as it is telling: "I'm cooking up," he says matter-of-factly. The distraught mother joins him. And why not? Again, if reality isn't to your liking, just snuff it out.

Eventually the law catches up with them. Spud goes to prison, and Mark gets remanded to a state-run rehab at a methadone clinic. But it's like putting a bandage on a severed limb to stop the bleeding. Mark relapses in spectacular fashion, and overdoses. The scenes of him descending into oblivion—the carpet swallowing him in on both sides—is both hilarious and frightful. Boyle, who had no special effects budget to speak of, is a master in the use of quirky camera angles and fish-eye lenses to convey Mark's semi-conscious disorientation throughout the ordeal. But it's when Mark gets locked in his childhood room to suffer withdrawals that Boyle's low-tech cinematic wizardry really comes into its own. If you've watched the film, you know the scene I'm referring to. It makes the alcohol detox ward in ***The Lost Weekend*** seem like a trip to Legoland. It lays waste to any argument that Boyle "glamorized" heroin use. Mark's withdrawal is so harrowing to watch it probably could have been multi-purposed as a high school anti-drug campaign.

Eventually free of heroin, Mark grapples with the fact that he has no way of escaping reality anymore. Yay, he got his life back! But now he faces the daunting prospect of actually having to live it. Boyle perfectly captures Mark's despair in a timelapse scene at a local bingo parlor. While his parents enjoy the evening out, he's trapped in super slo-mo as the mundane trappings of lower-middle-class Scottish life speedily happen all around him. Anybody in recovery can relate to this problem of time dilation. Gravity affects sober people differently. Time passes slower. Reality is heavier. I wouldn't be surprised if Einstein was high when he came up with Special Relativity. Getting high certainly made it easier for me and my friends to understand it in physics class.

But Mark does what any person in recovery must do: live life. Perhaps not to the "fullest" as he once did with heroin, but hey, them's the breaks. He moves to London, rents a flat, gets a job, and creates reality on his own terms. Anybody who has overcome addiction has experienced this. I've experienced this. And while difficult and awkward at first, creating a new and better existence without addictive substances is the basic end-goal of recovery. As Mark tells us, "I was content for the first time in my adult life." And good for him. I'll take content and sober over happy and addicted any day of the week. As the quote often attributed to John Lennon says, "Life is what happens to you when you're busy making other plans."

But sober life is not without its challenges either, and Mark's new straight-and-narrow thing is suddenly threatened when Begbie—played with psychopathic intensity by Robert Carlyle—comes to crash at his place. Carlyle steals the movie in many respects. Even U.K. audiences needed subtitles to understand what he was saying. Eventually Mark's other lads show up too, lured by the possibility of a quick score if they sell a kilo of heroin they've inadvertently come across. But of course, the merchandise should be sampled first, so Mark heroically volunteers to ruin his life all over again and sample it for purity. But it's just "one last time," he insists.

And, miraculously, it ends up being just that. The lads finally consummate their drug deal and end up going their separate ways. Mark takes his last hit of heroin almost like a romantic last-weekend-in-Paris goodbye with the true love of his life. The experience is amazing, and he wishes it could continue forever, but he knows all great things must come to an end. And in declaring an end to it, Mark finally experiences what it is to be fully human. Anyone in recovery can attest to that *moment* when they finally *get it*. The realization that reality can never be the same, and that's *totally fine*. He made the choice; reality didn't make the choice for him. This is true freedom. As Mark says in closing: "Choose life!"

By ending **Trainspotting** on such a positive note, Boyle was able to have his cautionary movie cake and eat it too. It would have been a waste of his immense talent if he had made just another cookie-cutter anti-drug movie. Instead, he gave audiences an honest, balanced look at why drugs have the appeal that they do. Audiences could make their own obvious conclusions about the downsides of addiction. Yes, the characters in **Trainspotting** are doing some crazy shit, but it allows us to see heroin addicts as multi-dimensional human beings instead of mere cookie-cutter "junkies."

The result is a better understanding of not just the drugs, but the deepest desires and metaphysical challenges of the individuals who take them. Better understanding leads to empathy, and empathy allows us as a society to reach out to addicted individuals and help them where they are—not where we expect them to be. This leads to better care and better outcomes.

Darren Aronofsky is an acquired taste. His movies aren't for everyone, which is probably why he hasn't met with much commercial box-office success. The critics love him, at least those who actually understand his films. They're intellectual exercises in many respects, and like a James Joyce novel, his films must be watched several times to make sense out of them. But even then, they still don't make total sense. Even to Aronofsky, perhaps. And that's part of his appeal. Not understanding everything leaves open the potential of considering anything, which is why many YouTubers have made a great living making "what it all means" videos about his films.

Requiem for a Dream, made in 2000, was Aronofsky's first "studio film" in the sense that it was fully financed and he didn't have to do it on a shoestring budget ($60,000) like his debut feature *Pi*, which he sold to Artisan Entertainment for $1 million. Artisan is one of those companies that no longer exists (its library was swallowed up by Lionsgate) that had real moxie when it came to supporting movies every other studio was afraid of. They were the geniuses behind *Blair Witch Project*, a home video masquerading as a movie that still holds one of the all-time records of biggest return on investment ($35,000 budget versus $225 million at the box office).

I remember speaking with Artisan Entertainment's head of production about Aronofsky's *Requiem for a Dream* right after it was greenlit. He agreed that the subject matter was completely depressing, but there was no way he *couldn't* support Aronofsky. That's what great production executives do, really. They support truly creative people first, and figure out the economics later. Aronofsky clearly had a bright future ahead of him, and Artisan was content to let him "just get this story out of his system."

And luckily he did, because it ended up being an important film featuring powerful insights into the nature of addiction and the mental problems that precipitate it and exacerbate it. To call it cautionary is really an understatement, but the caution is not against taking the drugs themselves, but rather the tragic mindsets of the people who indulge in them. Aronofsky taps into a basic human foible we all have: the endless capacity for self-delusion. It's usually a victimless crime. Everybody lies to themselves to one degree or another. Avoiding blame, or the need to qualify your existence, is one of the many inherent biases people have as they try to navigate through the complexities of life. But when coupled with addictive substances, self-delusion becomes weaponized to such a degree that its sufferers are no longer inhabiting the same universe as the rest of us. This is the universe Aronofsky set out to explore.

From the opening minute of the film, you know you're going to be in for a distressing experience. Not so much from the visuals, although yes, you're about to get assaulted by them too. More so by the haunting music score by Clint Mansell and his Kronos Quartet. Deep and somber cellos and high-pitched violins mixed with electronic beat tracks and sampling effects create a symphonic hellscape within which no good can come. It *sounds* like a Greek or Shakespearean tragedy, and all we can do is sit back and watch fate run its terrible course.

Aronofsky tells the story through three interlaced narratives. The first is centered around Harry (played by Jared Leto), a "good kid" from Brooklyn who periodically visits his elderly mother, Sara (played by Ellen Burstyn, who was nominated for an Academy Award for her performance). What's heartbreaking is that this "good kid" isn't there to actually visit his mother, he's there to try to steal her television set so he can score some heroin. Sarah has already put locks on the door to stop him from robbing her blind. But she's so lonely and desperate for company that she'll let him take the TV, only to buy it back from the same pawn shop after he unloads it, as she has many times before.

Harry's girlfriend Marion, played by the frequently underrated actress Jennifer Connelly, is the centerpiece of the film's second storyline. She's also a "good girl" who's pretty, clever, and has limitless potential. The problem is, she's in a ménage-à-trois with Harry and his heroin addiction. Connelly is a method actress, and to prepare for the role she attended Narcotics Anonymous meetings, talked to addicts, and isolated herself in an apartment she rented on location.

Similarly, Jared Leto and his heroin dealing sidekick Marlon Wayans (playing the role of Tyrone) both lost substantial amounts of weight and swore off sex and sugar in order to appear haggard and desperate. In Marion's case, she looks more motivationally emaciated than anything else. Aronofsky paints her as a party girl who's leveraged her looks to move ahead in her world. But, as a result, that world ultimately views her as a commodity. Much more so as the story progresses, her addiction to heroin worsens, and the compromises she's willing to make to avoid withdrawal become increasingly dangerous and perverse.

The third storyline, involving Harry's mother Sara Goldfarb (Burstyn), is the most harrowing of the three—in my opinion—and could have formed the basis of an utterly depressing film in and of itself. Her journey downhill begins when she receives a call to tell her she's been selected to appear on a TV show. She's elated, suddenly validated as a human being. "I'm gonna be on television," she proudly tells Harry. But the "TV show" is nothing more than a 24-hour infomercial scam to hawk a motivational program hosted by gaudy pitchman Tappy Tibbons (played by the always kinda creepy Christopher McDonald). The only thing separating her from her 15 minutes of fame is a red dress that's too tight to fit into.

And so everyone's slow descent into the hell of addiction begins. It starts innocuously at first. Always does. Harry and Tyrone seem to have their shit together, dealing some small quantities of heroin on the streets of Brooklyn, staying relatively clean. Then they get handed the opportunity to sell a large supply of heroin for a local dealer. Things are looking up. Money starts flowing in. Aronofsky's editor Jay Rabinowitz wonderfully captures their manic activity with hundreds of jump cuts and split screens (the average movie contains 500 cuts;

Requiem for a Dream has over 2,000) as they ply their trade at a corner food stall. But the guys can't help themselves; they break the cardinal rule of drug dealing: Never get high on your own supply.

With enough cash flow left over after shooting up, Harry can now buy his poor mom a big screen TV, take Marion out on dates, and rent an apartment. Harry and Marion can live like "normal" people. But "normal" to them includes heroin. Aronofsky renders this stage of their downward spiral through the rose-colored glasses of heroin-addict fantasyland: glamor shots of blissful walks on the pier, lying together on the grass, looking deeply into each other's eyes, both professing deep love to the other—all precious moments made better (or possible?) with heroin.

It's at this point, when they feel the happiest, that addiction fantasyland fully subsumes reality. Harry and Marion actually believe their perfect life with heroin can continue forever. In fact, their perfect life *requires* heroin. But they're not unique in thinking this. All other addicts on the planet share some aspects of this delusion to some degree. The heavy drinker who manages to hold down a great six-figure job and provide for his family also thinks he can do this forever. Cocaine and meth addicts buy into the idea that using gives them a competitive edge in the workplace. In my own case, I happily bought into the notion that heavy drinking with fellow producers and screenwriters would help advance my career in Hollywood. But this kind of thinking is clearly ridiculous. Put in another context, it's like a serial killer imagining he can engage in a lifelong crime spree without ever getting caught.

Similarly, Sara begins to live in a fantasyland, albeit of a different sort. She's become addicted to an idea, a delusion, not a substance. But that will change shortly. The notion of appearing on television has legitimized her existence, given her a purpose, earned her status among her elderly widowed friends. She visits a doctor to help her lose weight so she can fit into that red dress. She begins taking "diet pills," ostensibly uppers or Fen-Phen, or perhaps some sort of amphetamine. One pill still leaves her hungry, so she doubles the dose. She begins to lose some weight. Paranoia sets in. Her refrigerator and TV come alive and attack her. It's literally dieting hell, rendered masterfully by Aronofsky's go-to cinematographer Matthew Libatique via distorted lenses, unsettling camera angles, and timelapse photography.

Things eventually go south for Harry, Tyrone, and Marion when their main heroin wholesaler gets killed. Supplies around the city dry up. Their business implodes. Withdrawal and desperation set in. And it's at this point of the downward spiral that Aronofsky deftly lays bare one of the most sinister parts about addiction fantasyland—the act of doubling down. Some call it the Gambler's Fallacy[9]. It's that point in addiction where, despite all reason and experience, the addict truly believes that something unprecedented will happen and turn everything around; much like a gambler believes his luck will suddenly change.

There's no going back. Only forward. The pain of not using (in the gambler's case, folding) seems so unbearable that all the misery that will come from continuation actually seems endurable, even magically surmountable. But this requires that additional delusions be layered on top of the ones that already exist. Terrible compromises must be made, leading to even greater erosion of the addict's last remaining self-respect and human dignity. The downward spiral is now a black hole. No logic or reason can escape.

With heroin unavailable to even those who have money to buy it, Marion must resort to bartering her body to procure it. Sleeping with a sugar daddy, or a random drug dealer—a non-starter only a few days earlier—suddenly seems like a perfectly good idea. Again, the pain of not using seems worse than the degradation of sleeping with men she finds physically repulsive. Even Harry's natural feelings of jealousy

---

[9] The very human tendency to continue a course of action because so much has already been invested in it, even though the odds of success are slim.

seem like the lesser of two evils. Not only does he have to endure Marion prostituting herself; he must also live with the guilt of having convinced her to do so to begin with. This episode in Marion's story only hints at the degradation many addicted women must submit to in real life in order to feed their habit. Few filmmakers have dared to explore this sad dynamic.

Sara's choice between the lesser of two evils is more complex. Harry, Tyrone, and Marion are young. They can choose to quit heroin and live a life full of whatever meaning they can find or create. But Sara is old. She had already bought into the delusion that her life was meaningless before getting that phone call from the infomercial producers. Addiction to uppers is just an unfortunate accident brought on by a careless doctor who over-prescribed. Is Sara wrong to think she's reached her metaphysical sell-by date? Some facts can't be sugar-coated. She's lonely. Has nobody to care for, nobody to care for her. Nobody visits her. Why wash the dishes? Why make the bed? What's the point of continuing to live at all?

Ellen Burstyn's monologue as she poses these questions to Harry is among the saddest moments ever committed to film, and probably the reason why she was nominated for an Oscar. But, as tragic as it sounds, Sara's position is not too far removed from reality. Many older people decide that the effort to find any motivation or create new sources of meaning in their lives is simply too much work. You don't find a lot of self-help books in nursing homes. In the year before her death, my own mother—a very religious person—asked me: "Why am I still here? I've lived a great life. What else does life expect of me?" I would try to give her a pep talk about all of life's infinite possibilities, but even I didn't believe what I was saying.

You can find the same form of defeatism in many individuals in advanced stages of addiction. At a local park here in Southern California where I live, I would frequently chat with a homeless man named Chris. His addiction to alcohol had completely destroyed his marriage and career. He admitted as much. Each time he wound up in the hospital with alcohol poisoning, social workers would offer him an apartment, job training, and all manner of recovery services. I tried to help him imagine a future where he could be a happy, healthy, engaged member of society and develop a feeling of purpose and meaning. Chris' response each time was the same: "It's just too much work." Chris had made a rational decision that his eventual death due to alcohol was the lesser of two evils. And he got his wish a few months later.

Having made essentially the same decision as Chris, all of **Requiem for a Dream's** characters' fortunes go from bad to worse. If you have seen the film, you know I can't do justice in summarizing how horribly it all plays out. And if you haven't seen the film, be forewarned that it's difficult to watch. Each character holds on to their delusions all the way to the bitter end, until their lives collide head-on with reality. It's tragic. But unlike in classical Greek tragedy, the outcomes were not pre-ordained by fate. Each of the characters had several opportunities to act differently, but their delusions were too pleasant to abandon. They weren't just addicted to drugs; they were addicted to their false realities. And this is what Aronofsky apparently set out to explore by making this film:

> *Requiem for a Dream is not about heroin or about drugs. The Harry-Tyrone-Marion story is a very traditional heroin story. But putting it side by side with the Sara story, we suddenly say, "Oh, my God, what is a drug?" The idea that the same inner monologue goes through a person's head when they're trying to quit drugs, as with cigarettes, as when they're trying to not eat food so they can lose 20 pounds, was really fascinating to me. I thought it was an idea that we hadn't seen on film and I wanted to bring it up on the screen.*

If ***Requiem for a Dream*** doesn't make you uneasy about getting addicted to heroin, probably nothing will. And although making a cautionary tale about heroin wasn't Aronofsky's primary intent, the film graphically illustrates just some of its disastrous consequences. But did it move the needle when it came to lessening the amount of new heroin converts? We'll probably never know. Did Nancy Reagan's "Just Say No" campaign curb drug use in the '80s? No, quite the opposite. Films can certainly take on the role of public service campaigns, but that doesn't mean they *should*. ***Triumph of the Will*** was a public service campaign after all.

I don't know whether high schools do this anymore, but back in the '80s as part of driver's ed class we had to sit through blood-soaked footage of fatal car crashes caused by drunk drivers. I'm sure it made some people think twice. But scare tactics can also backfire. Tell a teenager they can't do something and it often makes them want to do it even more. Remember the Law of Unintended Consequences? ***Reefer Madness*** utterly failed to scare American youth about the dangers of pot, and instead became a sexploitation flick. A few decades later it became a midnight movie cult classic that inspired a whole generation to toke up and laugh themselves silly. ***Trainspotting*** actually made me want to try heroin. But the film also reminded me how I would be surrendering my life to the drug if I did so. At the end of the day, there's little evidence to prove that cautionary films about addiction make people stop using drugs, any more so than ***Jaws*** made people swear off swimming or ***Alien*** made people sour on intergalactic space travel.

Another question is whether graphic depictions of drug use are helpful in any cautionary context. Shows like ***Intervention*** have made "addict porn" into more of a carnival sideshow than a serious exploration of how to help people recover from addiction. It's like stopping to gawk at that traffic accident on the 405 Freeway I alluded to in the Introduction. Sure, it piques your curiosity, but does it make you a better driver? Graphic depictions also further reinforce unhelpful stereotypes about addicted individuals, leading to further stigmatization. Scare tactics can seem useful at the time, but as **Reefer Madness** shows, when they are coupled with a political agenda with racist underpinnings, they can also create tremendous collateral damage.

Regardless, we are all fortunate that films and TV shows have been (and will continue to be) produced that explore addiction and recovery from a balanced, well-informed, unsanctimonious point of view. If they didn't, this book would be a pretty brisk read. Cautionary films may or may not be the best way of achieving this, so cautionary films should be viewed…well, with caution.

CHAPTER 5
God It's Tough Being a Supermodel
Gia

If you're jonesing for some hardcore '80s visual nostalgia, scenes of everybody doing blow at Studio 54, a killer '80s MTV soundtrack, and generous amounts of full-frontal nudity, look no further than 1998's ***Gia***—an HBO film based on the true story of supermodel Gia Carangi. It's an emotionally powerful period drama, and a perennially relevant cautionary tale about how a simple coping mechanism can turn into a macro-addiction and kill the person you'd least expect to have a problem.

Gia is a young lady from a lower-middle-class-home in Philly who skyrockets to international fame and fortune and becomes the first "supermodel." Then loses it all to heroin. Carangi is played superbly by Angelina Jolie, a role which made her into a superstar.

As previously noted, actors and actresses assume huge risks when they take on these kinds of roles, but the payoffs can be massive. And playing Gia certainly became a career windfall for Jolie. Few people could have predicted that she would eventually catapult to her current level of stardom. Yeah, she was beautiful, and talented, and it didn't hurt that she was Jon Voight's daughter. (I actually interviewed Voight at the 1989 Deauville American Film Festival when I was a TV reporter. He was delightfully insane.)

Four years after meeting Voight, I interacted with his daughter Angelina briefly during the sale of **Cyborg 2**, her first real movie gig. This is back when I worked for an international film distribution company. Note to the gentle reader: There are only three Great Satans in the world: Organized Crime, Scientific Illiteracy, and International Film Distributors. At any rate, nobody thought Jolie would make it. I can't say I did either. But **Gia** proved us all very wrong.

The film is a wonderful representation of what I call the "Poor Billionaire's Dilemma." Movies in this category include **A Star is Born** (all four versions, which we'll review later), **Walk the Line**, and **Ray**, among others. The central construct is that, for some people—despite the fame and fortune and plethora of God-given talents they possess—life is still monumentally unsatisfying for them. Interesting, right? Because if making $100,000 a second, flying to exotic destinations on a G5, and having millions of fans love and adore you is your definition of unsatisfying, I'm dying to know what you consider "satisfying."

But therein lies the point. Nothing will ever satisfy some people. At least nothing in the material world. Hence they need drugs and/or alcohol to fill the void. And hence a movie like **Gia**.

I must admit, watching **Gia** made me wax nostalgic. I need to come clean. I was a male model in the late '80s. Exactly like Gia, except I didn't make nearly as much money, and I didn't take heroin. And, yes, what you've heard is all true. But since I don't know what you've heard, I'll just say modeling makes no demands on your intellect, strains your patience, and thoroughly decimates your feelings of self-worth. On the flip-side, the money is ridiculous. Graduate school at USC is really expensive. I paid for my whole master's degree with one TV commercial.

I might as well make another confession: I was a "Booker." No, not a "Hooker," a "Booker." A "flesh-peddler" for a modeling agency in Madrid. So Gia's story is familiar to me, and I felt a great deal of empathy for her as I read about her decline in real life, and as I watched her spiral in the film decades later. I'll get to some of the challenges that may have led to Gia's heroin addiction, but for now just know this about models: Parading around semi-naked, along with 100 other pretty girls, like chattel, in front of a sleazy photographer—the only person standing between you and a hot meal—has got to take a toll on anyone's mental health. Especially a girl who's body conscious.

Gia made it through these indignities and found great success. But that doesn't mean she wasn't affected by them. Modeling and acting can take a personal toll in other ways besides the objectification of one's body. Gia, clearly a highly intelligent and prideful young woman, is told early on by her agent and mentor, Wilhelmina Cooper (played by the always amazing Faye Dunaway[10]): "Talking in this profession is not encouraged." This can't be a positive thing to internalize, any more than an actor—even a superstar—realizing that they are never paid to speak their own words, but rather words written for them.

As a TV reporter (yes, I have worn many hats in my career) I often interviewed movie stars during press junkets for the upcoming release of their films. Often these stars had "minders" around to make sure they didn't say things that would hurt the film or tarnish the brand. Things like how they were really feeling, or what they really thought about the film they were mindlessly promoting. Think about this for a

---

10 Faye Dunaway is a lovely person in person. I met her at Cannes several times, had cocktails, and she was always so pleased to see me and tell me her crazy Hollywood stories.

second. A person whose job it is to make sure an actor or actress never acts like themselves.

And it's because actors—and models—are not paid to think. But to think is to live. And as one of Gia's photographers and mentors said after noticing her disaffection with her modeling career midway through the film, "Work now; live later." It's an interesting aphorism for the rest of us to consider carefully as well, lest we become one of those people who, as Thoreau said, "lead lives of quiet desperation."

The filmmakers manage to make Gia appear quite sympathetic from the get-go. This is no easy task given that a large part of her allure and success was due to her outlandish (sometimes obnoxious) behavior. The future supermodel's fractured childhood is told in flashback with a splendid Mila Kunis as a younger Gia,[11] playing opposite the always excellent but frequently off-kilter Mercedes Ruehl as Gia's mom Kathleen Carangi.

Gia's parents, Kathleen and her husband Louis (both portrayed as heavy drinkers), have terrible fights in front of their daughter, and Gia's mother eventually leaves. This appears to generate strong abandonment issues for Gia that will surface later on in the film. We can add this to the list of possible factors that led to her eventual addiction to heroin.

We are also told by narrators early in the film that Gia hated people taking photographs of her. If this was true, the rest of this poor woman's life in front of the cameras 12 hours a day, 360 days a year, was probably a complete nightmare. Add this to the list as well.

Next, we can add ambiguous sexuality. The film doesn't mince frames in showing us Gia's preference for women—or sex in general for that matter—although those same narrators tell us that "it was never about sex" with Gia. Which is strange, because her first amateur photo shoot turns into a threesome with her milquetoast "boyfriend"

---

[11] Kunis holds the record for the actress appearing in the most films discussed in this book.

Cole and another girl. And then another guy. Her first professional photo shoot—the one that would eventually rocket her to fame—starts innocently enough with her standing naked behind a wire gate, then goes all in flagrante delicto with her and a designer named Linda, played by Elizabeth Mitchell (of subsequent **Lost** TV fame).

Gia's relationship with Linda is the emotional centerpiece of the film, but Linda is a closeted lesbian (or perhaps bisexual) who has a boyfriend and can't be with Gia in the way she would like. Add the pain of unrequited love to the list of factors contributing to Gia's addiction. As a narrator reminds us of the period, "sex was easy; it was love that was hard to find."

To this must be added the stress Gia likely felt in having to hide her true sexuality—in all of its diverse expressions. As much as the film may try to show us how permissive the late '80s was when it came to same-sex attraction, remember that Ellen's coming out on primetime TV was still a decade away—and I can tell you from professional experience that nobody at that time would book a $1-million-an-hour supermodel who was an avowed lesbian.

Even though we know there won't be a happy ending here, it's fun to watch Gia go from rags to riches. She moves to New York and gets a snazzy apartment, but barely furnishes it because she's never there. She buys herself an MG convertible, but rarely drives it because she's always stuck on first class flights going to international photo shoots. I know, life is rough.

But as her success increases, so do the demands. Early on, Gia's agent Wilhelmina gives her Nembutal to help her sleep before a big photo shoot. For those who don't follow this kind of stuff, Nembutal is a little pill, also known as Pentobarbital, and it is a barbiturate. Later, Gia transitions to cocaine—like practically everyone else—when she parties at Studio 54. Heroin is quick to follow—first as a snort in the back of a limo after a long day making too much money, then "chasing the dragon" (smoking it) alone in her apartment, and eventually taking it intravenously in a back alley with homeless people.

And to think this whole human tragedy may have started with *one* little sleeping pill. But the thing is, that's usually how it happens.

Inevitable decline follows, and while it was fun to watch her rise, it's difficult to watch her fall. But I think it's important for audiences to see how it plays out. Carangi becomes model kryptonite. Nobody will hire her. And like so many people macro-addicted to drugs, she tries to kick the habit. She moves in with her mother, she's reduced to working retail, goes to a methadone clinic, goes to mutual support meetings, and does the hard work of recovery. We see her trying. We want her to succeed.

But it's obviously not easy. Living with your mom? Trigger. Folding clothes at The Gap? Probably another trigger. Going to meetings? Made me want to relapse. Total trigger. Like in a brutal scene at a Narcotics Anonymous meeting, where one of the female participants rips Gia a new one for simply doing her job. She's accused of being a walking poster child for a venal modeling industry that profits from negative body images and causes body dysmorphia.

Can't say I disagree.

Sadly (or inevitably?) Gia relapses. Again and again. She tries to reclaim the love that was denied to her by Linda, who by now has come out and no longer has a boyfriend. But in a sad yet telling scene, Linda can only offer Gia a simple choice: me or heroin. Guess who wins.

At this point, Gia's kinda-boyfriend Cole tries to stage an intervention by showing up at her apartment—only to find it, and her, in pestilent disrepair. She offers to have sex with him in exchange for a few bucks to buy smack. It's a sad precursor to what is rumored to have happened to Carangi in real life as she was reduced to prostitution to support her habit in its end stages.

Speaking of end stages, Gia also contracts AIDS from a dirty needle. At the time, she was the first female celebrity to get this (then) mysterious disease, alongside male celebrities like Rock Hudson and

Freddie Mercury. This fact alone—and not her heroin addiction—is probably (and sadly) the reason why she's remembered in popular culture at all. She died too early to leave any real legacy besides the pointlessness of her death. But all AIDS-related deaths were—and are—pointless.

Looking back at Carangi's life, it's hard to explain why she derailed so spectacularly. It's a cliché to say this, but she literally Had It All. In a parallel world she never took the Red Pill (a supposedly innocent little Nembutal). She never became a heroin addict. She went on to an amazing career in acting. And she became a strong, heroic voice for charitable causes around the world. Much like the little-known actress I met 35 years ago named Angelina Jolie who went on to prove everybody wrong.

But that's not what happened. Gia *did* take the Red Pill. But is that pill at fault? No. The pill is just a pill. Gia's addiction seems to have been "caused" or "hastened" (I need to choose my words carefully here) by a myriad of factors. Also, keep in mind that the reasons people start using are different than why they keep using. They keep using because they get hooked.

But it's worth taking a closer look as to the "why's." On one level we have Gia's fractured childhood. A lot of people have a fractured childhood, even a horribly abusive childhood, but they don't become addicted to drugs. I had an amazing, totally unfractured childhood, and yet I ended up addicted to alcohol. So let's scratch that from the list. And basically everybody I know has some abandonment issues in their story. Maybe it's just feeling lonely. So let's strike that too.

Sexual identity issues? No disagreement there. Closeted gay teens are a gazillion times more likely than their non-gay peers to become homeless, self-injure (cutting, burning, etc.), and commit suicide. But many people have successfully come out as gay and lived to tell the tale. In fact, some might say Carangi's ambiguous sexuality actually helped her career in some respects. Unlike with men, fluid female sexuality can be seen as open-minded and "progressive" by the culture generally, and highly popular with the millions of "straight" men who watch girl-on-girl porn specifically.

This brings us back to the "Poor Billionaire's Dilemma." Gia had wealth and celebrity, arguably two of the most coveted commodities in the known universe besides a stable Wifi connection. Sure, she had a few emotional issues, and came from a broken home. But so do many people. So why her?

But the bigger question should be: Why *not* her?

We see over and over how macro-addiction is an equal opportunity affliction. Plenty of billionaires have drinking problems. I know some. Plenty of millionaires have compulsive gambling problems and are no longer millionaires as a result. An overwhelming majority of SuperLotto winners report major depression, and some even commit suicide after becoming instant millionaires.

The larger issue **Gia** also has us consider is that regardless of how little the rich and famous seem to deserve any sympathy, they need it just as much as anyone else. Addiction doesn't discriminate; why should we?

Gia's mentor tells her repeatedly, "You have everything; you have nothing." So perhaps remember that no matter how much money or how many Instagram followers you have, you can always fall prey to that harshest critic, that bad influence your parents always warned you about, that most cruel of mistresses: *yourself.*

CHAPTER 6
Mammas Don't Let Your Babies Grow Up to be Country Music Stars
Crazy Heart
A Star is Born

The question is as old as time and will never be answered: Does art imitate life, or does life mimic art? Posed differently for the purposes of this chapter: Does listening to country music make people sad, or do they listen to country music *because* they're sad? The correlation between country music and ennui is not just the butt of jokes but also a well-researched cultural phenomenon. A study of 49 metropolitan areas showed that among white people the more time people spent listening to country music, the higher the suicide rate.

There are books and articles going back decades that talk about how country music's popularity derived from white lower middle class social angst, economic uncertainty, marital infidelity, alienation at work, and alcohol abuse. The correlation between country music and alcohol was memorialized in Hank Williams' famous song *There's a Tear in My Beer* which he recorded in 1951 and was released posthumously by his son in 1989. Williams died in 1953 at the tender age of 29 of a heart attack brought on by years of alcohol and drug abuse.

In any other societal context, Williams' death would be seen as a cautionary tale about the dangers of alcohol addiction. But the United States is not your typical societal context. The principle of "American Exceptionalism" mixed with the oft-cited Law of Unintended Consequences meant that alcohol would become a celebrated—and even foundational—part of country music as an art form. The so-called "Hank Williams Syndrome" was nothing short of the mythologizing of alcoholism itself. Notable country stars like Waylon Jennings and Keith Whitley paid the ultimate price. Said Whitley once, "You couldn't put that soul into your singing unless you were three sheets to the wind." It's like walking into a burning building with a smile on your face.

Sadly, Jennings' and Whitley's untimely deaths only enhanced their hard drinkin' bad boy cult status, with most up-and-coming country music performers under pressure to emulate their behavior in order to achieve success. They don't just have to drink a lot of alcohol—they have to sing about it too. A study found that over 40% of country songs mention alcohol in their lyrics. Two content analysis studies done by Northwestern University and Johns Hopkins found that country music songs have the second highest level of mentions of alcohol (after hip-hop). But you can't blame the performers. Alcohol brands are their willing enablers. Country concert acts today have multi-million-dollar sponsorship deals with beer and hard liquor companies. Country stars like Blake Shelton, who claims publicly that he "never drinks vodka before noon," own their own liquor brands and bar chains.

To explore the unhealthy relationship between alcohol and country music, let's discuss two exceptional films: **Crazy Heart** and **A Star is**

Born (the Bradley Cooper/Lady Gaga version). The central character in each film is addicted to alcohol, but for very different reasons and at very different points in their respective careers. ***A Star Is Born's*** Jackson Maine—played by Bradley Cooper—is at the height of his country music career, playing to thousands of devoted fans in sold-out stadiums. In contrast, ***Crazy Heart's*** Otis "Bad" Blake—played by Jeff Bridges—is desperately clinging to what's left of his career, barely able to fill bowling alleys and seedy back-country bars.

What I find interesting here is how these contrasting stories allow us to study the role alcohol plays in coping with musical success and/or failure in the booze-soaked world of country music specifically, but also in the performing arts and celebrity culture in general.

Crazy Heart was theatrically released in 2009. Written and directed by Scott Cooper (no relation to Bradley), and based on the eponymous 1987 novel by Thomas Cobb, the film is a now-all-too-rare example of how one lucky film screening can change the course of movie history, especially for the film's star—in this case, Jeff Bridges. ***Crazy Heart*** was originally planned as a direct-to-video/cable release by Paramount, owners of the film's production company, Country Music Television. At that stage of a film's exploitation cycle, it is very rare for a distributor to step in and purchase theatrical rights. Video and cable revenues were already spoken for and could not be used to amortize the cost of an expensive theatrical run.

But Searchlight Pictures—a 20th Century Fox division known for taking gambles on high quality "boutique" films—attended a screening hosted by ICM, the film's packaging and sales agent, and realized the film had Oscar potential. And they[12] were right. The film ended up earning respectable box office revenues in a market saturated

---

12 I worked with Searchlight executives on several film projects, including ***Snowflower and the Secret Fan***, which I associate produced. I have to say they were the nicest, smartest, gutsiest bunch of people I ever ran across over my 20 years in Hollywood.

by big studio tentpole titles, as well as a Best Actor Oscar for Jeff Bridges.

Bridges plays Otis "Bad" Blake, a country music crooner whose best days as a songwriter and performer are behind him. He drives an old truck from one crappy gig to another, survives paycheck to paycheck, and imprisons himself with a cheap bottle of whiskey in a different ugly motel room every night. He's broken, cynical, and totally alone. Bridges inhabits the rough-scrabble personality so completely it's hard to imagine anyone else playing the role. His performance is the perfect balance of quiet confidence and nonchalance with an irascible edginess and vulnerability. Whereas hard drinking may have once been a critical part of his popular appeal, now it's a major handicap that has destroyed his ability to write new songs and renders his performances sloppy and painful to watch.

But his audiences still seem to love him. Drunk and all. Probably because they're just as blasted as he is. As long as Bad can keep a tune and remember the lyrics, the pickup bands at each gig are sober and professional enough to belt out his popular favorites. And the hard-drinkin' country star mythology is the perfect cover if he flubs a song. To a point. And Bad is reaching that point. They're not difficult songs, mind you, and he's played them a billion times. It seems to boil down to the "soulful" delivery. And people certainly feel more "soulful" when they're blitzed. Perhaps Keith Whitley was right: You need to be drunk to play country music. My mother said you'd have to be drunk just to listen to it.

Mom also shared a wonderful Castilian saying with me: "Once you get famous, you can go to sleep."[13] Bad's previous fame earned him near-legendary status, so there's really little additional effort required to keep his career alive, and no incentive to quit drinking—even though it is slowly destroying his life. In fact, the mythology demands that he *keep* drinking. But fame is not a perpetual motion

---

13 The exact quote in Spanish is "*Créate fama y échate a dormir.*"

machine. The second law of thermodynamics still applies. Disorder (entropy) must always increase over time. Fame inevitably dissolves. And nothing hastens dissolution quite like alcohol. It is, after all, a solvent.

Fate throws Bad the first of several lifelines in the form of Jean, played by Maggie Gyllenhaal, a single mother who wants to write an article about him for a local newspaper. Gyllenhaal plays the role to perfection. She appears naive enough to have bought into the whole country music bad boy mythology and finds it seductive. But she also conveys the seriousness of a single mom who recently dumped her husband because of his drinking. She has everything to lose by falling in love with Bad, knows exactly what she's getting herself into, but walks right into that burning building anyway. Countless women (and men) do the same thing in real life all the time. She literally likes "Bad" boys.

As Jean's relationship with Bad deepens, her newspaper interview becomes a device for us to find out more about how he got to this sad point in his life. A spate of broken marriages, a son he never knew, and unrequited dreams of pro baseball superstardom. Because those who can, do. Those who can't play pro baseball become country music stars. It seems silly and ironic to feel sorry for a guy who had to "settle" for fame and fortune, especially given the extraordinary focus, luck, and determination required to achieve these things to begin with. But that's one of the cruel ironies of life, isn't it? No matter what we get, we *always* feel that we want more. Elon Musk isn't going to wake up some morning and think, "Wow, I've achieved everything I ever wanted in life. Time to clock out." Is Bad, holed up with his whiskey bottle in an ugly hotel room, really any different? No, but Musk probably doesn't drown whatever sorrows he may have in alcohol, either. Bad could make better a choices for how to cope with his lost dreams, yet he chooses to self-medicate with alcohol.

While Jean uses Bad to get a newspaper article and some casual sex, Bad uses Jean to "play normal"—i.e. ignore the billion pound elephant in the room and pretend to be a normal person doing normal things. Like being a pretend boyfriend who's kind and attentive to help him forget the last four marriages where he wasn't. He strikes up a sweet relationship with Jean's four-year-old son, Buddy.

He gets to be a pretend father and have a pretend son to distract himself from the fact that he hasn't seen his real son in a quarter century. But he's living in sobriety fantasyland. A delusion. Yes, he's currently sober. And "normal." But both these states are unsustainable. So he doubles down on the delusion. He can be even better at being normal *if* he drinks. But Bad's pink cloud will instantly evaporate the minute he does. And he'll end up right where he started: drunk and alone.

But fate intervenes with another lifeline in the form of Tommy Sweet, Bad's former bandmate and now a huge country music star in his own right. Tommy is played by Colin Farrell, an unlikely choice given he's Irish. But Farrell pulls it off brilliantly, country twang and all. Bad is offered the chance to be the opening act for Sweet, and initially refuses, until his agent (played by the wonderfully quirky Paul Herman) convinces him to put his vanity aside.

Tommy is incredibly gracious, publicly credits Bad for helping launch his career, and even sings a duet with him. Best of all, he hires Bad to write new songs for him. It's really nice to see country stars looking out for each other, and I'm told this kind of camaraderie exists in real life too. Perhaps it's why duets are so common in that industry. I think it's a wholesome distraction away from the blood feuds fans are subjected to in the rock and hip-hop industries.

With renewed validation of his talents as a songwriter, plus the income to match, plus a beautiful (much younger) girlfriend, Bad's fortunes appear to have turned. But as Louis Pasteur once said, "Fortune favors the prepared mind." Alcohol is so ingrained in his day-to-day reality that Bad's simply not in the head space to fully appreciate the breaks life has given him. Or perhaps he feels he didn't earn them or doesn't deserve them (more on that in a bit). Either way, instead of gratitude and calm, his brain only knows urgency and want. He gets drunk, drives his truck off the side of the road, and gets seriously injured.

But ironically, fate throws him a third lifeline: an understanding of his own mortality. While in the hospital the physician makes it very clear that Bad needs to quit drinking and smoking and lose 25 pounds or he won't make it a day past 60 (he's 57 then). You'll frequently find people in recovery saying that a terrible traffic accident or arrest or health scare was the best thing that could have ever happened to them. And assuming nobody else was hurt in the process, perhaps that's true in some circumstances. But addiction professionals will also tell you that an individual's greatest odds of long-term recovery success are when they actively choose to stop drinking instead of the choice being forced upon them. As we'll discuss in other chapters, this may partly explain the high relapse and recycle rates of individuals (especially the young) who have been subjected to interventions and forced into rehab, however well-intentioned the aims of the people who orchestrated them.

In Bad's case, the accident does give him some food for thought. Great. But thoughts don't always lead to decisions, and even less so to concrete actions. And actions are the only stable currency that matters here. At this point in the story, Bad knows full well he has to stop drinking, but he can't. Or won't. So once again, he pretends his way through life. He invites Jean and Buddy to come stay with him and play "pretend family." But he can't even last an afternoon out at the park with Buddy without getting the shakes and hitting the hip flask upon his return home. He reaches out to his estranged son who he hasn't spoken to in 25 years, pretending he suddenly cares about him and now wants a relationship. But he doesn't understand that (un) loved ones don't suddenly forgive a lifetime of neglect just because you randomly pick up the phone and ask them to.

Bad's sobriety fantasyland eventually comes crashing down when he loses track of Buddy at a mall because he's too busy getting drunk at a bar. Jean's been to this barbecue too many times. Burned once, shame on him. Burned twice, shame on her. She bails before hers and Buddy's lives go up in flames along with Bad's. And as is so common in these kinds of rock bottoms, Bad leverages his resulting pain into yet *another* reason to self-medicate so he doesn't have to feel the loss. In a rare moment of clarity after waking up on the floor covered in his own vomit, he reaches out to his friend Wayne, played by Robert Duvall, and finally declares, "I want to get sober."

Wayne now becomes a pivotal character in the story, and although Duvall has relatively few lines in the whole movie, every ounce of dialogue that comes out of his mouth is immensely powerful. Duvall has the same gravitas in real life, too. I had the pleasure of interviewing him at the Deauville American Film Festival for a Spanish TV show I was producing (where I also interviewed Jon Voight). Here's a guy who's been through the Hollywood meat grinder for half a century, and yet he never loses hope that film can be an instrument of transformative change. It's probably the reason he produced this film and was instrumental in its development and financing. His simple yet profound advice to Bad in his rare moment of clarity is, "It's never too late."

I believe truer words have never been spoken, both when it comes to recovery specifically and overcoming any of life's challenges in general. Entropy and dissolution can always be reversed; it just takes a little bit of elbow grease and good fortune (for the prepared mind).

The third act of the film sees Bad checking himself into rehab and doing the hard work of recovery. He changes his name to Otis, his given name, as a way to move beyond the hard-drinking country legend persona he's used to justify his behavior throughout his hard drinking career. He unconditionally accepts himself, his life, and others in it. Yes, he still has regrets, but he'll learn how to process them. He realizes—contrary to Hank Williams Syndrome and country music mythology—that he doesn't need to get drunk to be a great songwriter and performer. And when Wayne picks him up after his stint in rehab, he's reminded that although there will still be rough roads ahead, he has friends who care about him. Fans who care about him. And a universe willing to give him anything as long as he cares about himself.

Sound too much like a Hollywood ending? Sure. In real life the odds of a guy like Bad succeeding at sobriety are depressingly slim. But life is full of outliers. Without them we wouldn't experience miracles. Thomas Cobb, the author of the book upon which the film is based, wrote a completely different ending. In the film, Bad's career is back on track, his songwriting royalty checks are pouring in, and his manager is booking new concert gigs aplenty. He meets up with Jean after a concert, and realizes she's remarried and moved on with her life. And that's okay. Them's the breaks. But in the book, Bad relapses, has a heart attack, and dies. Yes, the book version is way more plausible, but plausible can be rather depressing, and glimmers of hope in the form of great movie endings like **Crazy Heart's** can go a really long way in inspiring people to follow a great example.

A Star Is Born is based on a timeless story of love, redemption, and self-destruction. So timeless, in fact, that a total of four iterations of the film have been made over the years—most recently 2018's Bradley Cooper/Lady Gaga version. The story stayed basically the same through all four versions, although Lady Gaga and Cooper's version is set in the world of country music. It's arguably the best if you factor in the number of Academy Award nominations it received.

Personally, I prefer the Kris Kristofferson/Barbra Streisand version. Kristofferson was a real life alcoholic rockstar playing a movie alcoholic rockstar, and he inhabits the role as completely as Bridges does in ***Crazy Heart***. It was also written by the late-great Joan Didion, whose accomplishments as a writer and thinker (and apparently also Hollywood screenwriter) are seldom paralleled. There's a great documentary about her life on Netflix called ***The Center Will Not Hold***.

But there's another reason I prefer the Kristofferson-Streisand version. I vividly remember seeing the film without adult supervision as a naive, impressionable 12-year-old when it was released in 1976. I lived in Seoul, Korea, on a diplomatic compound (my father was a Foreign Service Officer), and the U.S. Army base nearby would screen every single movie made by every Hollywood studio and major independent label, regardless of whether they were R-rated or not. My parents never caught onto this fact, so I saw a lot of things I probably shouldn't have.

One of those things was Kris Kristofferson getting shitfaced and ruining his life. I didn't know that was possible. My parents had been throwing cocktail parties almost every month since I was born. When you're a diplomat, it's a big part of the job. I had no idea alcohol could be a problem. I asked my parents about this. They hemmed and hawed and quickly changed the subject. My curiosity got the better of me, and I ended up getting plastered for my very first time at a friend's New Year's Eve party. So thank you Kris Kristofferson. My former alcohol addiction and the very existence of this book is all your fault.

Addicted in Film

But there was another question I couldn't quite answer. Kristofferson has it all. He's a sold-out rock star. Millions in the bank. Fast cars. Easy access to an abundant supply of beautiful sexual partners. He's even nabbed Babs, for God's sake. *"What the fuck is his problem?"* Same question for Bradley Cooper. As we briefly touched upon in our previous chapter about **Gia**, it's kind of hard to muster up much empathy for incredibly rich, successful people who actively choose to sabotage their careers. I guess there are aspects of the experience that are so utterly horrible they need to self-medicate in order to cope. Demi Lovato and Steven Tyler, I'm talking to you.

The various explanations for why fame presents addiction challenges to rock and hip-hop stars and Hollywood celebrities are non-clinical, anecdotal, and seldom very convincing. There aren't any Hollywood feature films made about this, probably because these kinds of music celebrities would probably rather sell records than their life stories. However, in the documentary space I do highly recommend **Kurt Cobain: Montage of Heck** about Cobain's struggles with stardom and drugs, and **Amy**, about Amy Winehouse's battle with alcohol.[14]

There also aren't any Hollywood movies about Hollywood celebrities auto-destructing either. I suspect this is because Hollywood studios have no interest in biting the hand that feeds them with a roman à clef about themselves. But country music is different. So many addiction tell-alls centered around the industry's hard drinking and drugging mythology came out (**Walk the Line**, **Coal Miner's Daughter**, etc.) that a film parody was produced called **Walk Hard: The Dewey Cox Story**. It's absolutely hilarious.

Whereas alcohol abuse was the cause of (and way to cope with) Bad's waning fame in **Crazy Heart**, Jackson Maine ("Jack") is at the top of his game in **A Star Is Born**. So why is he self-medicating? What's

---

14 Unfortunately Kurt and Amy had to die before anyone could tell that side of their story in film.

his *problem*? The film actually provides very few clues. But those that do emerge are telling. We meet Jack after a sold-out performance attended by thousands of adoring fans. Jack should be happy about this. Ask any performer and they'll usually tell you that—regardless of the size of the audience—it's absolutely amazing to have people clap and cheer after you sing or act or joke your guts out.

It must unleash one of the most powerfully positive feedback loops a brain can experience naturally. But for Jack it doesn't. And that's probably because any feedback loop, repeated enough times, gets old. Jack's built up a tolerance to all the adulation. He'd have to increase the size of his audiences or the frequency of his performances in order to chase the same high. And that's not possible. So he's likely substituted an alcohol feedback loop to supplement or replace the adulation feedback loop that no longer works for him anymore.

But this explanation is too simplistic. We all know there's more to addiction than just feedback loops. Emotions and feelings factor in as well. And the minute Jack's safely ensconced in his limousine and reaches for that bottle of gin, he looks like the loneliest guy in the world. It's the same loneliness Bad experienced in **Crazy Heart**—albeit at the nadir of his career, not the apex. Yes, there are thousands of fans who love Jack, but he doesn't have any real human connection with any of them. They are the "people out there." He is an object to them. A commodity they have bought and paid for. Even trying to get close to his fans physically would be dangerous. Perhaps even deadly. At the height of their fame, I'm quite certain that without protection the Beatles would have been torn into tiny little bloody pieces for teenage girls to treasure as keepsakes.

I experienced something similar in my career as a public speaker (at a significantly lower scale, and minus the part about being torn to pieces). I started out giving a few two-day seminars about film financing to about 20 would-be producers and screenwriters in a small library. I basked in their applause and loved and appreciated all the attention as they asked for help in getting their movie projects financed.

But as my seminars started to catch on and become more popular, the audience sizes grew into the hundreds—the libraries became large auditoriums, and something began to change. I started to become estranged from my audience. One smiling face melded into another. I stopped appreciating or even listening to the applause. The requests for help became tedious and intrusive. I didn't feel like anybody actually liked *me*. I felt they were just focused on what I represented, what I could do to help their careers. I felt objectified. A commodity. And after every seminar, I would take refuge in another ugly, lonely hotel room and drink until I passed out.

If this was my experience on such a modest scale, I can empathize with what celebrities must experience on much larger ones. Many will tell you they feel totally trapped by their fame, living in a bubble. They become the ultimate commodity, a business model, a value proposition, a brand. Everybody wants something from them, and everybody owns a piece of them. Something as banal as going out in public to grab a cup of coffee can be a life-or-death proposition.

The positive feedback loop derived from signing autographs has long since evaporated. It's no surprise that many of these celebrities opt for self-medication with drugs and alcohol, just like Jack does in ***A Star Is Born***. I dated a celebrity once, and she told me flat out that the whole fandom thing sometimes made her feel like she had made a Faustian bargain with the devil. She felt like suicide was her only way out. And, sadly, she successfully pursued this option later in her career.

But there is another aspect of celebrity—or indeed any type of success in life—that factors into Jack's alcohol abuse. It's the so-called "Imposter Syndrome." It becomes apparent when Jack stops at a local drag bar to grab a few drinks and meets Ally (played by Gaga). As they get to know each other, one of Jack's songs pops up in the jukebox. He's ashamed of the song and takes a big gulp of his drink. Like an imposter who has suddenly been exposed, he feels a need to defend his own celebrity: "Talent comes from everywhere, everybody's talented. I bet you, fucking everybody in this bar is talented…"

Jack insists that he's nothing special, a fluke perhaps, undeserving of the success he's achieved. Similarly, in **Crazy Heart** Bad asks Jean whether he is "less than you imagined me to be?"

I've run across the Imposter Syndrome many times in the mutual support meetings I've hosted for SMART Recovery over the years. The story is always the same. A person has achieved success in life, but still feels like they lied, cheated, or stole their way up the ladder—even if they didn't. There's the constant fear—terror sometimes—that someone, somewhere, sometime, likely very soon, will finally expose them as a total fraud. Their whole world will collapse like a house of cards. The constant stress and anxiety these individuals experience is substantial. It's no surprise many of them resort to alcohol or drugs (especially cocaine and meth) to get sudden—albeit artificial—boosts of self-confidence. My own father was a successful diplomat, did his fair share of drinking, and often told me he was just waiting for the other shoe to drop.

Jack finds the perfect antidote for his loneliness and celebrity angst in the form of Ally (Lady Gaga), a wanna-be singer working a dead-end job. She's the perfect mark for Jack—seemingly naive, impressionable, and awed by his celebrity. Or is it Jack who is the perfect mark for Ally? It's not overly cynical to assume Ally latches onto Jack because she knows he can help her career. She's well aware of his drinking problem. She tells her father as much. During their first night together, Jack passes out. It's just the first of many red flags.

She even receives an outright warning about his excessive drinking by his half-brother and tour manager Bobby (played by the perfectly-cast Sam Elliott). And yet, like Jean in **Crazy Heart**, Ally walks right into that burning building with a self-serving smile on her face.

Bobby is a peripheral character in what is predominantly a tragic love story between Jack and Ally. But Bobby's conflicts with Jack do reveal some other reasons why Jack abuses alcohol. There's the indication that they once had a band together, that Bobby yearned for stardom, had talent, but it was somehow eclipsed by Jack's. We learn that their father made Jack his drinking buddy, and that Jack once tried unsuccessfully to commit suicide when he was a teenager. These lingering traumas and underlying mental health challenges are certainly relevant to Jack's current alcohol problem, as they would be to anyone's. But we all know that self-medicating over these types of problems just pushes them back into the shadows of the subconscious where they continue to fester. Unfortunately, country music mythology probably also means never admitting you need help.

Ally eventually becomes a huge music star in her own right thanks to Jack's assistance. You would think that a guy like Jack would feel secure enough in his own career to not view Ally's success as a threat. But then again, if he felt even remotely secure generally, he might not be drinking the way he is. While the professional jealousy angle is a central plot point in the previous three iterations of the story, in this version Ally's success barely even seems to register with Jack. The only hint that he feels even remotely affected by her success is when he gushes over her accomplishments in private but can't manage to mutter a simple congratulations when they're in public.

Jealous or not, by this point in the story Jack is spiraling. Even a hastily arranged marriage, major TV appearances; and Ally's endless supply of love, compassion, and understanding can't seem to slow him down. It all comes to a head in a scene which is quite certainly the literal stuff of nightmares for any celebrity or performer. It's the ultimate form of humiliation, seen by millions. The imposter finally unmasked. Morally and physically exposed in public, laughed at, pitied. It's sad to watch, perhaps too over-the-top, but unfortunately relatable to anyone who never imagined they could go any lower on their way toward rock bottom yet went lower still.

There isn't a tidy Hollywood ending in **A Star Is Born**. Jack goes to rehab, tries 12-Step meetings, and begs Ally for forgiveness. But it's not enough. He commits suicide by the same method he tried and failed at when he was a teenager. Perhaps this was his plan all along. Perhaps his country music success distracted him just enough to not go through with it any sooner. And when that success got old, he turned to alcohol. And now with his career up in flames and alcohol seemingly off the table, there was nothing left to distract him from finally carrying out that plan. Not even Ally's love.

In both **Crazy Heart** and **A Star Is Born** the central "complication" in the protagonist's pre-existing drinking schedule is the sudden introduction of a love interest. But in both cases love clearly does not conquer all. And it's also clear that some people just can't bounce back from their rock bottoms. There's been too much collateral damage, resentments, regrets. Whereas Bad managed to make peace with the fact that he couldn't rewrite the past and right every wrong, Jack simply couldn't accept it. While **Crazy Heart** shows us that it's "never too late," **A Star Is Born** reminds us that some people simply will never change.

Both films are interesting because they don't just give us a true grit bird's-eye view of fame, fortune, and failure in the country music industry specifically; they also touch on more general themes of achievement, and what defines personal success to begin with. As both films show, the pursuit of/indifference to success is a major factor in each character's road to self-destruction with alcohol. And it's true in real life as well. While "achievements" can be quantifiable, "success" is an entirely subjective term. What or who defines success? And once "attained," what then? Will Jeff Bezos ever wake up and say, "Amazon is a success; it doesn't need to increase its profits anymore"? Success is like infinity. Once you reach it, you can always go to infinity plus one. Or as Charlie Sheen famously asks Michael Douglas in **Wall Street**, "How many yachts can you waterski behind? How much is enough?"

We may never know what is "enough," but part of the lure of fame and celebrity is the notion that celebrities actually do have "enough" success. That they're blissfully happy, rich, famous, beloved by millions. When it's revealed that some of them have serious drug or alcohol addictions, it's difficult for fans to process. Some think that celebrities don't deserve to have problems like addiction. They resent them for having any human foibles. Still others bask in celebrities' difficulties, getting massive jolts of schadenfreude every time they fail.

The entire yellow journalism industry is founded on it. In Latin America, one of the most popular TV series of all time is **Los Ricos También Lloran** (*The Rich Also Cry*). Overall, I think it's comforting to know that, yes, celebrities are just like us, addictions and all. And their triumphs over them are just as well deserved as anybody else's, if not more so because they're widely publicized and inspire others to seek help too.

Crazy Heart and **A Star Is Born** both also serve as cautionary tales about how alcohol's deep correlation to success can be perpetuated (in fact celebrated) by the cultural context that surrounds it. Heavy drinking seems to be part of the foundational myth of the entire country music industry. Its songs reflect it. Its fans emulate it. But this phenomenon is not unique to country music; it's just more blatantly obvious in those circles. Let's not forget the drug and alcohol-soaked excesses of rock and heavy metal legends. With the possible exception of the Arab world, alcohol is a part of the foundational myths of most cultures. French wine culture, American TGIF culture, Japanese corporate hazing culture, fraternity culture, German Oktoberfest, Russian fatalism, the Camba tribe in Bolivia; the list is endless.

These drug and alcohol myths are perpetuated by popular culture and advertising to such a degree that they have become cultural norms that nobody bothers to question. People celebrate their success with alcohol. They bemoan their lack of success with alcohol (Bad). They tolerate their success with alcohol (Jack). To be romantically successful you need to drink the right kind of alcohol. Advertisers even sell us the counterfactual argument that drinking actually *leads* to success.

When people hit happy hour after a stressful work day, one of the things they're seeking is a temporary relief from the constant stress of *always* having to be successful. Same reason people drink more during vacations. Alcohol's role in any and all situations, positive or negative, is staggering. When I naively asked my parents what Kris Kristofferson's *problem* was, I didn't realize how truly ubiquitous and universal the problem actually was. I sure as hell do now.

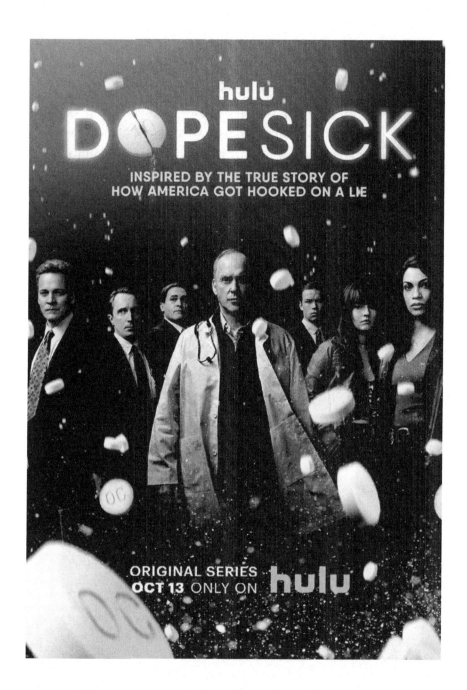

CHAPTER 7
Evil Incarnate: Purdue Pharma & OxyContin®
Dopesick

I'm the first to tell you that movies and TV shows are a business first and foremost—which is why most screenwriters and producers like me strive to make them as provocative, romantic, comedic, horrifying, and/or thrilling as possible.

Unfortunately, many media critics bemoan the negative impact of commercial imperatives on "quality" storytelling, and it's why Marvel superhero franchise films usually take the brunt of the criticism. But as I mentioned in the Introduction, Hollywood is also known to take chances from time to time, and some of its greatest artistic and public-service accomplishments have occurred when it dramatizes important current events. Hulu's original series ***Dopesick*** is a prime example of how producers endeavored to take on a difficult and challenging issue like the opioid epidemic and hit it out of the park.

It must have been no small undertaking. The now well-documented and exhaustively researched story of how Purdue Pharma and the Sackler family managed to flood the country with a highly addictive pain medication like OxyContin® could fill volumes. For an in-depth look, I highly recommend Patrick Radden Keefe's bestseller ***Empire of Pain: The Secret History of the Sackler Dynasty***. HBO also produced a powerful documentary on the subject called ***The Crime of the Century***. These two dispassionate takes on the story are vital to the national discourse on the topic, but with ***Dopesick*** the producers have managed to give this complex story a deeply human, very emotional dimension.

Dopesick tells the OxyContin® story from several different vantage points—from the coal mines of West Virginia to the boardrooms of Purdue Pharma to the halls of the FDA. The story is anchored around no-nonsense country doctor Samuel Finnix—played by Michael Keaton—in a role for which he won the 2022 Golden Globe Award for Best Performance by an Actor in a Miniseries, as well as the Emmy for Outstanding Lead Actor in a Limited Series. If you haven't seen his acceptance speeches for both wins, I highly recommend you watch them on YouTube. The series itself is an emotional rollercoaster; Keaton's speeches in real life take it to a whole other level.

Finnix is an everyman good guy family practitioner who dotes on his low-income patients in a small West Virginia mining town. Many come in for help with the injuries and associated chronic pain caused by hard physical labor in the mines. One of them is Betsy, played by Kaitlyn Dever, who suffered a back injury. Her physical pains are further compounded by the emotional stress of keeping her sexuality a secret from her Christian parents and community. Writer/producer Danny Strong made a wonderful decision to humanize Betsy in such a way that her subsequent fictional addiction to Oxy is caused by a multiplicity of factors (physical and emotional), just like addiction is in non-fictional real life.

Betsy's injury just happens to (unfortunately) coincide with the rollout of a new "miracle drug" pain medication called OxyContin®. Finnix learns about it when he receives a visit from a polished drug sales rep named Billy, played by Will Poulter. Billy's the pride of the Purdue Pharma sales and marketing department, a boiler-room that thrusts young and eager 20-something overachievers into every doctor's office in America to sell a lie: OxyContin® isn't addictive. While Finnix has enough common sense and medical knowledge to doubt this spurious claim, Billy's sales pitch does sound pretty compelling. So he writes Betsy a prescription for her pain. And to test OxyContin® out for himself, he tries one (but *just* one) pill from the countless samples Billy leaves behind as promotional freebies. You can guess where this is going.

The story then rewinds a few years to show the architect of all the ensuing misery, Richard Sackler, played with surreal creepiness by Michael Stuhlbarg. Somewhat miraculously, the writers have managed to humanize one of the most despicable characters in recent memory. Sackler comes off as a sad rich kid overshadowed by the achievements of his father and grandfather. OxyContin®—a new "blockbuster drug"—is his desperate attempt to earn his family's love and respect. So what if, for him to earn his gold star, it'll endanger and destroy the lives of hundreds of thousands of people? Ah, the banality of evil.

What is so striking about **Dopesick** is the way the story goes on to portray the complexity of how Sackler and his Purdue Pharma foot soldiers cleverly managed to manipulate, dupe, and/or bribe seemingly respectable doctors and medical opinion leaders into endorsing a product that even a first-year medical student could have told you would be highly addictive. Purdue even put one over on the FDA to keep OxyContin® off the list of heavily controlled substances. Equally fascinating (albeit horrifying) is how Purdue's sales teams continually doubled-down on the lies told by their sales reps every time anyone raised a red flag. And if that didn't work, they just doubled and quadrupled the dosages per pill in order to combat *"Breakthrough Pain,"* a made-up medical condition that was really just users building up a tolerance to the drug and needing higher and higher dosages so they wouldn't get literally dopesick. Talk about pouring gasoline on a fire.

With Sackler and Purdue firmly established as the ultimate Goliath, the story then introduces us to the Davids—no-nonsense country lawyers Richard Mountcastle (the always amazing Peter Sarsgaard) and Randy Ramseyer (John Hoogenakker). Their slow and methodical search for the truth, and their crusade to bring Purdue and the Sacklers to justice, plays out like an Agatha Christie mystery crossed with *Erin Brockovich*.

To call these two guys "heroes" is an understatement, both in the series and in real life. Mountcastle gives up any semblance of a personal life during his decades-long investigation. Ramseyer even goes so far as refusing to take OxyContin® to relieve the pain of his prostate cancer surgery. Not because he thinks he'll become addicted, but because it would put more blood money into Richard Sackler's pocket.

Equally heroic is Bridget Meyer—a scrappy, ambitious DEA agent played by Rosario Dawson. Dawson does a superb job of looking calm and collected (albeit indignant) as the OxyContin® catastrophe unfolds in plain sight all around her. Her sclerotic agency seems to be too afraid of intergovernmental red tape to do much about it, and she gets stonewalled at the FDA—an agency seemingly beset by an admixture of dark money influencers (mostly funded by Sackler) and unscrupulous regulators (many of whom went on to cushy six-figure jobs at—you guessed it—Purdue Pharma!).

As the conspiracy investigation unfolds, we eventually circle back around to Purdue's primary victims in the story, Dr. Finnix and his patient Betsy. Her well-intentioned effort to use OxyContin® "as prescribed" for pain quickly spirals out of control. She's reduced to turning tricks in seedy back alleys after she loses her job for being high.

Overly dramatic made-for-TV overkill? Not at all. Betsy's fictional story is similar to that of many people swept up in the opioid crisis in real life. Most had jobs, were well-educated, had families, paid their taxes, walked their dogs. The farthest thing from their mind was to become addicted to drugs. Problem is, they had pain.[15] Real physical pain. And for that they simply wanted help. But they got something else.

Finnix (Michael Keaton), the one guy you'd think would know better, quickly gets consumed by the drug as well. Desperate for money, he gets recruited into the Purdue Pharma "Speakers Series"—basically TEDTalks for OxyContin® apologists and liars. All he has to do is step in front of the mike, say he's an MD, and tell everyone the drug isn't addictive. And all of this as he himself is addicted and high as a kite. Granted, Finnix is a fictional character, but his path to the "dark side" mirrors that taken by countless other once-respectable medical professionals who the Sacklers bought off to help them overcome critics and move more inventory.

What makes **Dopesick** especially relevant to the overall conversation about recovery is just how difficult it was for treatment providers and mutual support groups to combat such an addictive drug. Betsy white-knuckles it at 12-Step meetings and attends group prayer at her church. But neither Narcotics Anonymous (NA) nor the Almighty seem to be any match for Purdue Pharma's "miracle pain reliever." While NA may have helped some individuals overcome their addiction, in Betsy's case her meetings turn out to be secret OxyContin® swap meets.

Finnix also tries rehab, but like many people legally mandated into recovery, his initial (defensive) reaction is to feel like an outsider.

---

15 There are other points of view on this profile of people who became addicted. Maia Szalavitz, a science writer and columnist for the New York Times shared this with me: "80% of those who got addicted were NOT patients and did not have a prescription; they were people who use other illicit drugs already." https://undark.org/2022/02/04/opinion-the-wrong-battle-against-opioids/

He's not addicted like "those people"—no sir! What's worse, he realizes that many of the other patients at the facility have cycled through several times before. Whatever it is that's supposed to be "working" in this rehab facility clearly isn't. But that could be said about many rehab facilities at that time. When it came to the fight against OxyContin® literally everyone in the recovery universe seemed to be boxing outside of their weight class. Such was the power of this drug. Finnix eventually leaves the facility, relapses, then seeks recovery help at a methadone clinic.

Dopesick culminates in Mountcastle and Ramseyer's successful prosecution of Purdue's deceptive marketing and business practices. This eventually led to Purdue's bankruptcy and multi-billion-dollar settlements (still in contention today). It's a satisfying ending to a sad story, but in many ways it's cold comfort. It took the U.S. judicial system more than a decade to put a halt to a tragedy that was blatantly obvious to anyone who cared to look. Thousands of people died needlessly. Entire communities were ravaged. All while the Sackler family made billions.

Was it only the Sacklers' fault? Well, yes and no. But mostly yes.

Dopesick lets us peel back the curtain and see all the moving parts of this consumer product catastrophe. It was a perfect storm of contributory negligence. Purdue's chemists knew the drug was highly addictive, so they bribed medical professionals to say it wasn't. They submitted skewed data-sets with sampling errors to regulators, whose job it was to *know* better. Purdue's legal team knew they would never pass muster with the FDA, so they rewarded the FDA chief (Curtis Wright) with a $400,000 a year job at Purdue if he would help them create a loophole. Purdue's marketing department knew the drug was addictive, so they paid users to say it wasn't in promotional videos. Purdue's sales department was under pressure to meet its targets, so they offered ridiculous commission structures to motivate its avaricious young sales teams. Yes, everyone at Purdue could say they were "just following orders." But that didn't work at Nuremberg, so why should it work here?

Not surprisingly, we see money at the root of this evil. A perverse amount of money. The financial incentives created by Purdue to market and sell the drug cascaded down the value chain. Small private pharmacies could mark up OxyContin® and make higher margins on its sales (but in all fairness, they were also afraid Purdue would sue them if they didn't sell their pills).[16] Medical and treatment professionals with prescription privileges stood to make a lot of money too. After all, they were helping people manage chronic pain, right? And thus the infamous "Pill-Mills" formed around the country. Watchdog groups could reap millions in off-the-books "sponsorship" revenue from Purdue if they looked the other way. If all of this doesn't smack of a criminal conspiracy, what does?

By revealing the interdependence of all these bad faith actors, **Dopesick** does a wonderful (if maddening) public service. It illustrates how *actual* conspiracies work. How criminality is allowed to fester in plain sight because it seems too outlandish to believe it's actually happening (I'm reminded of the quote attributed to Edmund Burke: "The only thing necessary for the triumph of evil is for good men to do nothing"). This situation demonstrates how a lie told enough times eventually becomes the truth. And if that doesn't work, just pay more people more money to parrot your talking points. These are painful lessons society seems to have to relearn over and over again.

I also think **Dopesick** is an important series to watch because it's an unflinching look at addiction in general, both what addiction is and what people *think and say* it is. OxyContin® is a case study in how real societal harm and death is caused by the language we use to describe and stigmatize individuals who suffer from addiction. We

---

16 Since lawsuits are probably now Purdue's only source of revenue, I have made sure to add the registered trademark logo after each mention of their stupid drug so as to not run afoul of their legal team.

often hear in church, "*Love the Sinner; Hate the Sin.*" Well, the Sacklers made billions and avoided criminal prosecution by just flipping the sentence around: "*Hate the addict, love the addiction.*" OxyContin® was harmless. The Sacklers were innocent victims of a vast left-wing anti-business conspiracy. It was all the "pill-heads'" fault. Sound crazy? No, not at all. The Sacklers were just channeling the idea that addiction is a moral failing, completely unmoored from any physiological or mental health considerations. This idea is out of date, it's wrong, and it's killing people.

While **Dopesick** spreads out culpability for the OxyContin® opioid epidemic among many participants and institutions, I'm reminded of something my father once told me: "*The fish rots from the head down.*" And in my mind, that rotten head was Richard Sackler's. He was the architect of the drug, the crimes, and the coverup. To date, he and his minions have avoided criminal prosecution in exchange for billions in civil settlement fines. As you read this, these settlements are still under review and appeal. On the one side, victims are demanding personal accountability from the Sacklers; on the other, states desperately need that settlement money to help clean up the mess they made. The Sacklers recently participated in a court proceeding where family members of OxyContin® victims were allowed to confront their tormentors. Richard Sackler joined via Zoom, but only because he was forced to. His camera was turned off.

CHAPTER 8
Parenthood is the Scariest 'Hood of All
Four Good Days
Beautiful Boy

Relationships present people with some of life's biggest challenges. Family dynamics can be particularly combustible. We're social animals and are sometimes forced to socialize with loved ones who can cause great harm to themselves and those around them. Not because they intend to cause harm necessarily, but because of the poor choices they've made. I'm reminded of Jean-Paul Sartre's famous quip from his 1944 philosophical play **No Exit** where he wrote "Hell is other people." And for millions of parents around the world, that hell can be very real if they care for an addicted son or daughter.

When I say "millions" I don't know the exact number; nobody does. Parents of addicted children are not exactly the types to race out and fill in a census form to spill their family secrets. A typical web search will tell you that 23 million Americans suffer from drug or alcohol addiction. A further search will tell you that the average person has 5 intimate bonds (usually family and relatives). Simple back-of-a-napkin math seems to suggest that over 100 million people (parents/relatives) in the U.S. have their mental health and well-being negatively impacted to some degree by a close family member's addiction.

One of the central questions with parents of addicts is this: What are they supposed to do to help their kids? Clinicians, therapists, and recovery professionals have widely divergent views on what constitutes "help," and even whether giving help might actually be counterproductive or harmful. For instance, for the last 35 years, we've been told that "tough love" is not just the best approach, it's the only approach. Parents and relatives should just let their loved ones hit rock bottom. In fact, they should try to hasten it. To do otherwise is to "enable" the addict. Those who don't practice tough love are labeled "codependent." They suffer from their own disease. They too require help.

But in addiction and recovery there are no absolutes. Long-held ideas about best practices are being reviewed, modified, and overturned as we speak. Every recovery situation is different, like every individual is different, and any path to recovery is valid if it gets the job done. Unfortunately, when it comes to family support, we have a fragmented and dysfunctional system where social, psychological, and ethical best practices have become polarized—even politicized in some cases. It's confusing to those who give help and need help and makes an already difficult problem even worse.

For instance, consider this thought experiment. In Scenario A:

Mary's son Bob is unemployed and doesn't like to look for work. He stopped going to church. He likes to party with his friends and eventually graduated from pot to heroin. To support his habit, he has stolen and pawned all of Mary's jewelry, and stripped the copper wiring from his neighbor's home. Mary fears Bob will come after her 401(k) and meager retirement savings next, so she considers two options 1) Gently urge Bob to quit heroin cold turkey (97% failure rate) and attend mutual support meetings; or 2) Call the cops, file a police report, get him busted for possession, have him do hard time, and cut off all communications until he can prove he's "clean."

Now consider this alternative Scenario B:

Mary's son Bob lives at home because he lost his job due to a back injury. He was prescribed pain pills, built up a tolerance, eventually started taking heroin, and is now addicted. He prays every day for God to help him quit, but he can't stomach the withdrawals—or the back pain. Mary is afraid he won't be able to come up with the money to buy heroin, and may turn to crime, so she considers two options: 1) Gently urge Bob to quit heroin cold turkey (97% failure rate) and attend mutual support meetings; or 2) Call the cops, file a police report, get him busted for possession, have him do hard time, and cut off all communications until he can prove he's "clean."

Of course, we know that the two options presented here are not the only options available. Medically-Assisted Treatment like methadone and suboxone can certainly help. Going to church might help. Meditation might help. The psychedelic drug Ibogaine might help. Doing absolutely nothing might help. However, if Mary has bought into the codependency model, what lies behind door #2 is *absolutely* the only way to "help" Bob—regardless of whether it's the "bad Bob" in Scenario A or the "good Bob" in Scenario B. Both need tough love.

Really? This sounds ludicrous because it is.

Would the calculus change if the "bad Bob" in Scenario A had been sexually molested as a kid? Or if Mary has a drinking problem herself? Or if all their forefathers were addicts? No, because we're dealing with absolutes. Extenuating circumstances are irrelevant. In both scenarios Mary must stop enabling Bob. He should go out and lie, cheat, and steal from others (perhaps violently so), experience homelessness, procure street heroin (potentially laced with deadly amounts of fentanyl), and hit whatever rock bottom awaits. That'll teach him.

Again, ludicrous.

This thought experiment is an oversimplification, but it nonetheless sheds light on just a few of the incredibly complex issues families navigate as they try to help their loved ones not just recover but also *survive*. They face daily choices that challenge their positions on morality, loyalty, guilt, attachment, privacy, betrayal, and simple common sense. They experience fear, pity, and bitter resentment. They're constantly forced to question basic assumptions about themselves: Are they good parents? Are they doing the right thing? Are they partly or fully to blame for what is happening? These questions don't have simple answers, or any answers. And depending on the severity of the addiction and the substances involved, this is all part of a family drama that plays out over years, even decades, for millions of people.

Many very thoughtful people have worked on these complex problems. I want to take a minute to give kudos to an excellent resource, the Community Reinforcement and Family Training (CRAFT) program, which forms the basis of SMART Recovery's Family & Friends Program. It is intended to help family members of people with a substance use disorder learn how to steer their loved one away from substance abuse and help them admit they have lost control. It takes the position that "tough love" rarely works and can actually be highly destructive. Everyone wants and needs love, and while parents can't be foolishly supportive, love and compassion build the inner strength needed for the addicted son or daughter to succeed long-term.

To do justice to these complex issues in filmic terms would likely require a 30-part miniseries, something Hollywood will likely never do. However, some very fine films have managed to tackle key segments of the story in various ways, and I will discuss two that stand out for different reasons. *Four Good Days* is a powerful mother-daughter drama that covers the tail end of an addiction and recovery story and pieces together the events that brought them both to this point. It is a contained, linear story that builds toward an uncertain, tension-filled climax. It all takes place over four days, hence the title.

Beautiful Boy is a father-son story that is more expansive and non-linear, using flashbacks to show the day-to-day struggles over years, not just days. While quite different in terms of narrative approach, both films are master classes on the complexities involved in helping loved ones suffering from addiction—and probably a great source of inspiration for those who do. If you thought basic parenting was hard…

Four Good Days was directed by Rodrigo García (of HBO's series *In Treatment*) and was co-written by Garcia and Eli Saslow. It stars Glenn Close as the estranged mother of a daughter (Mila Kunis) addicted to heroin who reluctantly agrees to quarantine her at home and keep her away from heroin long enough to safely get an injection of Vivitrol, an opioid antagonist that makes it impossible to get high. Molly has been through detox fourteen times. This is basically her Hail Mary.[17]

The fourteen times part is not just Hollywood hyperbole. The film is derived from Saslow's 2016 Washington Post article "How's

---

17 Vivitrol works better on alcohol use disorders and has limited efficacy in opioid addiction.

Amanda? A Story of Truth, Lies and an American Addiction" about real-life mother and daughter Libby Alexander and Amanda Wendler. The film premiered at Sundance in 2020, received a limited theatrical run, and is currently available on Hulu. Critics were ambivalent about the film, and a common criticism was that it didn't address the subject matter "authentically" enough and therefore devolved into a "bland" melodrama. But that is exactly what you would expect a critic to say if they had never been through addiction and recovery themselves, or never had to deal with a "Bob" in their lives.

The film begins as Deb (Close) answers a knock at her door late at night. She's nervous, and we soon see why. Her daughter Molly (Kunis) has come home after a long disappearance. This has obviously happened many times before, and judging from the expression on Deb's face, it never gets any easier. Molly has open sores all over her body, hasn't showered in weeks, and looks emaciated. Imagine the cognitive dissonance Deb must be experiencing. On the one hand she dreads Molly's return because it'll probably blow up her own life; yet on the other she's elated that Molly's even alive. This is the disjointed emotional calculus parents of addicts must face almost every day. Their instinct for self-preservation is pitted against their instincts to nurture and protect their children at all costs. And this is just the first three minutes of the film, mind you. Strap in.

Molly asks her mother why her key to the house doesn't work anymore. It's because Deb changed the locks. She also put in a home alarm system. Molly begs her mother for a safe place to stay, and promises she'll kick her heroin habit "this time." Because this time is "different." But Deb asks why "this time" will be any different than the dozens or hundreds of other times she's given her mother the same speech. It's a simple exchange in narrative terms, but highlights a central conundrum that family members face 24/7 in real life: What can a family member believe? What should they believe?

We all know lies are a common currency in addiction. There is the cynical Narcotics Anonymous joke: "How do you know a heroin addict is lying? Their lips are moving." In every addict's life there comes a point when reality catches up with them. And when it does, people who would otherwise be completely honest to a fault suddenly become bold-faced liars. I know this because when I had an active alcohol addiction, I was one of those people. It all starts with little "white lies" to answer questions like "Where have you been?" Later the lies become more complex, but still plausible. Last are the wildfire lies to explain the pink slips at work, wrecked cars, maxed-out credit cards, cuts and bruises, and needle marks. Deb has endured countless lies over the years, big and small. But regardless of the size, lies are still lies. And choosing to believe them or not can sometimes carry life-or-death consequences.

And it's not as simple as just distinguishing a lie from the truth, either. Addiction makes family members question who is actually doing the lying. When we fault people for lying to us, we assume they are rational agents and understand and respect the idea of quid pro quo. But addicted individuals are not rational agents. Addiction brings out their "evil" side. So in the same way that Christianity has Satan as an antagonist to God, family members bifurcate the addict into two distinct personas. There's the sober Bob and the using Bob. The Bob who exercises free will, and the Bob who has a "disease." Deep down Molly is a great gal, except for those times when she's a heroin zombie.

Deb falls prey to this fallacy several times later in the film where she talks about "the good Molly" and "the bad Molly." She tells her daughter that addicted Molly is "not who you really are." But what she's really doing is trying to sell herself on this delusion. The distinction is purely cosmetic anyway. Both versions of Molly constitute the same person. When Molly shows up on her door with the usual speech, Deb doesn't even have to hear it. She knows Molly's lying, unequivocally, and has no choice but to turn her away. And who could fault her for this?

But the gut-wrenching result is that Deb must sleep in her warm bed knowing the daughter she loves is left shivering on the front porch. Pretty rough, right? And yet "tough love" advocates would argue that Deb hasn't gone nearly far enough. Similar to "Bob" in the scenarios above, Deb should slam the door in Molly's face, call the police, have her arrested for theft, and file a restraining order. Wait, what? Since when did this become accepted wisdom?

The "tough love" paradigm became a foundational myth in addiction recovery with the publication of Melody Beattie's 1986 best seller **Codependent No More: How to Stop Controlling Others and Start Caring for Yourself**. It's no surprise that its zero-tolerance approach coincided with Reagan era mandatory minimum sentencing guidelines for drug offenses. The problem was that the codependency idea wasn't based on any actual data. The diagnosis itself was rejected by psychiatry's Diagnostic and Statistical Manual of Mental Disorders, or DSM—basically the bible of mental health diseases. *Real* diseases.

But whatever, right? This is the '80s, dude. "Pop Psychology" (a.k.a. Pseudoscience) was the hottest literary genre around. Past life regression cures depression. Recovered memories can be used in court to convict innocent people of incest and pedophilia. Smothering children in blankets to reenact a painful childbirth can make them better students. Little green men are not trying to fix your hemorrhoids; they want to control your mind.

As crazy as it sounds, the codependency paradigm is still as pervasive as ever. For some family members the tough love approach may have worked wonders. Perhaps performing oral sex on strangers in a back alley to score drugs is a great character building exercise. Homelessness can be a teachable moment. Debasement and humiliation build resilience. Painful lessons, sure, but nobody dies, right? Well this has all changed with fentanyl. You no longer hit rock bottom, rock bottom hits you first. Hundreds of families have tough-loved their sons and daughters to death. Lawsuits have, and are, being filed against treatment facilities and doctors charging wrongful death after they coerced parents into disengaging from their children at a time when they needed love and support the most.

You can imagine how torturous it must be for Deb to see Molly, curled up in a ball, shivering on her front porch. She's damned if she helps her; she's damned if she doesn't. It's not clear whether Deb knows what codependency or tough love is, but her sprawling 10-year struggle against Molly's heroin addiction has led her to make tough choices on her own. She's had to set bottom lines to ensure her own sanity and survival. (The real-life mother this story is based on became so desperate she almost committed suicide.) But any family member in a similar circumstance will tell you that love sometimes makes you do crazy things. If tough love were always practiced to the letter, we would have a homeless and prison population in the tens of millions. So Deb takes a flier and agrees to let Molly crash at her house for four days until she can get her Vivitrol injection. She's put up with so much already; why not try this "last" time? But is it ever really the "last time?" Here we see Deb falling prey to the Sunk Cost Fallacy[18] we all do at times, but sometimes it can actually be for the good. And to help Molly survive, this is one of those times.

With mother and daughter finally reunited and able to interact calmly over these four days, the filmmakers are able to fill in key details of a rich but troubled backstory. Something that surfaces repeatedly is Molly trying to transfer some of the blame for her addiction. We learn that she was over prescribed pain pills after a soccer injury. While that may be one of the reasons she became a heroin addict, it doesn't explain why she became a heroin addict. And Molly knows this. Like many addicts riddled with guilt, she digs up some dirt on her mother to spread some of the guilt around.

We learn that Deb walked out on the family when Molly was in high school, but eventually returned after the divorce to her first

---

18 As discussed previously in ***Requiem for a Dream.***

husband was finalized. It was an act of self-preservation. So sure, Molly can certainly claim to have suffered trauma as a result of her mother's actions. But is it fair to use this as a crutch to explain away 10 years of heroin addiction?[19] Most would argue that she's had plenty of time to process and overcome this. And she probably has. But it's more convenient to hold on to that trauma because it supplies an easy excuse for past behaviors, and a free pass to try to continue them. Granted, we all play the victim from time to time, but addicts like Molly take this kind of manipulation to another level.

Parents of addicts are especially susceptible to emotional blackmail. The fact that their son or daughter is an addict already has them on the defensive. How bad of a parent must they have been to raise a kid who shoots heroin? Putting actual child abuse aside—which I'm in no way discounting—kids don't understand just how many ways parents can be flawed and imperfect in raising them. Even well-intentioned parenting decisions can be taken as a terrible slight. Unremarkable moments that parents can't even remember get reinterpreted as life-changing trauma events. Like clever children who use tears or temper tantrums to get what they want, addicts then leverage guilt to weaken a parent's bottom lines so they can continue their bad behavior unchallenged. It's the reason why many support programs for families and friends of individuals with addiction problems focus on teaching self-love and self-acceptance first before they discuss strategies for helping others.

But Deb is wise to Molly's strategy and pushes back. She acknowledges that some harm has been done, but firmly reminds Molly that the past needs to stay in the past, and the next four days sober are the only thing that matters. But it soon becomes clear that these four days are a solo mission for Deb. She can't let Molly

---

[19] There is an important body of evidence to support the argument that past trauma informs addictive behaviors later in life. I highly recommend Gabor Maté's fine book ***In the Realm of Hungry Ghosts***.

out of her sight for even a second. Unfortunately, this is an almost insurmountable problem even in the best of times, but for parents to think they have to do all of this on their own is frequently a problem of their own making. A problem caused by shame.

As they sit together in Deb's garage, doing puzzles to pass the time, a few neighbors walk by and see Molly. They walk away quickly. Deb is ashamed. She has a right to be. But shame and addiction are a toxic combination. It's been called "*The Silent Killer*" in relationships. Research has linked it to violence, depression, sleep problems, eating disorders, anxiety, and—no surprise here—addiction. Shame stops parents from reaching out to others who could help them at a time when it literally "takes a village." They try to keep their son's or daughter's addiction a closely guarded family secret. Seeking professional help feels like a personal defeat. Or they can't afford it to begin with. While addiction slowly pushes the addict toward complete social isolation, shame does the same for those trying to help them.

When both child and parent get caught in the same shame spiral, things can go from bad to worse. The addict becomes so dependent that the parent(s) begin to treat them as helpless children. Everyone assumes rigid new roles: the authoritarian father; the nagging mother; the stubborn, ungrateful child. Parents who may have felt marginalized and forgotten as their kids grew up and left home now get a new sense of relevance and control when addiction forces those children to move back. They get to be the Alphas all over again, overprotective to the point of smothering. But by then so much resentment has built up that exercising that newfound control can slowly devolve into abuse.

In extreme cases, parents are left with so little of themselves that their sole sense of identity, their sole sense of purpose, derives from being an addiction caregiver. To stay continually relevant, they need to continually care, and anything that challenges that dynamic becomes an existential threat. Like the mental disease Munchausen Syndrome by Proxy, in some extreme cases parents may actually do everything in their power to keep their "patient" sick and dependent upon them. That includes supplying the substances to keep them addicted. When unemployment, disability, Social Security, and public assistance income is factored in, the need to keep their loved one perpetually sick becomes a financial imperative, too.

Deb is nowhere near this point with Molly, but there is an interesting exchange midway through the film that highlights another challenge for caregivers of addicts: loneliness. Despite everything Molly has put her through, Deb is happy that Molly has returned home. Empty nest syndrome might not be listed as a psychiatric disorder in the DSM, but it causes suffering nonetheless. When combined with (or caused by) social isolation, loneliness causes increased mortality. Loneliness is especially acute with the elderly, particularly widowers. Many are willing to make dramatic compromises just to have a loved one—in fact anyone—back in their lives, even if that loved one is an addict who is systematically depleting their retirement account.

It's astonishing what living situations some parents will tolerate just to have a son or daughter around for company. I had a little old lady neighbor once who allowed her daughter—a meth addict—to move back in with her. The daughter had turned to prostitution to support her habit and converted their small apartment into her personal brothel. I asked the lady why she would allow this, and her answer was quite simple: "Because I'm totally alone in the world and nobody cares about me anymore. I think my daughter does…"

These kinds of situations cause levels of cognitive dissonance that can threaten a parent's grip on reality. Utter despair fuels magical thinking that "things are not that bad," and the loved one will suddenly and miraculously get sober and live life happily ever after. We see the beginnings of this with Deb. Despite red flags everywhere (Molly getting mysterious phone calls, going out for unsupervised walks), Deb thinks her daughter is "really different this time." Hope encroaches on common sense. There's a powerful scene in the film where Deb asks Molly if she has ever resorted to prostitution. Molly's response: "I never had sex for money. But I have had sex for drugs." Deb's magical thinking response: "That's not prostitution. No, that's survival." Okay, but technically it still is prostitution, regardless of the consideration involved.

Caring for a loved one with an addiction also exerts tremendous negative pressure on what few relationships a parent may have left. In Deb's case she has remarried and lives with her new husband Chris—played by Stephen Root, my favorite character actor of all time (remember the "stapler guy" in *Office Space*?). Chris has a small part to play in the overall drama unfolding between Molly and Deb, but it's an important one. He loves and supports Deb's attempts to help her daughter.

But he also reminds her of her bottom lines, saying, "She won't walk if you carry her." Deb knows this; it's apparent that she and Chris have argued about this many times before. But from that moment on their relationship becomes visibly strained. The presence of Molly turns Deb defensive, agitated, insecure, and argumentative. Chris becomes her punching bag. It's a telling example of how addiction splits the defense, and sometimes forces impossible decisions between saving a marriage and saving an addict's life.

Unlike in other chapters, I don't want to give away too much about the ending of **Four Good Days**. Suffice it to say that the emotional and thematic climax of the film boils down to a scene where Deb realizes Molly has not been 100% honest about her actions during the four days leading up to her Vivitrol injection. She's used heroin and will fail her drug test. She asks her mother to provide her own urine in order to pass it. And in this subtle, well-acted scene, we see the harrowing choice parents of addicts may eventually face in real life. Do you take what's behind Door #1 or Door #2? Gullibly ignore all precedents, and try to help your son or daughter one last time, hoping for a miracle? Or stand by your guns, and let them dig their own grave?

Clearly there is no right answer. Addiction is as complex and nuanced as the family relationships it affects. That complexity is captured perfectly in the last scene of the film where Deb and Molly sit together in the garage where they've done the hard work of repairing their relationship. Molly looks sober, healthy, vibrant, committed. Is she off heroin forever? No way of knowing. There never is. Hence the popular 12-Step motto, "*One day at a time.*"

Deb and Molly look down at the complicated puzzle they have managed to finish over the last four days. And in a wonderful visual metaphor that perfectly underscores the fact that addiction is a complication that will never go away, they rip the puzzle apart and begin to piece it together all over again. Day by day.

Beautiful Boy is a very different film than *Four Good Days* insofar as it covers a much larger time period of its protagonist's recovery journey, not just the final days. It's based on the best sellers ***Beautiful Boy: A Father's Journey Through His Son's Addiction*** by David Sheff and ***Tweak: Growing Up on Methamphetamines*** by Nic Sheff.

The book rights were acquired in 2008 by Paramount Pictures and the film spent nine years in development with several Hollywood elites circling the project, including Cameron Crowe (***Jerry Maguire***, ***Almost Famous***) to direct, and actor Mark Wahlberg attached to play the role of David Sheff. Nine years is certainly a long time when you consider that the average time to get a book made into a film is around 800 days; however, it is understandable given the intensity of the subject matter, and the fact that Hollywood is justifiably nervous any time it makes films in this genre.

The project finally began to gel when Belgian director Felix Van Groeningen was brought on board to direct and co-write a new script along with Australian writer Luke Davies. It was very much a "dream team" in several respects. Davies had won great acclaim with his novel ***Candy: A Novel of Love and Addiction***, and Van Goeningen had been nominated for Best Foreign Language Film at the 86th Academy Awards for ***The Broken Circle Breakdown***. If you've seen the film, you know just how great of a dramatic storyteller van Groeningen is, and why he was the perfect choice to helm ***Beautiful Boy***.

An A-List cast quickly accreted around the project. Steve Carell (***The Office***) signed on to play David Sheff, and Timothée Chalamet was hired to play Nic. Casting Chalamet—who was blowing up into a megastar at that point following ***Call Me by Your Name***—was a lucky coincidence. Van Groeningen had selected him after passing on hundreds of other audition tapes, unaware of, and indifferent to, Chalamet's newfound fame. It's a rare case of actual acting talent taking precedence over box-office appeal. Rounding out the cast is Maura Tierney of ***ER*** fame, a versatile actress who deserves to be hired for more feature films.

Beautiful Boy touches on most of the thematic aspects of the loving-parent-addicted-child story we discussed in ***Four Good Days***, but because it covers several years of Nic's struggle with meth, it's able to do so in a more emotionally involving way. Whereas Deb (Glenn Close) channels a decade of struggles and disappointments into pained reactions to Molly's struggles in the moment, ***Beautiful Boy*** features flashbacks that let the audience live inside and experience David's struggles and disappointments with Nic over a span of years.

The main reason why each movie chose such different treatments of the same basic story is likely budgetary. ***Beautiful Boy*** was made for $25 million, while ***Four Good Days*** was made for under $5. With his budget Van Groeningen was able to stage elaborate flashbacks across multiple locations—captured lovingly by cinematographer Ruben Impens, internationally renowned for much more visceral works like ***Titane*** and ***Raw***. The budget also allowed for the use of numerous music tracks by popular artists old and new, some of which probably cost in the six-figures. But whatever was spent was well worth it; the music ends up being a key part of ***Beautiful Boy's*** overall emotional experience, and John Lennon's eponymous song is the basis of the title.

The story begins as David (Carell) meets with a clinician for guidance on his son Nic's meth addiction. But it goes beyond simply asking the same question parents are always desperate to have answered, "What can I do to help him?" It's also a fraught admission that he no longer even understands *who* he's trying to help. The bifurcation issue again. He tells the clinician, "There are moments that I look at him, this kid that I raised, who I thought I knew inside and out, and I wonder who he is."

David's subsequent personal odyssey throughout the film is an attempt to answer that question. His son was once happy, healthy, full of potential. Now he's a meth addict who's walking into that burning building. Which "version" of his son can be helped? Is it even possible to restore the previous version before addiction ruined everything?

To show the disconnect between what Nic once was and what he has become, Van Groeningen mixes flashback sequences of David and Nic's idyllic past father-son relationship intercut with the present-day reality of David calling hospitals to see if Nic has OD'd. In these flashbacks, it becomes clear how special their relationship is. It's "everything" to both of them (a word they always repeat to one another as an emotional coda). The scenes remind us just how profoundly, selflessly, and unconditionally parents love their children, despite their problems. It's a kind of love that's ineffable. When I was single, my friends who had children would try to explain it to me. I figured they were just high on oxytocin[20] or desperately trying to convince themselves that no sleep and dirty diapers was actually fun.

But now that I'm a parent, I get it. I implanted myself into those flashbacks with my nine-year-old daughter Quinn. I then flashed forward and put myself in David's position—not knowing where Quinn was, if she was safe, or if she was even alive. After bawling my eyes out, I suddenly became haunted by the fear that I might create the same conditions in Quinn's life that David had in Nic's. What would I need to do to prevent my own daughter from following down the same path? If I warn her about the dangers of meth, will it pique her interest, make her want to try it? If I intentionally get sloppy drunk around her, will it disgust her enough to never pick up a drink? If she breaks her back in a skiing accident, do I tell her to just suck it up without pain meds? I don't know the answers to these questions. When it comes to parenting, I don't even know what I don't know[21].

It is natural for David to try to seek some answers. What did he do, or not do, to cause Nic's addiction to meth? What *happened*? He goes to Nic's room, studies his paintings, reads his journal. Like a private eye, he's looking for his son's kidnappers. But can he ever find

---

20 Our bodies produce oxytocin when we fall in love or experience affection. That's why it has earned the nicknames "love hormone" and "cuddle hormone."

21 I recommend Stanton Peele's book ***Addiction Proof Your Child.***

them? And what value is there in emotional forensics at this point? As mentioned previously, there are so many ways for parents to screw up their parenting without actually doing anything wrong. So many contingencies play out over the first decade of a child's life, I'm sure most kids think their childhood is a nightmare on some level. Fact is, virtually *anything* can lead a "normal" kid to become addicted. Sometimes nothing does. Sometimes it just happens. And too many times parents like David try to make the problem all about them instead of focusing that energy on finding solutions.

Nic eventually returns home, broken and in withdrawal. And David does what most parents would and should do: get him into treatment. Nic pushes back, of course. His relapse was "just this one time," probably the most-repeated phrase in all of recovery after "I got this." But David persists, and Nic agrees, saying, "I'm doing it for you." That should have been the first red flag that rehab wasn't going to work. A person's odds of successful recovery are greatest when *they* want to change; not when they're forced to or feel like they're doing it for other people. But what other choice does David have but to throw down his credit card? Demand curves for rehab are not exactly elastic. When you need it, you need it *now*, regardless of the cost. Never mind that relapse rates for meth users are 61% in the first year after treatment.[22]

And relapse he will. It's easy to see why from Nic's perspective. There's a simple scene where he eats breakfast along with other patients at the rehab facility. He looks over and sees a haggard 70-year-old man who's in exactly the same mess he's in. God knows how many times the poor guy's been to this rodeo, and it still hasn't worked. Those of you (like me) who have faced a similar situation in your first rehab or recovery meetings know exactly what's going through Nic's mind right about now. If this is what a life in recovery looks like, if

---

[22] According to a National Institute of Health (NIH) study.

the next 50 years of white-knuckling it will lead me right back to this breakfast table looking like this guy—fuck it!—I may as well go right back to using. As terrible as it is to say, rehab isn't just part of the solution—it can also be part of the problem. Incurable disease? Lifelong abstinence? Bad rehab experiences can scare the living shit out of young people and prevent them from trying to get professional help ever again.

And so relapse Nic does. He flees the facility. David goes out looking and finds him in a seedy rain-soaked back alley, broken once again. Yet this time when he returns to treatment, he seems to understand that he's there to save himself, not just to please his father. The two of them have a come-to-Jesus moment, and David is shocked to learn Nic has been using drugs for several years. And of course, the question he's obsessed with is *why?* As if Nic simply answering that one question will somehow fix whatever's wrong with him. But try as they may, parents seldom find *the* smoking gun when it comes to addiction. And even if they did, it may be something as banal as when Nic says "[Meth] made me feel better than I ever did."

But there has to be more to it than that, right? Or does there? David may find it hard to accept, but Nic is not special. He's not an outlier. He's like billions of other people on the planet who think everyday reality is tedious. He just happens to be among those who found a chemically-induced alternative to it.[23]

But as Nic's recovery progresses, David begins to see light at the end of the tunnel. Nic gets meaningful periods of sobriety under his belt, wants to go to college, be independent, and flourish as a young adult. It's everything parents could ever want for their kids, everything they've saved up and planned for. This was the whole *point* of it all, right? But David is worried about letting Nic be on his own. He knows

---

23 There's a wonderful scene where Nic tries to get his father to smoke a joint with him. (I did the same thing with my dad once.) David asks him why he wants to smoke pot. Nic answers "[Because] it takes the edge off stupid everyday reality."

he might relapse. *Probably* will relapse. But the alternative is to keep him close to home, under control, financially dependent, smothered for his own good, but resentful of his captivity, frustrated, always on the verge of acting out.

If David's conundrum sounds familiar, it's probably because you've lived it as a parent of the child who has reached the ripe old age of eighteen and is about to strike out on their own for the first time. It's both terrifying and exhilarating. The minute after the final hug at that college dorm, bus stop, airport, or Armed Forces recruitment station, your sweet and beloved beautiful boy or girl is suddenly weak, vulnerable, and in imminent danger. But not necessarily from others. From themselves. Parents would be stunned to know even half of the crazy shit their kids got up to in high school, let alone college. At least David knows what Nic's capable of; it's the devil he knows. But it's the devil parents *don't* know that should keep them up at night. Newfound independence means kids are free to make terrible mistakes, including smoking meth, shooting heroin, or worse. And parents must accept the fact that they can't control whether these things happen or not.

This is what makes David's decision all the more excruciating, and why being the parent of a child with addiction issues feels sometimes close to impossible. Addiction or not, parents cannot protect their children indefinitely. Even if they try, they're damned if they do, damned if they don't. Most would agree with the statement, "Sometimes you need to let children fail on their own; it's the only way they'll learn." But doesn't that sound exactly like the "tough love" argument we discussed before? There is this immense gray area eighteen light years long called "parenting" where fathers and mothers live their whole lives hoping for good things for their children, but in the end it's all up for grabs.

Parents can and do make all the difference in the world. But they walk a tightrope between being too overprotective and too laissez-faire. I remember when my father (John Perkins) took me aside in

10th grade and told me he knew I was smoking pot. He was okay with that; everybody my age was doing it. But he also noticed that my grades sucked and that if I didn't get my act together, I was blowing any chance of getting into a decent university. But then he told me that he was okay with that too. It would save him a fortune in tuition, and he could spend the money on my sister's nursing school instead, and probably have enough left over to take my mom on a nice cruise every year for the rest of their lives. Guess who stopped smoking pot and started getting straight A's?

In retrospect I realize my father had psyched me out. He hated cruises. But his wise parenting achieved its intended result. Later during college, there were a few times during summer breaks where he must have noticed how much I was drinking. But he sometimes drank a lot too and decided not to take the hypocritical high road. I wish he had said something, given me a gentle warning. Who knows? It may have saved me a lot of trouble as my drinking behavior became more problematic over time. But maybe not. And that's why David's situation with Nic is so difficult. As he hugs his son one last time before leaving his college dorm room—just as my father did with me forty years ago—there is no way of knowing whether it's the start of something amazing, or a path toward destruction. Will he end up in that garage like Deb, hoping for one last miracle to save his son?

Nic seems to thrive in college—at first. He enjoys learning, wants to be a writer, and falls in love with a nice girl. It's everything that's *supposed* to happen. But again, when it comes to addiction, all bets are off. Nic finds some pain pills in his girlfriend's parents' medicine cabinet during Thanksgiving break. He takes a few of them. And then it's right back on the crazy train. He drops out of school, disappears back into the void, briefly reemerging to beg his father for money to leave San Francisco and start a "new life" in New York. But David's heard all these lies before. He keeps his bottom lines. So then, just like Molly did with Deb, Nic plays the guilt card: "You know," he tells his father sneeringly, "the more I think about it, Mom should have gotten custody."

David sees through this attempt at emotional blackmail, but it must be terribly painful to hear nonetheless. And Nic's insinuation that his parents' divorce "caused" his addiction is not necessarily far off. Children of divorced parents have nearly triple the amount of emotional problems, drug use, and arrests than children of intact families.[24] A sudden loss of security leads many to seek emotional coping mechanisms. Drugs and alcohol fit the bill nicely. But again, isn't this just *another* reason, among dozens of other reasons, or possibly no reasons, why Nic is addicted to meth? Nick can't change the past, but he can change what he believes about it. And some beliefs are better than others when it comes to successful recovery.

Predictable consequences follow, and Nic ODs. By this point David has started to realize he can't win. Nic's mother Vicki (played by the always versatile Amy Ryan) offers to step in and place him into rehab in Los Angeles. And for fourteen months he thrives, speaks at 12-Step meetings, and even works at a treatment center. Perhaps David was indeed part of the problem? Mothers and fathers have very different ways of influencing their children. Perhaps Nic was trying too hard to please his father, but always coming up short? Perhaps he felt overly judged, burdened by his father's lofty expectations of him? Perhaps...*perhaps?* But once again, there are a thousand contingencies, tons of blame to go around. All of it irrelevant by this point. What's done is done. The past is the past. It's the choices Nic makes *today* that matter.

And therein lies the rub. Today is too much like yesterday. Tomorrow will be more of the same. There is just so much *time* to fill when you're sober. And nothing to make the time go faster or seem more interesting. Oh wait, there is. The instant after Nic graduates

---

24 https://www.webmd.com/parenting/features/children-coping-with-divorce

from college, bids farewell to his family, and starts to drive off into the sunset, he's suddenly overcome by an idea. Those of you in recovery like me know the idea I'm referring to. It's the fantastical idea that reality is broken. Maybe it wasn't before, maybe it was always broken and Nic just had the bad luck of being born into it, or maybe he broke it after that first hit of meth. Whatever. The point is, there's only one way to fix it, and that's by using again.

Nic pulls over to the side of the road to think this through, even though his brain has already decided for him. He calls his AA sponsor, Spencer (played by Andre Royo), for support. One must go through the motions, after all. Spencer congratulates Nic for graduating college and says, "Welcome to the real world." And Nic's response pretty much sums it all up: "Oh, I don't want to live in the real world." And really, how can anyone argue with that? The claim that reality is broken is unfalsifiable. It may well be true. So as if parenting isn't difficult enough, let's add ontological debates to the list of challenges mothers and fathers need to overcome in order to help their kids recover.

Predictable consequences ensue. Nic hooks up with an old girlfriend, shoots up, has great sex, robs his dad's house, she ODs, and everybody spirals—including David, who by now is in full-on helpless mode and struggling to keep his new marriage and family from collapsing under the weight of Nic's addiction. He finally arrives at that terrible fork in the road that he'd been fighting all these years to avoid. No more compromises, no more bailouts, no more rescue squad. When Vicki calls to say Nic has been missing for several days, David finally resigns himself to that elemental truth no parent of an addict ever wants to admit: "I don't think you can save people."

Beautiful Boy did lackluster business at the box office but was well-liked by critics and film festivals. Chalamet's wonderful performance earned him nominations at the Golden Globes, Screen Actors Guild Awards, BAFTA Awards, and Critics' Choice Awards, among others. Given its theatrical roll-out and marketing campaign, I'm sure the producers were hoping the film would be a solid Oscar contender. They developed the project for years, nurtured it at every turn, had high expectations, overcame countless challenges, and were proud of how the film turned out. But the film won no Oscars. In fact, it wasn't even nominated in any categories. So in Hollywood, just like in parenting, you can plan and hope all you want—but in the end it's all up for grabs.

CHAPTER 9
Addiction as a Ménage à Trois
Days of Wine and Roses
When a Man Loves a Woman

I met the love of my life over the summer after my junior year of high school. Wow, we had a blast. She made me laugh, made all my friends laugh, and had this great way of making everybody feel awesome when she was around. She had this funny way of bringing out my good side, making me feel popular.
Things were getting pretty serious between us, and she ended up coming to college with me. I wanted to get great grades, so we didn't see much of each other during the week, but on the weekends we made up for lost time. I eventually joined a fraternity and of course all my frat brothers loved her too.
    As my career took off, we settled into a nice routine. She'd come with me on my business trips on private jet, and be my date at all the lavish

Hollywood parties. I had an expense account and spent a lot of it on her. Sometimes she got a little too clingy and I would break up with her for a few months just to get some space. I worried that I was too reliant on her for my happiness, fun, and success. But she was so captivating, so alluring, so available, anywhere and anytime, that eventually I would take her back and we'd pick up right where we left off.

She was also a really great "wingman" when it came to meeting women, and she encouraged us to have an open relationship. We had one threesome after another and it worked great most of the time. Occasionally the other woman would get jealous or think we were spending too much time together and leave us. Like any relationship, we had our share of breakups and reconciliations, and as I got older, I started to realize the relationship was in trouble. So after a really big fight where I ended up in jail, I knew I'd had enough.

Breaking up with her was probably the most difficult decision I'd ever faced. I missed her so much. She had been such an important part of my life and we'd had so many great times together that I felt like I had lost a key part of my identity. Nothing seemed as fun anymore. But over time, I realized that wasn't true. I'm having way more fun now without her. Sure, every now and then I really want to get back together. After all, I did love her. But it wasn't real love. It was a selfish love, a love based on possession. I just wanted to own her, but in the end, she owned me.

By now you might have figured out that the "love of my life" in this story was alcohol. The point I'm trying to underscore here is that people—like me, maybe like you—who get addicted to drugs and alcohol have an ongoing and important *relationship* with their substance of choice. It's a love affair that can span decades. And when you bring a partner or spouse who also drinks or uses into the equation, it becomes a ménage à trois with addiction.

Of course there is plenty of evidence—both practical and clinical—that says that the majority of these three-way relationships will eventually self-destruct. Addiction is clearly a key factor behind many failed marriages, including my own. But when it comes to alcohol, this generalization may not be totally true across the board. There's a University of Michigan Study that found that couples who drink together report higher levels of marital satisfaction.[25] Said the study's author, "We think that the takeaway is that it appears couples with similar drinking habits are less irritated with one another." But then again, take this with a grain of salt, because the report was published in Men's Journal and their whole revenue model revolves around ads for liquor and erectile dysfunction.

However, upon further investigation I found an actual scientific study[26] underwritten by the National Institutes of Health that concluded that people tend to drink more when they're with their spouses, and when they do, they report higher levels of marital satisfaction. An interesting caveat: Women who also drink with others outside their marriage report higher levels of satisfaction, but the same is not true of men. Maybe this explains why I was always happy when my wife went out with her wine-o-clock friends, but she wasn't too happy when I hung around with my beer buddies.

But again, these results only tell one side of the story because the study only captures a small snapshot in time. Over the course of a whole marriage, alcohol and substance use becomes increasingly problematic and destructive, especially when you throw kids into the mix. And also keep in mind these results are 15 years old. The pandemic changed everything. Married couples were forced to spend more time together in isolated, stressful, unstructured environments. Out-on-the-town fun and carefree drinking was replaced with at-home-bored and burned-out drinking. Divorce rates went up 34% during lockdown.

---

25 https://www.mensjournal.com/health-fitness/the-key-to-a-happy-marriage-drinking-together-w430182/

26 https://www.ncbi.nlm.nih.gov/pmc/articles/PMC6489547/

And this is not to say that relationships or marriages soaked in alcohol can't work at all. A former girlfriend of mine once took me home to meet her parents over Thanksgiving. I planned to be on my best behavior, but I realized much to my delight that mom and dad were living in a different booziverse. These were two very well-established, successful medical professionals who could drink me under the table.

Cocktails every weekday at 5pm sharp. Promptly starting at noon on the weekends. A wine cellar worth over a million dollars. A liquor "closet." They were perfect parents—happy and healthy, affectionate with one another, and still very much in love after 40 years of marriage. I'm sure they had their fair share of **Who's Afraid of Virginia Woolf?** moments after the guests had all gone home for the night. But from what I could gather, their ménage à trois with alcohol was an unqualified success. They were having their cake and eating it too. A *lot* of it. Every day. And I wanted what they had. I considered proposing to their daughter that very night.

Were they outliers? Not at all. Many successful marriages, like many a peace treaty or business deal, have alcohol to thank. Cynics would say you'd have to be drinking just to choose to get married to begin with. My own parents enjoyed a successful marriage where alcohol wasn't just part of their social lives, it was a key component of my father's career in the Foreign Service. He was paid to get foreign dignitaries drunk so our government could forge useful alliances with them—so-called "soft power."

Alcohol is so pervasive and socially acceptable that it's largely synonymous with love itself. You can buy T-shirts that read "Some people wait their whole lives to meet their drinking buddy. I married mine." Alcohol can certainly help couples feel less inhibited, more honest, more intimate, more "in love," but is this really the right kind of love? And is it actually love for the other person, or for the other person *and* their drinking habits?

To explore these questions, I chose two important films that take on the subject of alcohol use disorder in marriages. Released in 1962, **Days of Wine and Roses** explores the complete story cycle of alcohol addiction from the point of view of two people (played by Jack Lemmon and Lee Remick) who slowly go down the rabbit hole together. **When a Man Loves a Woman** is a 1994 film starring Meg Ryan and Andy García about a marriage that's being torn apart by only one spouse's drinking. Both of these films not only offer great insights into love's relationship to alcohol (and vice-versa) but force us to consider the very nature of love itself.

In the early '40s, Alcoholics Anonymous had been gaining traction thanks to the publication of a game-changing *Saturday Evening Post* article about it in 1941.[27] In 1945, **The Lost Weekend** cracked the window open on society's dirty, little secret of "alcoholism." Even though it went on to win a Best Picture Oscar, Hollywood was hesitant to roll the dice on another film about the controversial subject.

But with post-war prosperity and America in a generally festive mood, alcohol continued to take its toll, not just on individuals, but on family members too. AA founder Bill Wilson's wife set up Al-Anon in the early '50s to provide support for family members whose loved ones were struggling with alcohol. By 1962 the market was ready for (and probably needed) a film like **Days of Wine and Roses**. The pitch was simple: Alcohol and love don't mix. The producers went so far as to advertise that fact in their own marketing. Some versions of the movie posters read: "This, in its own terrifying way, is a love story."

Days of Wine and Roses was directed by Blake Edwards, whose body of work and influence in Hollywood can't be overstated. Edwards is remembered as a comedy film director, but when he made **Days of Wine and Roses** his hilarious **Pink Panther** films were still many years off. After **Breakfast at Tiffany's**, Edwards had the box-office clout to

---

27 https://www.saturdayeveningpost.com/2015/12/aa/

make films about subjects he cared about, and one of those subjects was alcohol abuse. I had dinner with Edwards and his wife, Julie Andrews, in the late '90s at some really expensive Italian restaurant in Brentwood, CA. I don't remember what project we were there to discuss; I just remember telling him how much he had influenced my career as a comedy writer. He seemed indifferent to the praise and told me he would rather I be inspired by his more serious films. I asked him which ones he recommended. He told me a few I hadn't seen and ended with **Days of Wine and Roses**. I distinctly remember the waiter coming by at that precise moment and asking us if we wanted to see a wine list. There was a brief pause, Edwards sighed, and then Andrews abruptly said "no."

A story about alcohol probably came naturally to Edwards because he already had a long-time pre-existing relationship with it. Joining the Coast Guard after high school, he got drunk and dove into a shallow swimming pool.[28] He narrowly avoided paralysis and spent five months in traction. He and Jack Lemmon drank heavily before and after the production of **Days of Wine and Roses**, and both ended up checking themselves into rehab about a year after it came out. Even after quitting, Blake maintained a nostalgic working relationship with alcohol, no more evident than in his film **10**, where Dudley Moore's character stays plastered for most of the film.[29] But it went a bit deeper than that. Blake had bouts with depression (then again anybody working in Hollywood probably does), and almost committed suicide on a beach in Malibu after a string of box-office failures. I wonder if his past relationship with alcohol or perhaps other palliatives had something to do with that.

---

28 I also did this once when I was in high school, and almost broke my neck. But I was tripping on acid, not drunk.

29 Moore's "adorable drunk" persona brought him tremendous box-office success two years later when he starred in **Arthur**. I sat next to him in British Airways First Class from Heathrow to L.A. once. He went through three bottles of wine all by himself.

Casting Jack Lemmon to play the part of hard-drinking PR executive Joe Clay must have been a difficult pill for Warner Bros to swallow at the time. Remember that Lemmon was a comedy juggernaut coming off two huge Billy Wilder hits, **Some Like it Hot** and **The Apartment**. It would be like having Jim Carrey do **Schindler's List** right after **Ace Ventura: Pet Detective**. The Studio brass feared that such a heavy drama might tarnish Lemmon's image, so they had him film a sit-down in-person pitch to audiences as part of the film's trailer.[30]

Lemmon, looking very earnest as he puffs on a cigarette, states that the film is very important to him, but stops well short of saying why—or ever once saying "alcohol."

Lemmon was probably attracted to the project because he too had a pre-existing relationship with alcohol. His struggles were a well-kept industry secret for years.

Perhaps this role was a way to process his issues, or to justify his continued behavior.[31] Either way, he delivered a searing performance for which he was nominated for an Academy Award for Best Actor. He later said it was one of his favorite roles in his career.

Lee Remick was also nominated in the Best Actress category for this film. Her performance as a level-headed secretary who crosses over to the dark side to find love is considered her absolute finest. To "act drunk" convincingly is harder than it seems. And Remick absolutely kills it. The authenticity of her performance may be due to the fact that Remick also had a pre-existing relationship with alcohol.[32]

---

30 The trailer can be found on the Apple iTunes store.

31 In interviews years later Lemmon spoke about his drinking issues and how they hit a head a few years after production of the film. Lemmon's challenges continued, however, and he was arrested for drunk driving in 1976.

32 There is a bizarre confluence of how both actors, the subject of alcohol, and me writing this book serendipitously intersect. Once, 20 years ago, when I went jogging in Beverly Hills, I came across Jack Lemmon, walking in the middle of the street, disoriented. I stopped to help him. He told me he couldn't remember the way home.

In another example of art imitating life imitating art, she also sought help for her drinking after the film—just like Lemmon and Blake did. Both Remick and Lemmon visited detox wards at state mental hospitals to prepare for their roles. Who knows, perhaps these experiences, and even acting in the film itself, were informing their own real-life recovery journeys as well?

The film starts with Joe Clay (Lemmon) living the life as a top executive for a public relations agency. At the time it was one of those new-fangled "communications" jobs that seemed sexy, cool, and mysterious—like being an advertising executive. And as **Mad Men** showed us in lovingly rendered detail, day drinking held an outsized profile in these industries. Back then pretty much every white-collar job carried with it the promise of the "three martini lunch."

Unlike blue collar types who had to stay sober to save their arms from getting chopped off in assembly lines, white collar types at most only risked getting their fingers caught in a pencil sharpener. A well-stocked bar used to be a given in every C-Suite. Now, it's cause for termination.

The film starts with Joe procuring beautiful single women for a rich client's yacht party. Basically, he's a glorified pimp in a toxic 1960s work culture drenched in male chauvinism and alcohol. Kirsten Arneson (Remick) joins the party, and Joe mistakenly assumes she's a member of the ad-hoc harem he's assembled. But it turns out she's his boss' secretary. He offers her a drink. She tells him she doesn't drink. Joe takes it as a challenge, an affront to his view of how reality should operate. And from that moment on he's on a mission to have Kirsten bend to that reality and join his ménage à trois with alcohol.

But Kirsten's no pushover, at least for now. Back at the office, hung over as usual, Joe tries to cajole her into a dinner date with a gift and some tired one-liners. When that doesn't work, he tries to cut her down a few notches: "I'll tell you what special qualifications you

---

I asked him if he had taken any medications or drunk alcohol. He said "No, I never drink." Separately, in high school, my first drinking buddy was Lee Remick's niece.

have," Joe says to her as they ride down an elevator, "You're pretty. [And your boss] loves to have you around to look at and lean on when he gets drunk, like he did last night, and who knows *what else*." Wow, how's that for mansplaining, 1960s style? Any girl who doesn't go out with him must be a prostitute, right? Kirsten lets him off easy with a bitch-slap to the face, the standard mid-century response to a guy getting "fresh." Today, a comment like that could get you jail time.[33]

For reasons that don't make sense until shortly afterwards, Kirsten actually takes Joe up on the dinner invitation and they go to a nice restaurant. But eating is the last thing on his mind. He's befuddled by the fact that she doesn't order a drink. Angered by it, in fact. So when he discovers that she actually has a vice, chocolate, he orders her a Brandy Alexander. She likes it but doesn't know it contains alcohol. It's basically the 1960s version of spiking a girl's drink or slipping her a roofie. Perhaps it's not entirely fair to paint Joe as a predator on the prowl for the perfect drinking buddy. He probably finds Kirsten to be intelligent, personable, and witty. But it's her unconditional acceptance of his drinking that makes him truly fall in love with her.

Fortunately for Joe (not so fortunate for Kirsten), his scheme works. Kirsten gets tipsy, loves the feeling booze gives her, and stays out late with Joe instead of going back to her roach-infested apartment. And it's then that we learn the reason why she'd go out to dinner with the same man she slapped in the elevator a few scenes earlier: simple loneliness. She grew up without a mother's love, her widowed father comes from emotionally constipated Scandinavian stock, and she's struggling to get by in the big city. But thanks to the magic of a few Brandy Alexanders, for once she doesn't feel isolated, physically objectified, or judged.

She finally feels heard as a woman, not spoken down to by a man. Alcohol does this. Why else would humans like to drink it so much?

---

33 When I watch these scenes today, I see how so much of the #MeToo Movement was probably fueled by decades of pent-up resentment resulting from millions of these kinds of microaggressions over time.

The feelings it enhances or disinhibits are all neurochemical precursors to falling in love. It's biology's favorite feedback loop. But is Kirsten actually falling in love with Joe the person, or the Joe who makes her feel less lonely and unloved when they drink together? Conversely, is Joe just falling in love with the Kirsten who'll never stand in the way of his drinking?

Regardless of what kind of love it is, they both fall into it. But for their relationship to really succeed, Kirsten's consumption has to catch up to Joe's. She needs to be groomed, slowly and purposefully, so that she can go from no drinking, to occasional drinking, to always drinking, to always drinking a lot. Feelings of "love" and intimacy are eventually only made possible by how much and how often they drink together. Alcohol has become their love tonic, aphrodisiac, and antidepressant. When they announce their marriage to Kirsten's father, Ellis (played by the grim-faced Charles Bickford), he rebuffs them. To overcome the pain, it's no surprise Kirsten wants to go drink.

Cut to a year later and they've had a baby. Kirsten is off the booze because she's lactating. Joe comes home drunk from a party and has a sloppy temper tantrum because she won't party with him. It seems the "fun" is out of their marriage. So he becomes her pusher again, just like on their first date. His message is clear: *If you don't drink with me, you don't love me.* Or is it *I don't love you unless you drink with me?* Lonely, financially dependent, and scared, Kirsten pours herself a drink and hops right back on the hamster wheel. And this is how it goes for many people who forfeit common sense for love. You finally give into the pusher. The pusher becomes your dealer. The dealer now owns you. Checkmate.

Predictable consequences follow. Joe's work performance suffers. He gets demoted to a crappy account and spends all his time traveling. Kirsten neglects her daughter, Debbie; drinks all day; falls asleep with a lit cigarette; and burns the apartment down. None of this is her fault, mind you. It's Joe's fault for being away on business all the time.

She's lonely. There's nobody to drink with. All the "love" has gone out of their relationship. Which means they'll just have to drink together again to rekindle it. And so on and so on…

With Joe eventually losing his job and Kirsten a danger to herself and her daughter, they finally arrive at a point of reckoning. I'm sure most couples with drinking problems end up in the same place eventually. I can tell you from experience, it's not a pretty place. Both spouses know they have to quit. They make solemn promises to themselves and each other. But now two people in the habit of enabling and excusing each other's addiction suddenly have to do the opposite. And let's not forget that they're in a ménage à trois with alcohol. This vertex point of the threesome will do everything in its power to split the defense and get everybody back together again. So actually quitting devolves into a childish game. *I'll quit if you quit. Will you quit if I quit? You stop drinking first. No, you stop drinking first.*

If they make it past this level in the game, the next level up is a tap dance around the truth with the help of confirmation bias—the tendency to only consider facts that agree with one's preexisting beliefs about reality. Adverse consequences of alcohol abuse are assigned different levels of "factiness," or discounted entirely. *I just burned our apartment down. But it doesn't mean I have a problem. These kinds of accidents happen all the time.*

Remarkably, Kirsten and Joe do manage to quit. They move in with Kirsten's father to work in his landscaping business and regroup financially. After two months sober, they seem to inhabit the same pink cloud, chase each other around like children, and make out on a haystack in the barn. It's their little sober wonderland, with a side of bucolic. Alcohol seems to be the farthest thing from their minds. Joe kisses Kirsten tenderly, and for the first time in the movie he appears to feel love, genuine non-artificially-induced love.

"I can't remember us ever feeling this way before," he says, brimming with hope.

"Except after a *couple of drinks…*" she answers.

And just like that, it happens. By equating love and alcohol, Kirsten opens that door juuuuuuuust a crack. Feelings of emotional love get replaced by that visceral hungering, the all-too-familiar craving for some*thing* you love instead of some*one* you love. Their sober wonderland facade begins to disintegrate, revealing a prison of abstinence behind it. And what's the point of prison if not to serve your time or escape from it?[34] So the little games start all over again. *Will she drink if I drink? Will I drink if she drinks? Will he relapse first? Or should I? We've been so good for two months. Don't we* deserve *it?* Yes, of course you both deserve it, alcohol kindly reminds them. And so the threesome is up and running again just like old times, and it's got a lot of catching up to do.

Needless to say, Joe and Kirsten get loaded and do stupid shit. Joe destroys his father-in-law's plant nursery in a frantic quest to find a bottle of whiskey he hid for later. Kirsten tries to make out with her own father and then slaps her daughter around. All terrible things, but amateur-hour stuff when compared to what happens every day in real life. Domestic spousal and child abuse—where alcohol plays a starring role—was another one of society's dirty, little secrets that wouldn't surface in the public discourse until the early '70s.[35] Hollywood finally tackled the subject in 1984's **The Burning Bed** with Farrah Fawcett. For **Days of Wine and Roses** to be truly authentic, we should have seen Joe drunkenly assault Kirsten, verbally or physically (or vice-versa). But hey, baby steps.

Joe ends up in a straitjacket in a detox ward. Lemmon channels Ray Milland's **The Lost Weekend** delirium tremens terror, but turns

---

[34] Joe and Kirsten joke around that they are "inmates" and Kirsten's father is the warden.

[35] The World Health Organization (WHO) estimates that roughly 55% of domestic abuse perpetrators were drinking alcohol prior to the assault. Women who are abused are 15 times more likely to abuse alcohol.

the volume up to 11 as he bites the orderlies and snarls like a vicious animal. It's all a bit over the top and veers into **Reefer Madness** hyper-alarmist territory when you consider that only 2% of people with severe alcohol use disorder ever experience the terrifying "little green men" hallucinations that Joe has.[36] Still, if one of the aims of the movie was to sound the general alarm about the dangers of alcohol addiction, this scene certainly does the trick.

Enter Jim Hungerford, played by America's favorite TV sportswriting slob and medical examiner Jack Klugman. He visits Joe in the rubber room, passes him a cigarette through the porthole,[37] and somberly announces he's from Alcoholics Anonymous. Who knew AA made house calls? But back in the day they did. Whereas today people from drug and DUI courts are funneled to AA meetings by default,[38] in the first decades after its founding the organization had not yet scaled, so it needed to actively recruit converts in detox wards, shelters, and hospitals. And good thing they did because before the mental health industries caught up with the problem, AA was really the only game in town besides the funny farm or prison. Klugman does a wonderful job as their brand ambassador: he introduces the disease concept, takes Joe to his first meeting (where he admits to being an alcoholic), and becomes his sponsor. The film is credited with greatly helping Alcoholics Anonymous to grow its worldwide reach and impact in the ensuing years.

Joe encourages Kirsten to follow down the 12-Step path that has allowed him to stay sober and begin to heal, but she refuses. Her reasons are reflective of the common objections people sometimes have to 12-Step programs: The label "alcoholic" doesn't sit well with her; she

---

36 https://www.ncbi.nlm.nih.gov/pmc/articles/PMC6286444

37 I'm convinced that this scene became the inspiration for an identical scene in **Apocalypse Now** between Dennis Hopper and Martin Sheen.

38 Several court rulings now mandate that evidence-based alternatives to AA be offered in drug and DUI sentencing.

believes she can achieve sobriety with her willpower alone (producers leave out any mention of a "Higher Power"), and she's simply too prideful to "degrade" herself in front of a bunch of strangers. JP Miller, the screenwriter of the film, is said to have consulted carefully with AA representatives to make sure the film conveyed these (valid) objections; otherwise it could have come off as one big puff piece.

But the biggest reason Kirsten doesn't want to try the program is that she simply doesn't want to quit drinking. Like Nic's relationship with meth in **Beautiful Boy**, she thinks reality is broken and will always stay that way unless she drinks. "The world looks so dirty to me when I'm not drinking," she tells Joe as he tries to rescue her from a cheap hotel room, her hair a mess, dress dirtied, and drool on her face. It's Kirsten who's broken, not her reality.

Like many spouses of people with alcohol use disorders, Joe thinks his love can save her. But he forgets that the anchor of their three-way relationship was, and still is, alcohol. "We always knew that we were in love," he tells Jim, "we just knew it; there was no doubt about it." Well, apparently there is, because Kirsten has replaced Joe with other more dependable drinking buddies. "She [only] loves the drunk you," Jim reminds him. And in typical deluded "alcoholic thinking," Joe completely forgets the fact that he pushed Kirsten to join his alcohol-centered reality from the get-go: "I just can't believe this is happening to me." He may as well have said, "I'm so pissed I got exactly what I wanted."

Days of Wine and Roses ends on both a high note and a low one. Joe chooses a life of total abstinence and a loving relationship with his daughter Debbie. His chances of a happy, healthy, sober life are as good as anyone's in recovery. But as much as he wants love, *real* love, and intimacy from Kirsten, both know she can't give him that unless she keeps drinking. So Joe issues the ultimatum: "Just room for you and me. No threesome." And sadly, Kirsten walks. She'll have to seek a new ménage à trois with someone else, and likely die trying. And this is how it goes for many marriages where alcohol is a key component. In the end, love can't conquer all unless it's the right kind of love from the very start.

———————

So what exactly is the "right" kind of love? That question—as well as many other aspects of the alcohol ménage à trois—are explored in **When a Man Loves a Woman**, starring Meg Ryan as a high school counselor with a severe drinking problem and Andy Garcia as an airline pilot forced to confront some difficult realities in his marriage as a result. The film grossed over $170 million in worldwide box-office revenue, which makes it by far the most commercially successful film we'll discuss in this book. The timing of the project could not have been more perfect in terms of packaging: Both actors were white hot at the time they signed on. Meg Ryan could do no wrong after her adorably effervescent performances in **When Harry Met Sally** and **Sleepless in Seattle**, and Garcia was a much-sought-after Oscar nominee whose star power went supernova with **The Godfather Part III**.

While Ryan's and Garcia's draw made the film successful, it was the chemistry between them that made it memorable. To help create that chemistry, Touchstone Pictures (a Disney film subsidiary in the '90s) turned to Luis Mandoki—perhaps the finest, most underrated romantic drama directors of his generation.

Originally from Mexico, Mandoki is a kind, graceful intellectual who seems out of place in Hollywood, but whose early successes helped pave the way for the careers of Guillermo Del Toro, Alfonso Cuarón, and Alejandro González Iñárritu. He's a very lyrical storyteller who wants every scene he shoots to be as beautiful and emotionally evocative as possible. When I was at Universal Pictures, Mandoki pitched me several films he wanted to do as part of a multi-picture deal we were negotiating. Each project was more romantically sprawling than the next. The guy was just born to tell stories about love. But as **When a Man Loves a Woman** clearly shows, it wasn't just romantic love that interested him.

From the first frame of the film, it's clear Alice (Ryan) and Michael (Garcia) are mad about each other. They engage in sexy role play at a local bar, and then make out like horny teenagers while all the patrons gawk. Back at home, they have the picture perfect family with two adorable young daughters Casey and Jess (the latter played by the incredibly talented child actor Tina Majorino). That night they go to a great restaurant, dance the night away, then return home and (at least try to) make sweet, passionate love. If perfect marriages looked like anything, this would be it.

But appearances deceive. Any marriage, no matter how seemingly "perfect," must conceal at least some cracks and fissures. And nothing smooths out the sharp edges of reality quite like love and alcohol. Because he's so smitten with Alice, Michael is willing to excuse her behavior later that night when she throws eggs at a neighbor's car because its alarm keeps going off. He even joins in the drunken revelry, albeit reluctantly because he drinks responsibly and probably wouldn't do crazy shit like that even if he were drunk. Cognitive dissonance kicks in. Alice isn't "too drunk," he's probably telling himself, "she's just adorably spontaneous and brave." Okay sure, we know Alice is too drunk, but when Alice is drunk Alice is cute, cuddly, frisky, and fun. She's the "awesome first date" version of his wife—except she's like that every night of the week thanks to alcohol. What husband wouldn't want his wife to be like Alice sometimes, or even all the time?

Welcome to the vast gray area of so-called "enabling" behavior. Whereas in **Days of Wine and Roses** Joe was actively pushing Kirsten to drink, in this film Michael is simply standing by and passively doing nothing to stop Alice from getting blitzed. Sure, he knows her drinking has become an issue, but until it causes any adverse consequences, who is he to try to change who she is and how she expresses herself? There's nothing wrong with him trying to maximize his "marital satisfaction," as cited in the study above. Her alcohol use has become a key part of how she "loves" him and is loved by him, emotionally and sexually. He feels needed every time he cleans up her messes and puts her to bed. It's the "spark" in their marriage. But a point is reached where for

Michael to stand by and let Alice self-destruct just so he can keep that spark alive would be selfish, irresponsible, and potentially dangerous.

The first breaking point comes when Alice gets drunk on a couples' vacation with Michael in Mexico, falls off a boat, and almost drowns. Both Alice and Michael see it as a positive outcome. The subject of her drinking has been broached, and now Michael doesn't look like "the bad guy" who challenges Alice on behavior that he himself has benefitted from emotionally. And Alice claims that the accident is the "best thing that could've happened to me," because it will force her to take stock of her problem. Focus on the word "force" here. While accidents and health scares are great motivators for change, they are still externalities that don't always affect whether the addict is prepared to change on the inside where it really counts.

And Alice is clearly not ready to change. Back at home, she makes a half-hearted attempt to throw out her secret stash of vodka, but then ends up drinking it instead. With Michael gone for work, she can really push the envelope. She returns home from a school happy hour completely tanked and orders their nanny (played gracefully by Lauren Tom) to go home. Now it's just her and the kids. They're part of the ménage à trois now too.

The scene that follows is heartbreaking to watch, but important to see. Alice's daughter Jess shows her a drawing she did on a computer. Alice drunkenly rebuffs her and orders her to do her homework. Jess is crestfallen. This is where "fun mom" ends and child abuse begins. Alice doesn't have to hit Jess (that happens a few scenes later) to abuse her. An equally sinister form of child abuse is neglect. And from the look on Jess' face, we can tell this neglect has been going on for some time.

It was brave but probably risky to include the subject of child abuse in such a mainstream Hollywood film. Depicting child abuse of any kind in films has long been considered taboo. No mainstream Hollywood studio film had ever dared broach the topic. But avoiding a topic doesn't make it go away. Whereas in ***Days of Wine and Roses*** Joe and Kirsten's daughter, Debbie, plays a very minor role, in this film Jess and her younger half-sister Casey (played by Mae Whitman) are central characters in the film. They are affected by their mother's drinking just as much (or more) than Michael is, and Mandoki doesn't shy away from showing us that. Seeing the unfolding drama through their eyes adds another much-needed-yet-seldom-seen dimension to the story.

The final breaking point comes when Alice slaps Jess and then drinks half a bottle of vodka to try to forget it ever happened. She passes out in the shower and crashes through the glass. Poor Jess has to call her father to tell him she thinks her own mother has died. You can imagine the effect this kind of trauma would have on a child in real life. There is already ample evidence that the addiction epidemic in America has created a mental health crisis among the children of addicts, many of whom—like Jess—find themselves dialing 911 when both their parents OD. Compounding the tragedy, in many cases the children of addicts turn to the very same substances to help them cope, and the cycle of addiction continues into the next generation. We will touch on some aspects of cross-generational addiction in our chapter about the documentary film ***Recovery Boys***.

Michael flies to Alice's hospital bedside and she finally reveals the truth about the extent of her drinking. All day, every day, a quart of vodka a day. "How come I couldn't see this?" Michael asks. "Because I hid it," Alice answers. And it's at this point that we realize how that gray area of enabling has come back to bite Michael in the ass. What sane husband doesn't notice when his own wife is drinking a quart of vodka a day? He had to have known. But he chose to do nothing about it. He put his own children's safety at risk in exchange for keeping the spark in his marriage. Michael is suffering from the same delusional thinking patterns that allowed Alice's addiction to flourish to begin with. In fact, in this moment of crisis where bottom lines should have been struck, Michael extends the delusion even further.

Jess just got smacked by her mother. But she's "fine," Michael tells Alice.

Um, no, she's not.

"We're gonna' get you better so it doesn't happen again," he continues.

It all sounds so easy, doesn't it? Like checking a box.

"Please don't hate me, because I'll die if you do," she continues.

"The thought would never enter my mind," Michael replies.

Really?

Here you begin to see just how surreal a ménage à trois with alcohol can become for everyone involved. It's magical thinking on steroids. Michael immediately tries to sweep the last five years of their marriage under the carpet. He doesn't even stop to ask Alice why she drank a quart of vodka a day. Not because it doesn't matter, but because he knows it *should* have mattered, and he should have done something about it—way before it got to this point. To deflect his own guilt, he turns this whole mess into a quick cleanup on aisle three. He can fix anything that's broken, even Alice. "I'm going to find you the best treatment; the best in the fucking world," he tells her, as if that's something he even understands, much less totally controls.

This is a key point in the story where the focus turns away from Alice's problems and begins to reveal Michael's as well. The way he relates to Alice while she's in rehab paints a picture of a man who's impatient, overconfident, and unwilling to accept the complexity of the problem he had a part in creating. When Alice calls him after detox, he doesn't ask her how she's doing; he's just happy the "hard part's over." He defaults to his winning formula of sexy role play, imagining that she's naked, desperate to rekindle the spark in their physical relationship that's under threat now that Alice is sober. As she hangs up the phone, Alice looks like she wants to jump out of her own skin.

It would have been easier to keep the focus on Alice as she goes through rehab and emerges right as rain on the other side. But instead, screenwriters Ron Bass (**Rain Man**) and Al Franken (yes, *Senator* Al Franken) take us on a much more emotionally complex recovery journey that examines the tumultuous interpersonal dynamics in the time period after Alice completes rehab. This had never been explored in a mainstream film before, but it's the most important part of a person's recovery. Rehab is the easy part. Afterward, the real work begins. And it's hard work, not just for Alice, but for Michael too. Film critic Roger Ebert—himself in recovery from alcohol—said of the film, "It's about Michael's recovery from Alice's recovery."

The first warning signs of a post-rehab shake up in their relationship come as Michael goes to pick her up at the completion of her program. What becomes immediately apparent: She doesn't need him. Her focus is primarily on her daughters. He seems completely out of place and irrelevant as he wanders the grounds, in control of nothing. More unsettling still is the fact that Alice has forged deep and meaningful friendships at the rehab facility—including one with Gary, played by Philip Seymour Hoffman (sadly, in another life-imitating-art moment, Hoffman would die from a heroin overdose twenty years later). Michael is clearly jealous of Gary, but not in any romantic context. It's because he and all of Alice's new friends threaten to kill his starring role as her savior, protector, and clean-up crew. When Alice tells Michael how much these people mean to her recovery, he tells her she can now talk to him instead. She's less than thrilled.

I don't want it to sound like Michael is the antagonist in this film. Let's not forget he was the guy holding down the fort while Alice was in rehab. He took care of the kids, supported them as they cried themselves to sleep, changed his whole work schedule around them, risked his career, and paid all the bills after Alice lost her job. He has every right to feel angry and resentful for what Alice has put the family through. But the Alice who's come home after rehab is not the same person who went in. He'll have to communicate with her in a whole new way, without alcohol to smooth out her rough edges. He's now a vital part of her recovery, but just not under the terms he believes he's entitled to—with entitlement being the operative term here.

The period after a spouse returns from treatment is easily the most difficult part of their recovery. Yes, overcoming urges and reassimilation into sober life are challenging, but the greatest threat to success can sometimes come from their spouse, who feels entitled to an explanation for what has happened. But sometimes there isn't one. Or the explanations come off as petty excuses. They feel entitled to some sort of repayment of an emotional debt for the damage that's been done. But this puts even more pressure on the spouse in recovery. They feel entitled to an apology, but no apology seems genuine enough. I've experienced all these things firsthand in my own relationship. It's quite common for people to relapse due to the stresses created by their spouse's demands for closure, reciprocity, and proper atonement. With so much pressure being applied, it can sometimes feel like the spouse *wants* their partner to relapse.

In Michael's case he feels like Alice is rejecting him, physically and emotionally. She won't reciprocate his physical advances, a key ingredient of the spark their marriage once had. And when he offers to help, it comes off as too controlling. Because it is. Often, spouses automatically assume their partner needs and wants their help, and when they don't accept it, resentment builds even further. But a person in recovery is under no obligation to follow their spouse's advice, or even listen to it. Yes, Michael can feel Alice is ungrateful for everything he's done to help her so far, but that doesn't entitle him to control her recovery process going forward. Healing will conform to Alice's timeline, not his. He needs to let Alice do Alice and realize that this new version of Alice doesn't need him to pick up the pieces anymore.

As their marriage deteriorates, Alice suggests they try couple's counseling. It doesn't go well. They both realize there needs to be more to their relationship than just physical intimacy. Their total reliance on that winning formula no longer works. For too long Michael has used it as a way to gloss over all the problems in their marriage, in the same way Alice used alcohol to ignore or forget them. Alice herself says, "Maybe I should start to learn to live in reality instead of trying to escape from it." But reality has jagged little edges. Sanding down those edges takes time and hard work. And since Michael can't control that process, he feels ambushed. Alice feels unheard.

Next he tries going to an Al-Anon meeting. That goes just as badly. Michael simply can't understand how people in these meetings feel a need to talk about their feelings instead of acting on them. He views their lack of control as a weakness. For him it's all black or white. No gray area. Do or do not, there is no try. But as family support programs always remind us, control over another person's addiction is an illusion. Trying to control a person's recovery is toxic. Control is one of the problems that has led Alice and Michael to this place to begin with. During a fight that almost turns violent, Alice says it best, "I think I could love you again if you could just once say 'I don't know.'" Instead, Michael packs his bags and the couple separates.

To say this is a painful point in the story is an understatement. I know because I've lived through it. Physical separation is hard enough, but the recriminations, resentments, should-have-could-haves, feelings of being unheard, being taken totally for granted, the guilt—it all comes barreling at you at once at 500 miles an hour. And then throw in having to explain everything to the kids. How should you explain "alcoholism" to a six-year-old? Do you? Is there any way to sugarcoat a divorce? Mandoki includes several touching scenes of Michael struggling to explain some of these things to Jess. He tells her "Life isn't fair," probably one of the most oft used phrases in parenting. Or at least it should be.

Unfortunately, this is how it ends for many marriages built upon a shaky foundation where love, intimacy and nitty-gritty real-world problem solving are mediated by one or both spouses' addiction. The rough edges lead to cracks that cannot ever be repaired. But **When a Man Loves a Woman** is a Hollywood film, after all. And while perhaps improbable in real life, creating a happy Hollywood ending where Michael and Alice reconcile is a tremendously satisfying resolution that teaches us quite a bit about how to end the addiction ménage à trois gracefully and definitively.

One of Michael's epiphanies comes in the form of a group share in an Al-Anon meeting. He tells the group that he "can't get a handle on things. Everything is loose and fuzzy." By saying this, he's finally acknowledging that he has lost control, or perhaps never had it. And that's okay. He has come to accept that he needs to be loved for who he is, not whether or not he can fix everything.

Alice's epiphanies come out in an emotional six-months-of-sobriety speech at her 12-Step meeting. She finally reveals how her father's alcohol problem and her mother's emotional abuse factored into her own addiction. But she doesn't blame them for her problems; she accepts responsibility for her own choices. She confesses a deep truth about her relationship with Michael and why she chose to stay medicated throughout it: "I knew if he ever really saw the real me, who I was inside, he wouldn't love me."

Michael's in the audience and has heard all of this. They come together to talk. Both of their hard-earned epiphanies have opened up the possibility of unconditional forgiveness, atonement, empathy, and trust. But more importantly, they have created a space in which to build a new relationship upon the foundations of unconditional, selfless love. They kiss each other passionately, just like they kissed at the bar at the beginning of the film, but without the bar this time.

It may sound trite to say that Alice's alcohol addiction is the best thing that ever happened to them, but maybe it is. Yes, addiction is terrible, but it can also be transformational. It pushes couples to an unavoidable fork in the road that can't be ignored or glossed over with alcohol or drugs. Recovery forces spouses to confront who they really were so they can create the person they want to be. They have to create a whole new life. That includes a factory reset on who they want to love, how they want to love, and how they want to be loved. Without drugs and alcohol, a clearer picture of what real love is begins to emerge.

PART II: MICRO-ADDICTIONS
Hopefully Not Deadly; Frequently Problematic: Other Addictions That Cause Chaos

CHAPTER 10
The Good, The Bad, & The Downright Yucky of Sex Addiction
A Dirty Shame
Boy Erased
Shame

Like many other potentially addictive activities, sex between consenting adults creates a very positive feedback loop. It's really the most powerful feedback loop we have. And it's one of the oldest too. Over two billion years ago simple forms of bacteria started exchanging genes through intercourse as a way to gain a competitive survival advantage over those more "square" bacteria that did it the old-fashion way through mitosis. And everything just went downhill from there, culminating in what we now know as divorce court. And for the purposes of this chapter, Sex Addiction.

The jury is still out as to whether sex addiction is actually a "disease" in a clinical sense, or just an opportunistic "affliction" men suddenly suffer from when their girlfriends catch them cheating—

AKA the "Tiger Woods Defense."[39] From a diagnostic point of view, there is little clarity or consensus. According to Google, sex addiction is "a state characterized by compulsive participation or engagement in sexual activity, particularly sexual intercourse, despite negative consequences."

Okay, sex addiction is a thing. But is it harmful? Sometimes. Deadly? Not usually. Annoying? Probably. And again, we must ask: Negative consequences for whom, exactly? Do those who are addicted to sex have a serious problem? How serious?

In this chapter we will do our best to address these questions from the perspectives of three very different films on the topic. One, a lighthearted satire (the "Good"); the second, a melodrama (the "Bad"); and the third, a brutally serious exposé (the "Downright Yucky"). I will try to show that when it comes to sex addiction, people's understanding is heavily biased by their views on morality, religion, and free will. Sex as a "problem" really boils down to perspective. Films and other narrative media help provide that perspective.

But so does nature. If we were to look at sex addiction from the perspective of the "selfish gene"—a term biologist and public intellectual Richard Dawkins coined in his eponymous book—we would be forced to conclude that sex addiction is DNA's version of reproductive Blitzkrieg. Our ancestors who had the proclivity to engage in a lot of sex (who defines "*a lot?*") tended to create more offspring. And this made their selfish genes extremely happy because they accomplished what natural selection required of them: replication. So in a strictly Darwinian sense, sex "addicts" enjoyed a reproductive advantage over those who were "normal." Viewed from this isolated perspective, we might also conclude that sex addiction is a major reason life flourished on the planet to begin with.

---

39 I highly recommend **South Park** Season 14 Episode 1 for a hilariously savage takedown of Mr. Woods, as well as the idea of sex addiction generally. Apparently Matt and Trey are having none of it.

That said, a reproductive advantage is different from a survival advantage. The subject of survival advantage in humans has more to do with social evolution, i.e. how humans interact with each other and either cooperate or try to kill one another. In this context, while sex addiction might confer a reproductive advantage, it could also exert a negative survival advantage. The sex addict hunter-gatherer who seduced or raped a man's "mate" faced the risk of jealous retribution by the individual or the clan. The fling that just got him killed can be seen as an evolutionary Hail Mary in the game of life. If the defilement resulted in a successful pregnancy, that game ended in a tie.

The very notion of sex as an "addiction" seems to be a very recent phenomenon. When I was in high school in suburban Virginia in the late '70s, all my guy friends would have met the clinical definition of a "sex addict," but we were just called "horny teenagers." Instead of Pornhub, we had these things called "magazines" like Playboy. The only term we knew related to aberrant sexual behavior was "pervert." Perverts were the guys who wore trench coats and exposed themselves to little girls at the park or hung out in downtown D.C. at triple X "peep show" parlors. Quaint term, right? One day, a friend and I decided it would be fun to drop acid and check them out—the parlors, not the perverts. There was a lot more than "peeping" going on, so my friend and I bailed before having a really bad trip.

In the same way the average college age male thinks about sex two gazillion times an hour, human beings have been obsessed with the topic of sex since time immemorial. It may have even been a central driver in humans' adoption of language itself. Sure, being able to communicate helped our ancestors successfully hunt in groups and forge the earliest non-aggression pacts, but it also enabled people to engage in an important human bonding ritual: gossip. And gossip is a perfect way for people to covertly discuss who's sleeping with whom, who's cheated on whom, and which potential mate has the most promising genes. Gossip is humanity's way of fostering intergroup reproductive success, anticipating jealousies, predicting sexual rivalries, and mitigating potentially violent retribution.

But talking about sex, and who was doing it with whom, was just the tip of the narrative iceberg. Humans have also always been fascinated by *how* other people do it. Both the act itself, and the human stories surrounding it. The Sanskrit classic **Kama Sutra** was written in 400 BCE and features incredibly graphic descriptions of various positions for sexual intercourse. After reading the book, I had the privilege of touring the erotic temple sculptures in Khajuraho, India, and was amazed to see how limber the Hindu "Kama" practitioners were back in the day. Unless you're a gymnast, do not try these positions at home. Oh, what the hell—try them at home.

But Kama was more than just the mechanics of intercourse. It was also a fascinating exploration of how passion and eroticism are an essential part of an emotionally fulfilling life. This is a surprisingly "modern" and candid way of looking at a very basic human function, divorced from the damper of shame that Christianity would impose upon it five centuries later.

Speaking about modern, we cannot forget the wonderful narrative contributions to the topic of sex made by the ancient Greeks. The poet-playwright Sophocles made incest the climax of his classic **Oedipus** in the 5th century BCE. In 411 BC, Aristophanes' comedy **Lysistrata** recounted how the wives and mistresses of Greek soldiers all went on a sex strike to try to end the Peloponnesian War between the Greek city states. It's arguably the world's first crack at Feminist Literature.

The Greek poets Straton of Sardis, Sappho of Lesbos, and Archilochus wrote erotic poems—some filled with "obscene" and erotic imagery that would have made even the Hindis blush. The Romans didn't disappoint either. The highly erotic poems of an anonymous writer in the first century CE were culled together to produce the **Priapeia**, named after the penis god Priapus. Priapism is now a medical term for a painful erection that just won't go away. It's to the sex addict what owning a liquor store is to the alcoholic.

After Christianity killed everybody's buzz, writing about sex went underground. Few people could read or write during the Middle Ages anyway, so a lot of the writing about sex was done by priests who delighted in chronicling women's infidelities in divorce cases in church logs. The infidelity was always the women's fault, of course. They were invariably portrayed as lustful, conniving, and duplicitous. These traits were eventually rendered incarnate in the form of "witches" who could then be burned at the stake for the "crime" of being "lustful." They were arguably some of history's first convicted "sex addicts." This sad double standard-based form of misogyny fermented over time to reinforce harmful female stereotypes that still live today.

The stereotype of the "lustful maiden" was the highlight of Geoffrey Chaucer's 14th century classic **The Canterbury Tales**. There's nothing quite as riveting as reading about naughty sex in Middle English. Highlighting the sexy parts was the only way our college professor could get us to actually read it. Chapters like The Miller's Tale and The Wife of Bath feature hush-hush body parts, prostitution, and—sadly—lustful, objectified women.

Stories involving sex and passion gradually eked out of the shadows of the Dark Ages thanks to various liberalizing forces like the Renaissance, the Protestant Reformation, and more open-minded English monarchs. By then there were printing presses, so more people could read. But most people couldn't afford to buy books. So they turned to cheap erotica in the form of pamphlets sold in seedy back alleys. "Kitchen prose and gutter rhyme" as my favorite flute-wielding rockstar, Ian Anderson of Jethro Tull, called it. Those pamphlets were precursors to the "Penny Press," and eventually led to magazines and newspapers. They were also the world's first mass-produced pornography. Isn't it funny how the mass adoption of a new medium owes much of its success to sex? Just look at what porn did for the Internet.

Clearly our fascination with sex has fueled literature and the arts for centuries. But the idea of sex as an addiction is relatively new.

Sexual deviancy was a thing, thanks to weirdos like the Marquis de Sade and Roman Emperors like Caligula. But addiction? Not really. The roots of society's discontent with overactive libidos stems less from intercourse and more from masturbation. Jerking off has been driving civil societies crazy for centuries. Not by actually doing it, but the thought of *others* doing it.

Victorian England was totally obsessed with masturbation, probably because its Wealth of Empire afforded it so much free time on its hands. The country plowed massive resources into public service campaigns to overcome the destabilizing power of so-called self-abuse. Way more resources, in fact, than were ever devoted to real public health problems like, say, disease. For a simple habit that takes place in private and hurts no one, you'd think the English were fighting World War III. Such was the plague of self-abuse.

Even though there is nothing in the monotheistic "sacred texts" to indicate otherwise, generations of church leaders from virtually all faiths have railed against the foul practice of rubbing one out. For reasons that remain a mystery, masturbation was seen as A Great Evil. So the *habit* of masturbation (and addiction thereof) must have been the handiwork of the Great Satan. Anti-jerk-off contraptions that resembled Inquisition-era torture devices were no joke to the poor horny teenagers who were forced to wear them—often under penalty of further torture with professional-grade torture devices. Those who did despoil themselves faced severe consequences. Guys were given a good talking to; girls were burned at the stake.

But back to intercourse. Yes, adultery can be seen as having a destabilizing impact on individuals and society. Broken families, divorce, domestic violence, etc. But sex outside of marriage? Less so. So it's no surprise that it's this kind of sex that gets everybody all excited, and the Church up in arms. For as long as I can remember, Western society expected everybody to be virgins on their wedding nights. In some parts of Islam, if you aren't, you're in deep shit (but only if you're a girl). Even today, people in the U.S. Bible Belt take abstinence pledges. Hymens are subject to inspection in Sub-Saharan Africa. Normal people have gone on with their lives in practice. But the "problem" of sex out of wedlock, and the public's fascination with it, will never go away in theory.

And that's where movies come in!

Hollywood has known how to mine the vast commercial gold mine that is sex for over a century. Sex may even be an important reason movies exist at all. The first moving pictures were seen on kinetoscopes, these clunky devices invented by Thomas Edison. People had to look through a peephole to see a short film made out of a sequence of pictures on a carousel. This is likely where the early XXX term "peepshow" came from because many of the early kinetoscope shows featured pornography. Just another example of how a new technology evolved because of people's demand for sexual content.

From the minute Hollywood became Hollywood, sex was known to be a powerful selling point. Executives knew that graphic nudity and on-screen sex would get them in hot water, so they pushed the envelope as much as possible through suggestive imagery, tantalizing movie posters, and dialogue littered with graphic double-entendres. Eventually they broke the envelope, and in the early '20s Hollywood went on trial in the court of popular opinion after a few lurid real-life scandals broke—one involving murder, another a Coke bottle.[40]

With no First Amendment Right of Free Speech afforded to films, and faced with censorship laws in multiple states, the studio heads all agreed to clean up their acts and adopt The Hays Code in the early 1930s. Sex was censored by an uptight prude named Will H. Hays who (you guessed it!) was a highly religious Presbyterian elder in his free time. Hollywood adapted, of course, and gradually films started to push the envelope all over again. The studios just had to get a lot more ingenious in the way they went about it. And this forced

---

40 i.e. Fatty Arbuckle

ingenuity led to some of the greatest films ever made in Hollywood, with frothy eroticism bubbling just beneath the surface.

In the mid-'50s there was the gradual rise of the "B-Movie" circuit—films produced with independent non-studio financing. Less beholden to the Hays Code, and with sexual norms gradually softening after World War II, producers began to take calculated risks with more salacious content. Drive-in movie posters featured Amazonian priestess nymphomaniacs and freshly defiled scantily clad women in torn clothing. Foreign independent films like **Last Tango in Paris** in the '70s helped further inure the public to in-your-face eroticism. Then **Deep Throat** came out in 1972 and blew apart any lingering public notion of "decency."

In the '80s and '90s Hollywood quickly capitalized with a string of sex-centered comedies like **Porky's, Fast Times at Ridgemont High**, and **Risky Business**—to name but a few. It was boobs-a-plenty, and an occasional full frontal. **Basic Instinct** and **Blue Velvet** pushed the envelope on the vulvar side of things, while **Bad Lieutenant** and **Monty Python's Life of Brian** made inroads on the penile. All this, combined with the success of *Hustler* magazine and the explosive growth of the porn industry, led to moral outrage, of course. A minority of prudes branded themselves a "majority," cozied up with Ronald Reagan, and achieved absolutely nothing. As we look back on it all now it seems so quaint—what with the son of the movement's lead architect Jerry Falwell now revealed to be such a major perv.

It was only a matter of time before "aberrant" (usually European) sex got screen time alongside "normal" red-blooded American sex. Films like **Belle de Jour** and **The Night Porter** broke hallowed ground in their depiction of S&M in the '60s and '70s. Adrian Lyne gave us **9½ Weeks** in the '80s, and then filmmakers went on to explore all kinds of sex-related kinkiness in films like **Fatal Attraction, Indecent Proposal**, and the unnecessary remake of Vladimir Nabokov's pedophilic classic **Lolita**. Kinky sex (but fun kinky, not gross kinky) went mainstream in the early 2000s with **Secretary**, and the sexual deviancy sub-genre saw its most morally acceptable commercial expression in the S&M popcorn-movie classic **50 Shades of Grey** in 2015.

In short, the topic of sex (both in theory and in actual practice) has been explored ad nauseam by the film industry. Unless you're an uptight Mormon housewife on Prozac, sex in movies wasn't a serious problem. Movies could have even featured way more sex were it not for the need to accommodate these distracting elements like "characters" and "plot." In fact, if you look at the amount of nudity in films twenty years ago, you'll notice how much tamer movies are now. We hardly ever get a good sorority house shower scene anymore. Penises seem to be out of the question. Why did this happen? Who or what took the mojo out of America's greatest cultural export? Simple answer: China.

When I worked at Universal in the late '90s I developed one of the first-ever co-productions with the state-controlled monopoly China Film. The first thing the officials made perfectly clear to me about the project was that sex of any kind would not be tolerated. I remember making a joke about how sex couldn't be all that problematic in a nation of 1.6 billion. Nobody laughed. As the Chinese film market grew exponentially in the years that followed, Hollywood realized that eroticism in movies would lead to censorship in other countries and a huge forfeiture of potential revenue. Today big studio movies are only greenlit if they can make it past the Chinese censors. So thank you China. You killed the sorority house shower scene.

To be fair, however, despite China, Hollywood had already become a marketing-driven product. The marketing "pitch" was everything, less so the story, and often at the studios we wouldn't even bother to read the script. Character and story were an afterthought. Sex was still a big selling point, but a PG-13 rating (available since 1984) could mean 50% more at the box-office and a huge upside in merchandising than an R rating.

Marvel superheroes are tailor-made for this income stream. Movies with a lot of sex, not so much. Did you ever see a **Last Tango in Paris** play set, or a **9½ Weeks** lunchbox? As great as sex was, it has nearly stopped being a selling point in movies. Except when it's weird, like in **50 Shades of Grey**. Which, of course, was not released in China.

It's no surprise that Hollywood came to see movies about sex addiction as commercial Kryptonite. When projects about sex addicts were pitched to us at the studios, we always asked, "Why would we make a movie about people becoming addicted *to* sex when we're having enough trouble making films *with* sex? Talk about biting the hand that feeds you. *"Oh look, here's a sex addict pleasuring himself in a dark alley right before he commits suicide!"* Theaters want to encourage people to buy popcorn, not throw it up.

But thanks to some very persistent and creative producers, films about sex addiction eventually got their day in court. But keep in mind there are very few. And the majority weren't marketed as movies about sex addiction at all. Even into the late 20th century, the term itself was still in its infancy from a clinical perspective. It wasn't until the early 2000s that the term was even used in the marketing of a film. But once it was, the problem went so mainstream that four movies about it were released back to back.

First came **Shame**, starring Michael Fassbender, a 2011 film we will discuss shortly. Next came **Thanks for Sharing**, starring Gwyneth Paltrow and Mark Ruffalo—the first studio film to specifically say "This is a movie about sex addicts" in its marketing materials. (In my opinion, this was a false flag operation. The film is really about recovery from addiction in general, which is why we will discuss it in a separate chapter.) Hot on the heels of that film's relative success in 2012, audiences were then treated to 2013's **Don Jon** starring the ever-vibrant Scarlett Johansson, and then Danish *infant terrible* Lars von Trier's **Nymphomaniac** with Stellan Skarsgård. The less said about that film the better. Von Trier is an acquired taste.

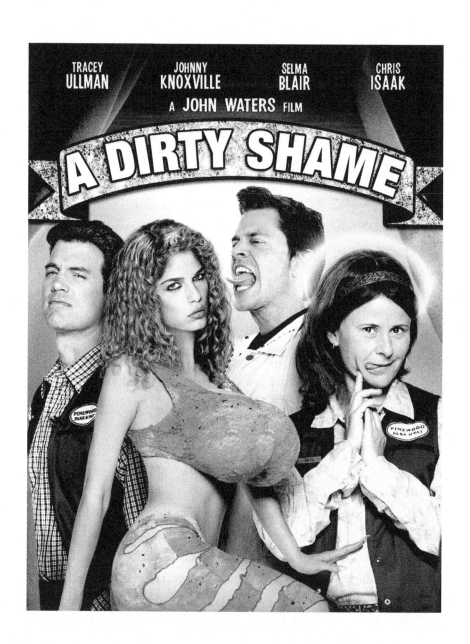

First up in our analysis of sex addiction in movies is 2004's ***A Dirty Shame*** directed by John Waters. If you've never seen a John Waters film, now is either a good time or bad time to start, depending on your sensitivity to moral outrage and poor taste. For some of us who grew up in the '70s and '80s, he was a counter-culture hero—a sort of "anti-movie" movie maker—whose low-budget films were required viewing at weekend midnight movie screenings at seedy downtown theaters.

His early works like ***Pink Flamingos*** and ***Female Trouble*** were dubbed "Transgressive Cult Films" and featured a stable of nutty "actors" like Divine and Mink Stole. I put the term "actors" in quotes because the acting was so bad it was great. But that was the selling point. And then there was the bad sex too. Waters delighted in shocking the "holier-than-thou" crowd, and if there is a hell for televangelists who steal money from little old ladies, I hope it's a John Waters film festival they can never leave—running all his movies on an infinite loop for eternity.

Waters eventually went "mainstream" with his effervescent movie musical ***Hairspray***, but he never lost his taste for shock and moral outrage, as ***A Dirty Shame*** amply demonstrates. But it's outrage with a purpose: to expose moral hypocrisy and rip apart sexual mores. Waters is out and proud and reminds us all that we either take sex *way* too seriously or we're probably not doing it right. By examining sexuality from the positions (no pun intended) of grotesque anti-movie extremes, his final studio opus is actually one of the most insightful films about sex addiction ever made.

The story begins with Tracey Ullman as a lower-middle-class housewife, Sylvia Stickles (even the names are in poor taste), cooking breakfast scrapple for her horny husband Vaughn, played by ***Twin Peaks'*** mesmerizing title track musician Chris Isaak. He makes a bungled attempt to get some hot pre-breakfast action, but Sylvia blows him off. With typical John-Waters-intentionally-bad-dialogue,

Vaughn tells her "*There's something wrong with your vagina,*" then takes care of business by jerking off in the bathroom to a handy copy of *Sex Addict* magazine. What other options does he have? Sylvia is "sexually repressed."

I put "sexually repressed" in quotes because I once spoke at length to Waters about this topic over cocktails at the British Airways First Class Lounge in New York while we were both on our way to the Cannes Film Festival. He explained that repression implies a belief or desire that is being kept in check. Sylvia isn't repressing a secret desire for sex at all—she simply has no interest in it, period. She's asexual. Society casts asexual women as "prudes" or "frigid," a deeply ingrained misogynistic attitude that assumes all women secretly "want it." When a man doesn't want sex, he needs to see a doctor right away; when a woman doesn't want it, she's just "repressed."

Waters creates a perfect foil to Sylvia's asexuality in the form of her daughter Caprice, played by multiple sclerosis awareness advocate and alcohol use disorder survivor Selma Blair. In the film, she goes by the stripper stage name Ursula Udders thanks to her 102 Triple-Z fake breasts. Sylvia has placed her under lock-and-key house arrest because of indecent exposure and her over-the-top libido. If Sylvia is at Absolute Zero Kelvin on the sex addict temperature scale, Caprice probably clocks in at 5,000 degrees—a level shared with Jeffrey Epstein and your typical G-type yellow-dwarf main sequence star.

Waters also populates Sylvia's neighborhood with other "deviants" including tacky neighbors who are swingers, a paperboy with wandering eyes, and a group of "bears" who are moving into the house at the end of the street. (For those of you who don't know what "bears" are, they're guys who look like Paul Bunyan and happen to be gay.)

But Sylvia doesn't stay "repressed" for long. On her trip to the store, she accidentally bumps her head and—voila!—suddenly has interest in sex. A lot of it. All the time. Enter Johnny Knoxville as Ray-Ray Perkins (no relation, but I wish)—a local mechanic and "sex saint"—who becomes Sylvia's new sensual messiah. He leads an underground cult of sex addicts headquartered out of his garage. Their mission: to boldly go where no orgasms have gone before. But they're not just some lunatic fringe. This is Baltimore, after all. Sex addicts are *everywhere*, and, like evangelicals, they're on the hunt for converts.

"*Pretty soon, this town will be OURS!*" shouts Ray-Ray with Messianic zeal, "*Let's go sexin'!*"

But alas, every great sex-addicts-taking-over-the-town movie needs a good nemesis, and Waters doesn't disappoint in the casting of Suzanne Shepherd. You may remember her from her hilarious performance as Lorraine Bracco's mom in **Goodfellas**. Shephard plays Sylvia's uptight mother-in-law Big Ethel, a Ninja-level zealot, or as Ray-Ray and his gang like to call her and those like her— "Neuters."

Big Ethel's attempts at moral policing are as futile as our military's nation building efforts in Afghanistan. And Waters blesses her with some of the best anti-dialogue dialogue in the film: "Lesbians have taken over the softball field!" she cries, just after lamenting that "somebody left a dildo in my neighbor's wishing well." "Only you can prevent fornication!" she chants, desperate to reverse the creeping tide of smut. Given how anti-sexual she is, it's amazing Big Ethel managed to have children at all. Luckily she raised them right, at least by her estimation: "My daughter is a good girl. She hates sex," she proudly declares.

Meanwhile, Sylvia seems to enjoy her newfound sexual liberation, plying her pudenda on a bus full of disapproving neuters, and visiting a nursing home where she does things with a water bottle that can never go unseen. But alas, there is so much more to learn than simple hip thrusts. And when the student is ready, the master will appear. So Ray-Ray takes Sylvia to his garage to train with his team of fellow sex addicts.

It's here that the film takes a U-turn and goes from dirty eye candy to a master class in sexual "aberration." Ray-Ray's crew of paraphiliacs includes a dude who's turned on by eating soil and licking the pavement. There's a middle-aged businessman who gets off by dressing up as a toddler, sucking on a pacifier as he rides a hobby horse, and crawling around in a baby pen. And let's not forget the woman who's into "sploshing"—or the erotic pleasure derived from dumping leftovers on one's privates. The aforementioned are all actual fetishes, not just John Waters movie fetishes, and comprise but a small fraction of the many other modalities of sexual expression clinicians have cataloged.

And this is what makes Waters' film so unique and relevant to the conversation about sex addiction. No other film I've ever seen covers the gamut of sexual "addictions" from such a clinical and value-neutral perspective. Every other film on the topic, including the one we will discuss shortly (**Shame**), portrays sex addiction as deviant, harmful, self-indulgent: compulsive masturbation every four hours to internet porn, prostitutes on speed dial, and degrading oneself in dirty dark alleys with the town wino. Waters shows us that it's not even fair to lump Ray-Ray's club's paraphilia into the sex addiction conversation to begin with. They're really just innocuous fetishes that harm nobody and are emotionally fulfilling for their practitioners. Why so much angst about what sex should be as opposed to what it is? Or could be? Ray-Ray's gang of "pervs" are just doing their thing. Let's let them do their thing.

And now that Sylvia is a sex addict, doing her thing opens up a new realm of possibilities—and not just sexual. Just like drinking alcohol can be a social lubricant to solidify friendships or close a big business deal, a shared interest in sexuality becomes a way for Sylvia to bond with her daughter—who apparently was also rendered a sex addict because of a blow to the head years ago. Sylvia releases Caprice from house arrest and the two finally have the freedom to chat frankly about penis sizes and the myriad approaches to cunnilingus. And what could possibly be wrong with that? Why should *Sex and the City* have a monopoly on women having salacious conversations about sex?

"I'm a sex addict and an exhibitionist," Caprice tells her mother, their strained mother-daughter relationship now healed. Sylvia answers, "Great, let's go down to the Holiday House and fuck the whole bar!"

Who knew Waters was such a romantic?

But Sylvia and Caprice go a bit overboard, so Vaughn and his mother Big Ethel stage an intervention. Caprice is given Prozac to kill her sex drive. Mother and daughter are forced to attend a 12-Step meeting of "Sex Addicts Anonymous" led by former Symbionese Liberation Army hostage-cum-bank-robber and Waters entourage member Patty Hearst. Hearst is not an actress, but she plays one on TV. It's anti-acting at its finest. But she has some choice lines like telling Sylvia, "You have a runaway vagina."

Waters lightly mocks the 12-Step traditions when Sylvia shares at the meeting: "I'm Sylvia, and my clitoris is in crisis. *Hellooooo, clitoris in crisis.*" And then, in typical John Waters anarchic style, the meeting quickly devolves into a defacto orgy because, hey, they're all sex addicts.

Speaking of anarchy, Ray-Ray and his crew have in the meanwhile managed to bonk everybody over the head and turn the citizens of their straight laced little town into erotic zombies marching down main street looking to fuck anything that moves. It's a satisfying climax (no pun intended) to a zany film that tickled a few funny bones, horrified some, confounded critics, and yet ultimately managed to say some interesting things about sex, sex addiction, gender, morality, and hypocrisy along the way.

And speaking of hypocrisy, the MPAA slapped **A Dirty Shame** with an NC-17 rating in the same year that it gave R ratings to films with over-the-top graphic violence like **Collateral** and **Man on Fire**. Waters tried to appeal the ruling, but to no avail. The hypocrisy he mocks in his films is no match for hypocrisy in real life. **A Dirty Shame** lost money and Waters was sent to movie jail. He never made another studio movie again. And that's what I would call a dirty shame.

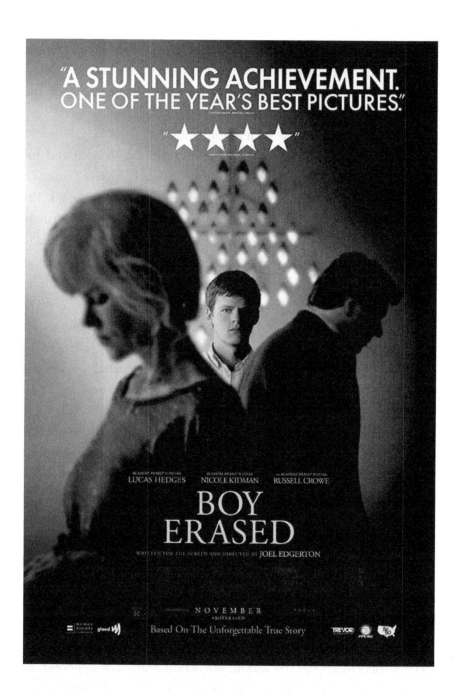

In my search for films about sex addiction I found several examples of characters in the throes of their problem, but none about treatment options available to help them. There are no "sex addict nails rehab" movies that do for sex what **28 Days** or **Clean and Sober**[41] did for drugs and alcohol. This is probably because sex addiction is relatively new to the addiction and recovery conversation, and Hollywood needs time to catch up. Keep in mind there was a four-decade lag between **The Lost Weekend** and **Clean and Sober**.

Luckily, Hollywood did take on the sex-addiction recovery story again, albeit from a different yet equally relevant vantage point. The therapy involved wasn't to help a person having too much sex, just the wrong kind. I'm speaking about gay "conversion" therapy—an attempt by Christian evangelicals to insert magical thinking into psychotherapy the same way the Intelligent Design movement tried with biology. Netflix offers a great documentary on the subject called **Pray Away**. Watching it, I found it hard not to feel a perverse satisfaction at seeing all the leaders of the movement condemn everything it stood for and admit they were gay all along. But the schadenfreude is short-lived. Some teenagers committed suicide as a result of this "therapy."

The "bad" film in our Good-Bad-Yucky analysis trilogy is 2018's **Boy Erased**, a great film about a really, really bad idea. Based on the memoir of the same name written by LGBTQ activist Garrard Conley, the film is a jeremiad against the faith-based conversion therapy movement. Which is not to say that faith isn't and can't be an important part of successful recovery, generally. AA, NA, and other 12-Step programs have helped millions of people when it comes to alcohol and substance use disorders. But as this movie shows, sex is a very different disorder, and religion and sex make for strange bedfellows (pun intended).

Boy Erased boasts an A-List cast, meaning in this case all Australians playing people with heavy Southern accents from

---
41 More on these films in later chapters.

Arkansas. This kind of linguistic feat only happens in the movies. Joel Edgerton directs Nicole Kidman and Russell Crowe as the concerned evangelical parents of gay teenager Jared Eamons, played by Lucas Hedges. Edgerton also plays Victor Sykes, the director of the recovery camp called Love in Action. Sykes is based on a real person who ran a real camp, John Smid. He eventually disavowed gay conversion, apologized for the harm his program caused, wrote a tell-all book (adding personal profit to misery), and married his boyfriend.

The plot of the film is quite simple. Boy gets outed, goes to a conversion camp, escapes the conversion camp, writes a book about it. Lucas Hedges does a wonderful job depicting a young man trying to unpack his sexuality, only to be condemned and punished before actually picking a team. Or even having sex for that matter. For all we know, he could be straight, but he claims to occasionally have "thoughts about men" (which studies have shown describes a large percentage of men, although they'll never admit to it). Of course, in Bible Belt America, this is tantamount to Orwellian Thoughtcrime. And since Hedges hasn't even acted on those thoughts yet—for you Philip K. Dick fans out there—his parents' intervention amounts to an arrest by the Precrime Unit.

And so Jared is sent to Love in Action where everyone is taught to hate themselves, wear crisp white shirts, pray to Jesus, and try not to be gay anymore. In many ways it's like a high-security prison. All personal effects are confiscated, especially cell phones, and there can be no contact with the outside world. Jared's mother (played by Kidman) isn't allowed to see the inside of the facility, and Jared isn't supposed to tell her what happens inside either. That should have been the first of several red flags.

But to be fair, various forms and degrees of isolation are not uncommon in the recovery world, and some can be helpful. Inpatient rehab facilities insist that patients stay on the premises. Some restrict cell phone access in order to separate patients from toxic co-enablers, or stop addicts who have their drug dealers on speed dial. Some private drug rehab isolation methods overseas are draconian, many verging on abusive, and some are downright criminal. Does isolation help addicts recover? Maybe for the length of the treatment. It's re-entry to the real world that's the problem. In **Boy Erased**, one of the most powerful pieces of advice Jared receives from a fellow inmate is *"You really have to think about what you're gonna' do when you get out of here…"*

What is certain is that most gay conversion therapies try to isolate individuals from outside influences under the faulty premise that outside influences are to blame for a person's homosexuality. At Love in Action, the program's no-no list is quite extensive: no magazines, non-religious books, TV, internet porn (or just internet), solo trips to the bathroom, lit syllabi from liberal arts colleges, and of course no masturbation. Ah yes. We all know how world peace and infinite prosperity could be ours for the taking, were it not for masturbation.

But this is the first of several questionable therapeutic premises in action in this film. Another is the quite comical idea that a person's physical actions can somehow cure their homosexuality. Sykes convenes a firm manly handshake training seminar for the kids. If only the guys would stand up straight, un-slouch their shoulders, stop crossing their legs, firm up their wrists, and play a little bit more baseball, they'd be cured! And for the lesbians, if only they would slip into a 1950s housecoat and slippers, slap on some curlers, grab a vacuum, and do some light housework, we could all go home and live happily ever after.

Okay, yes, epigenetics has shown that behaviors and environment can cause changes that affect the way a person's genes work. But magically turning a gay person's DNA straight? Seems like a real long shot. Then again, so is the whole premise of conversion therapy to begin with. Plus, according to its Christian inventors and practitioners, genes have nothing to do with being gay anyway. Being gay is a choice, right?

This makes the next phase of Love in Action's curriculum seem even more bizarre and contradictory. The kids are all asked to do a "genogram"—basically a family tree that points a finger at every ancestor who was ever an alcoholic, addict, adulterer, had an abortion, played slots, liked John Waters movies, or donated to NPR. As if the sins of their forefathers were to blame for the kid's same-sex attraction. What "choice" did these kids have here? Nature-nurture debates about our genes' influence on personal choice happen in the drug and alcohol addiction world all the time, but why not when it comes to a sexual addiction? Isn't sex the basic mechanistic foundation of genetics to begin with?

The last questionable premise worth covering is not exclusive to gay conversion therapy, and in fact underlies many addiction treatment programs around the world. It's the quasi-Freudian notion that forcing people to address memories of past trauma holds the key to their successful recovery. In **Boy Erased**, this takes the form of a nutty role play exercise where the kids are forced to tell their (absent) fathers that they hate them. As if parents were to blame for inflicting some past deep emotional pain that caused their son or daughter to be gay. If only that pain were addressed, reconciled, and forgiven, the gay would magically go away. But we all know it won't.

And yet, the same cannot be said about traditional drug and alcohol therapy. Successful addiction therapy does frequently involve an honest look at a person's past, and its effect on their mental health. Childhood trauma and poverty are known factors for a person's predisposition to addiction in later life. Same goes for anxiety and depression, and even Tourette Syndrome.

Unfortunately, there is a widely-held assumption—even by non-religious people—that, like alcoholics and addicts, gays are "missing something" in their lives, masking some terrible experience from their past, using gay sex to fill some deep dark chasm in their psyche. It can never be as simple as "I just prefer gay sex," right? Why must being gay be a "response" to something? People of both sexes often assume a homely woman chooses to become a lesbian because she can't get a man. Gay conversion therapy assumes its patients are gay because they are bereft of Jesus' love. A large percentage of religious people would agree with the statement that "a boy who is sexually abused is more likely to develop into a homosexual later in life." And yet these are many of the same people who looked the other way when their own priests were engaging in that abuse.

What's missing from this psychoanalytic paradigm is the fact that some people with addictions (sexual or otherwise) simply have no past trauma to address.[42] I'm one of those people. I drank because it felt great, not to cope with any pain. I grew up in a middle-class utopia and wanted for nothing. There was no deep underlying issue with my mother or father at play, no repressed memories of sexual abuse. Sure, my ancestry is part British, and my people have been known to quaff pints aplenty, but I would never blame any external factors like these for my drinking problem. But that's just me. The problem is that many people still assume being gay must be due to external pressures, not a freely chosen preference based on biological factors.

We should also keep in mind that addiction can be situational, not chronic. Some people become addicted because of life challenges, and then once those challenges are overcome their addiction ceases. A great example of this is the well-documented case of American soldiers in Vietnam who became heroin addicts to cope with the horrors of war. As soon as they shipped home and got away from those horrors, their addictions stopped. But in gay conversion, it's the reverse. Love in Action's program director Sykes tells the kids that homosexuality is a modifiable situational affliction governed by choice, not an endemic chronic disease caused by external factors beyond their control. But let's be clear: *Being* gay is "chronic"; *acting* gay can be situational. Like

---

[42] Traditional talk therapy doesn't always help people with addictions anyway.

in prison, for instance. Or for bisexuals. Or the so-called "bi-curious." Either way, or both ways, it's all good.

Another important theme of the film is the "fake it 'til you make it" paradigm of recovery. One of the most important moments of the film is when a fellow inmate, Gary, tells Jared to go through the motions or else risk prolonged internment at the camp. It's like a prisoner quietly doing their time in prison, hoping to get out early on good behavior—but with every intention of returning to a life of crime. The same thing happens in traditional drug and alcohol treatment centers. "Recycling," or the need to readmit addicts into rehab programs over and over, is the unfortunate result.

This phenomenon is especially true of young people in traditional recovery, partly because of how they got there to begin with. Like Jared—whose father threatens to completely cut him off financially, excommunicate him from their church, and kick him out of the house unless he goes to a gay conversion camp—many young people with addiction problems are forced into rehab through similar interventions and threats. But experts will tell you: For people to change they have to want to change. The problem is that young people rarely know what they want. Many barely even know *who* they are yet.

Think about it: You're forcing a confused, angry teenager into a rehab facility where they are immediately told they must assume a new identity of alcoholic and/or addict. In most 12-Step programs, the label implies a lifelong sentence without the possibility of parole. They will be in recovery *forever*. It's no wonder young people go through the motions, fake it, but have no intention of actually making it. Most just want to get the hell out of there. Some aren't even true alcoholics or addicts to begin with; they just screwed up a few times like most teenagers do, and are now labeled for life.

This personality rebranding process must be even more difficult for gay kids in conversion therapy. Imagine how horrific the assumption of a new sexual identity would be if articulated in reverse at a "Straight

Conversion Camp": *Even though you love women and want to have sex with them, that has to stop right now. From now on, you can't love them, or have sex with them, and probably shouldn't even look at them. From now on, and for the rest of your life, you can only be attracted to men (even though you aren't), and can only have sex with men (even though you find it repulsive),* etc. Let's face it, people will confess to just about anything if they're tortured long enough. And forced confessions are extremely unreliable.

So what happens to all the real-life, brave gay teens who don't take the blue pill and re-enter the Matrix (AKA "The Closet")? Those who own up to their sexuality publicly, refused to endure pseudoscientific brainwashing, and get cut off from their family's love and resources? Sadly, many wind up homeless on the streets of big cities having to rely on prostitution in order to survive. I can't think of a more tragic example of the cure being worse than the disease.

Clearly, **Boy Erased** has much to teach us about the fallacy of gay conversion therapy and the squishy terrain of sex-related therapy in general. But it also shows how both operate under some of the same questionable assumptions applied in conventional drug and alcohol recovery. The wild card in all of this is the role of faith. Sex is burdened with so much religiously inspired taboos and hang-ups. And whereas drug- and alcohol-related interventions on young people are meant to save their lives, gay conversion interventions are meant to save their souls. Many may disagree, but I think recovery and salvation are two entirely different things.

Closing out our sex addiction film analysis trilogy is **Shame**—a 2011 film directed by Steve McQueen, starring Michael Fassbender as the dashing oversexed New York City ad agency exec Brandon Sullivan. It is generally considered the first and most accurate examination of sex addiction as a serious behavioral disorder. However, like (the very few) other films about this topic, it only focuses on "icky" expressions of the disorder, not any treatments for it.

Hollywood hasn't made a "sex addict succeeds at recovery" film yet. And to do so was clearly not McQueen's intent with this film. Instead, he takes us on a graphic tour of Brandon's private sexual hellscape in action. And what is immediately apparent is how transactional sex has become for him. Paying for sex with a prostitute, subscribing to online porn channels: all repetitive transactions devoid of any emotion or real meaning. Everything's about getting that fix, and then planning for the next one.

But this sad feedback loop is true for all addictions. Drinking starts out as a highly romanticized pursuit. Toasting business deals. Awesome one-night stands. Tearful family toasts at Thanksgiving dinner. But before you know it, shaken not stirred at the Ritz Carlton Bar with that hot guy turns into a Saucey app delivery at 7:00am so your neighbors won't see. Same with most heavy drugs. The first time is transcendent: Lou Reed is so cool, coke puts girls in the mood, you get instant membership to a fantastic club full of awesome new friends. And we all know the rest.

Michael Fassbender does a great job portraying a man completely devoid of emotion yet somehow channeling inner torment in every frame. The very idea of passion and romance seems lost on him. Sex is just sex. But who ever said that sex needs to or should be passionate or romantic? Romance is a purely human construct. Centuries of art, literature, and now films and TV shows have imbued it with almost mythical qualities, an aura of transcendence. Orgasm is almost beside the point. Everyone is so used to everything *else* built up around sex that when we see Brandon's sex life denuded to its base primordiality, it's hard to look at. But it's also hard to look away.

People don't realize to what extent fictional narratives running in their minds influence the sex they're having with their bodies. I like to use movies as analogies. For an 18-year-old sorority pledge at her first frat party, sex takes on the aura of a **Mad Max** movie, where she's the supertanker full of gasoline being chased by frenzied guys in muscle cars.

For a sexually experienced man at a cocktail party beguiled by a self-conscious ingenue, he's Valmont from **Dangerous Liaisons**. Some women experience sex through the lens of a Jackie Collins novel. For others it's **50 Shades of Grey**. For most guys it's probably every James Bond movie, with **Debbie Does Dallas** a close runner up.

McQueen also shows us how Brandon is just as consumed with thoughts about sex as he is with the sex itself. Like the heavy drinker who ruminates over their next drink, or the drug addict over their next fix, Brandon's daily experience of the world seems entirely guided by simmering lust. There's a key scene at the beginning of the film where he stares at an attractive married woman on the subway. His laser-focus on a desired outcome seems all-consuming. His eyes project the cold intentionality of a tiger about to pounce on a gazelle. He's always on the hunt. At its mercy, if you will. But this is true of all addicts. Once rich intellectual and emotional worlds slowly collapse into two mental singularities: using or thinking about using.

Brandon's external reality seems to be slowly collapsing as well. He has no friends. Doesn't really go out. At work, his computer is confiscated because it's littered with hard-core pornography. It's almost like he's begging to get caught. And perhaps he is. Many addicts who can't make the hard choice to quit on their own will aim for a rock-bottom in the hopes that reality will make the choice for them. Luckily, Brandon's boss David covers for him, but there's a quid pro quo. David (married with kids) uses Brandon as a "wing-man" to help him pick up women at bars. So add "pimp" to the list of compromises Brandon must make in order to enable and sustain his addiction.

This all changes when Brandon's sister Sissy (played by the always wonderful Carey Mulligan) comes to town and crashes at his place. He finds her in the shower, completely nude. There is not even a hint of modesty; Sissy doesn't bother covering up for the entire length of the two-minute scene. It's the first of several hints that Brandon and Sissy may have had an incestuous relationship at some time in the past. Could Brandon's sex addiction be a response to that guilt? Possibly. Interestingly, McQueen sets Brandon and Sissy on opposite sides of a neurologically parallel feedback loop. Brandon's a sex addict; Sissy is addicted to love. She grovels on the phone for her ex-boyfriend to take her back, even though he's bad news. God knows many people are addicted to toxic relationships.

It's this dichotomy between love and lust that makes the story really come alive in the second act. While Sissy is capable and wanting of love, Brandon clearly is not. He asks a co-worker, Marianne (played by the ravishing Nicole Beharie), out for dinner, ready to apply his customary capture-and-kill strategy. But much to Brandon's dismay, Marianne is a complex, emotionally grounded woman with healthy feelings of self-worth. She doesn't want sex; she wants a relationship, a meaningful commitment. Brandon goes home from the date empty-handed. It's the coke addict's equivalent of buying an eight ball of blow that turns out to be baking soda.

Okay, Brandon has a hard time committing. So what? Most guys in their early 30s do. But in his case the question is: Has his fear of commitment made him into a sex addict? Or has sex addiction caused him to fear commitment? It's the same tail-wagging-the-dog question that alcohol and drug addicts ask themselves about their loneliness and depression. With Brandon we come to realize it's the former. He hooks up with Marianne on another date to seal the deal, but he can't perform. Brandon's addiction has robbed him of the ability to feel honest love and affection. After Marianne leaves, he hires a prostitute and his mojo returns in full force. Like any addict, he's trapped in a closed feedback loop that revolves around degradation and…*shame*.

Faced with this sad reality and unwilling to accept genuine love and support from his sister, Brandon goes on a sexual bender. It's graphic. Likely one of the several reasons the film received an NC-17 rating. Respecting art over commerce, Fox Searchlight Pictures didn't appeal the rating. As difficult as these scenes may be for some to see, they are true to the subject matter. McQueen doesn't compromise. Fassbender goes all out. There is no way to sugarcoat the deeper recesses of human lust. It's all out there on the table. And we can either feel disgust or pity.

It's easy to discount Brandon as a dissolute pervert with no self-control, but people forget there is a human being hiding beneath every addiction. Unfortunately, McQueen doesn't show us any part of Brandon's human side until the very end when he breaks down and cries following Sissy's failed suicide attempt. But by then it's too late, and we know too little about Brandon's past to feel any real sympathy for him. Whatever events from his past brought him to this point are anyone's guess. But also none of our business. We are all too biased by our own sexual mores to judge Brandon anyway.

Because, as the three films we've analyzed about sex addiction clearly demonstrate, when it comes to the good, bad, and the downright yucky, it all boils down to perspective. From John Waters' perspective, sex is taken way too seriously by repressed people who should mind their own business and let people follow their sexual bliss. As long as they're not hurting others or themselves, sex "addiction" isn't even a real thing.

From the gay conversion perspective, only the "wrong kind" of sex (i.e. gay) is the problem. Oh, and masturbation too. And porn. And just about everything non-missionary-position as well, I suppose. For a great book on the subject, I highly recommend Darrel Ray's *Sex & God: How Religion Distorts Sexuality*.

And lastly, from Steve McQueen's perspective, sex addiction is a very real thing that causes very real suffering in some people. Maybe it's brought on from past trauma, maybe due to fear of commitment, or maybe just because sex is a damn good feedback loop. Like with any good feedback loop, it opens up the possibility for addiction. But as interesting and romanticized as sex is, it's just like any other loop we all live with. So get used to it. And enjoy it while you still can.

CHAPTER 11
Gambling Addiction & Luck Cosmologies
The Gambler
Uncut Gems

Gambling addiction is a curious beast in the behavioral addiction universe. It clearly has negative consequences—as we'll see amply demonstrated shortly as we discuss two fine films on the subject, **The Gambler** starring James Caan, and **Uncut Gems** starring Adam Sandler. Unlike alcohol and drug use, gambling doesn't have any health consequences, unless you consider getting whacked by your bookie a health consequence. You can't overdose on gambling; your money just runs out. There are no physical withdrawals, only psychological ones, like regret and self-loathing. And you can be a gambling addict and still be a great parent, drive a car, go to church, pay your taxes, even be President of the United States.[43] That said,

[43] https://nativenewsonline.net/advertise/branded-voices/four-american-presidents-who-were-famous-poker-fans

pathological gambling costs the U.S. economy billions of dollars a year, has tremendous social costs, and destroys individuals and their families.

But gambling isn't just Las Vegas casinos and online poker. Gambling is just one mechanical expression of the much broader human tendency to bet. Betting on the future is something we all do, all day, every day. Because we can visualize possible futures in our heads and evaluate likely outcomes, we make decisions on how to act based on desired outcomes. In other words, human existence is a series of bets. We were born to bet. Some bets are life-changing, most are mundane. When I try to decide whether to drive an extra mile to get a better deal on toilet paper at Target, I'm placing a bet. If I win, I save money and pat myself on the back. If I lose, I waste gas money schlepping to Target.

Betting doesn't have to involve money, but it does always involve some form of tangible or intangible assets. When I write a Hollywood movie script hoping to sell it, I'm not risking any of my own money, but I am risking the 100 hours of lost labor if it doesn't sell. When a parent pays to put their kid through college, they're betting four years of tuition and living expenses that their kid will get a great job so they don't end up working at Target and living in the family basement. I'm placing a very large time commitment bet by writing this book and hoping people like it. You're betting the money you spent to buy the book, plus your valuable time reading it, in the hopes that you'll enjoy it. I hope both of us win our respective bets.

Betting is just another way of saying "planning," but planning sounds better because it seems to involve…well…planning. But perfect planning is impossible. Life is chaotic and unpredictable, especially over long periods. But this doesn't stop people from placing massive long-term bets every time they switch jobs, start businesses, or get married. The outcomes (desired or not) take decades to manifest. But here's the funny part: The amazing fulfillment and reward somebody gets when their huge long-term bet on the future pays off is neurochemically indistinguishable from the short-term "high" a gambler gets when he wins a hand of blackjack.

We engage in daily betting unconsciously for the most part, and 99% of these bets have trivial outcomes, like me saving money on toilet paper. But it wasn't always like this. Betting used to be a life or death proposition. Our hominid ancestors survived because they evolved large enough brains to create detailed models of the future in their heads, run cost/benefit analyses, then make decisions and act accordingly. The first models probably went something like this:

Hungry...family hungry...must leave cave to find food...risky bet...saber-toothed tiger attacks me...I get eaten...entire clan next, probably...I lose bet...bummer...my existence had no point...

Versus

Hungry...family hungry...must leave cave to find food...risky bet...saber-toothed tiger busy eating someone else (hopefully some Neanderthal)...I don't get eaten...I bring food home to clan...I win bet...awesome...females think I'm a bad-ass...I procreate...that is the whole point of my existence...

These kinds of mental models had to be running 24/7 for our ancestors to make it through another day without dying. Epigenetics[44] then took over, and the continuous act of mental modeling became a useful addiction that would be passed on for generations to come.

As human brains evolved further (thanks to the survival of those making more good bets over bad ones), the models got more complex and spanned greater lengths of time. Hunter-gatherers had to make bets on rainfall, animal migration patterns, and whether or not to wipe out a neighboring tribe first before they did the same to them. Most

---

44 https://www.cdc.gov/genomics/disease/epigenetics.htm

contingencies were known, but nature was still very unpredictable and poorly understood. So, humans also developed the ability to create mental models of third-party supernatural agents that affected the outcomes of their bets. This gave rise to superstitions, animism, ghosts, and spirits—all precursors to religion.

As language evolved, so did the ability for our ancestors to create and share mental models of future events amongst themselves. Collectively visualizing and predicting what would happen on a hunting expedition, for instance, led to better bets. Each mental modeler in the clan had different levels of highly relevant betting experience to share. Occasionally a member of the clan would pitch a crazy mental model like, "Hey, instead of killing the buffaloes with spears, why not run the whole herd off a cliff?" Think of it as the ancient equivalent of a fourth and down huddle with five seconds left on the clock where somebody comes up with an impossible Hail Mary. We will discuss these kinds of "*so crazy it* has *to work*" mental models shortly.

When a person's mental model of the future led to a great bet that paid off, it resulted in a highly pleasurable feedback loop. A wonderful brain cocktail of adrenaline and dopamine awaited any clan member who accurately predicted where a delicious wooly mammoth happened to be grazing. There were social rewards as well—including elevated status, access to more sexual partners to procreate with, and a larger share of the meat they helped hunt. Once again, these pleasurable feedback loops nourished a highly useful and adaptive addiction to mental modeling. It was iterative. Sometimes the hunter became the hunted. Those who weren't eaten shared their more successful bets with others, which resulted in "learning."

With the advent of agriculture, the food supply stabilized enough for humans to experience leisure time. There was less of a demand for mental modeling to ensure basic survival. Problem was, and still is today, that you can't just turn the mental machinery off. Modeling is a process running rampant in our brains all the time. Isn't the act of "thinking" really shorthand for mental modeling? When we think, we either remember the past or model the future. When this process causes stress and anxiety—which it did and still does—we call it "worrying."

But some mental modeling was pleasurable, especially when people shared their predictions about the future with others. Individuals could make their leisure time and social bonding really fun by comparing their models to one another's, and arguing over which one was better or more likely to pan out.[45] By choosing any causal event to bet on, humans could generate positive feedback loops if they won a bet over their competitors. And by shortening the time spans over which their resulting bets played out, they could enjoy more and better feedback loops over and over. In other words, reality could be gamified.

All that was needed next was to add physical representations to codify the bets, and tokens to symbolize the reward an individual would obtain from winning a bet over his/her competitors. There is evidence that early paleolithic humans kept track of their bets by drawing on cave walls. By 2300 BC the ancient Chinese were using keno slips. Fifteen centuries later they invented the idea of "money," tokenized in the form of copper and bronze coins.

And voila! Gambling was born!

Ancient Greeks were playing craps in 500 BC. The Romans loved gambling, especially in the gladiatorial games, which gave them an arm's-length proximity to primordial violence. Rudimentary poker was invented by the Chinese in the 10th century AD, and the Persians apparently perfected it by the 16th century. There are wonderful books about the history of gambling that make for fun reading. They are, in effect, psychosocial histories of humanity's increasingly ingenious forms of mental modeling and its ongoing affinity for magical thinking. Because, let's face it, the history of humanity is as much a

---

45 Instead of arguing, writers and artists created physical representations of their elaborate mental models that they then sold for profit. As a screenwriter, I'm just a modeler.

study in human foibles as it is human greatness...and when it comes to foibles, nothing gets the job done quite like magical thinking.

Some anthropologists say the brain is hard-wired for magical thinking, to believe in supernatural beings like gods, angels, and unicorns. I don't think that idea is far off, but it is debatable. As I mentioned above, mental modeling not only tried to predict the future, it also populated the models with supernatural agents to account for causalities that weren't understood. Belief in the supernatural took on its most powerful cultural expression in the form of organized monotheistic religion. But less organized, more deeply personal links to the supernatural could still be had. The most culturally universal of these was through the concept of Luck.

Luck is a fascinating subject in and of itself, and unavoidable in any discussion about gambling. Gambling is all about Luck. In fact, I would go a step further and say that gambling has little to do with the mechanics of gambling, and everything to do with how those mechanics are influenced by that powerful hidden force called Luck. Nobody goes to Vegas to test out the invariability of Bayesian statistics. They go there to "try their luck." For anybody who knows the basics of statistics and probability, gambling is nothing more than an entertaining way to lose money. But if Luck is involved, a whole new world of infinite possibilities opens up, a world steeped in myths and legends.

Luck is like Dark Matter. Nobody knows what the hell it is or what it's made of; we can't see it; we just know it's out there because of its effect on those things we can see, like this sweet poker hand we're holding. Luck is that special sauce you add to your mental model when the Debbie-Downer of common sense tells you the model won't work. Luck's been anthropomorphized as "Lady Luck" and those terrifying leprechauns. The Irish have co-opted it as a symbol of national identity in the "Luck-o-the-Irish" although I haven't found any empirical evidence for this phenomenon. Then again, words like "empirical" are total buzzkills in Luck mythology. Luck defies all attempts by science to measure its qualities; it's unfalsifiable[46] so no need to even debate it. Luck is not an "it"—it just *is*.

For something inherently supernatural, I'm surprised Luck didn't get a worse rap during the Middle Ages. Luck feeds off of various occult ideas like numerology, divination, fortune-telling, incantation, and sorcery. It even shares some ideas with witchcraft, but nobody ever got burned at the stake for being too lucky. If they had, they wouldn't be in that kind of predicament anyway, right? And getting burned at the stake would be such bad luck it would be proof of innocence.

Then again, witch hunts weren't known for their evidentiary precision. If a woman was suspected of being a witch, she would be thrown into a river. If she floated, she was a witch and would be executed. If she sank to the bottom of the river and died, she was innocent. Especially interesting is the history of organized religions' ever-changing, hypocritical attitudes about gambling over the centuries. Equally if not more so is the influence religious faith has had on problematic gambling behavior.[47]

Luck feeds into a deeply human desire to be special, to deviate from the norm, to temporarily ignore reality and dogma in favor of a unique and highly personalized Luck cosmology—with its own proprietary rules and exceptions. It's customizable kismet, guided serendipity, the illusion of control over the material world. Think of it as DIY spiritualism where people can imagine they are lesser gods affecting the outcome of their entire universe. They don't have to share this providence with anybody else; it only works for *them*. When anybody dares question it, it's because they just "don't get it," ain't got it, and they wish they had it. It's a feeling, a superpower, like The Force. It's deeply personal and treasured, yet also fragile and capricious. Rules and rituals must be observed at all times to keep the "mojo" from drying up. Like a jealous god, Luck must be constantly

---

46 https://en.wikipedia.org/wiki/Falsifiability

47 https://www.ncbi.nlm.nih.gov/pmc/articles/PMC6174594/

worshiped via verbal incantations, repetitive gestures, talismans, and supplications.[48]

Luck has also played a huge role in social history. In old-world aristocracies, it didn't matter how much work or ingenuity you put forth, you were still considered part of the "great unwashed."[49] Before Marx and Engels called everybody out and told the proletariat to rise up and dissolve social hierarchies, Luck was one of the only ways for people to move up the ladder. Gambling and lotteries gave Joe and Jane-Q-Sixpack a quick, effort-free avenue to riches unobtainable by traditional means. Aristocracies are largely gone, but the idea of Luck as the key ingredient in social mobility still persists. Granted, the landed gentry will still look down on you as nouveau riche, but who cares? They just inherited their money—you at least won yours.

Luck and gambling were also great ways for ordinary, cautious, law-abiding people to access dangerous, illegal, forbidden worlds. In the same way Romans loved to bet on gladiatorial death and dismemberment, gambling gives people an arm's-length proximity to rampant lawlessness, unthinkable violence, the mob, and bookies who break kneecaps. Famous poker players today dress and act like criminals and gangsters as part of their brand "mystique." Winning a huge bet feels like you "took the house for everything it's worth," got something for nothing, and "made away with it." The rush of adrenaline and dopamine is identical to that experienced by kleptomaniacs, bank robbers, and first-time skydivers who land safely. I felt it when I ran with the bulls in Pamplona. It's the euphoric feeling of having cheated death, bent causality to your unique purposes, taken down "the man," and outwitted all the criminals at their own game. Who couldn't get addicted to that?

---

48 To see a great example of this in action, I highly recommend **Silver Linings Playbook** where Robert DeNiro has a whole set of hilarious rituals and behaviors to "guarantee" that the Eagles win a football game.

49 https://en.wiktionary.org/wiki/great_unwashed

To see many of these ideas about betting, gambling, and Luck come to life, let's review two films on the topic, *The Gambler* (the original version, not the Mark Wahlberg remake) released in 1974, and *Uncut Gems* released in 2019. Even though there are over a dozen fine films on the subject of gambling, I chose these two because I think they speak most directly to the ideas of gambling addiction as a pathology. They are also wonderful explorations of magical thinking and the mythology of Luck. Both films give us insight into human fallibility and courage, as well as the creative and destructive power of hoping against all odds.

The Gambler was written by James Toback, who achieved artistic prominence as the Oscar-nominated screenwriter of 1991's *Bugsy*. It was directed by Czech-born Karel Reisz, the acclaimed director of 1981's *The French Lieutenant's Woman*. The subsequent careers of both men never rose to the level of their achievements with the above mentioned films, especially Toback, whose contributions are now overshadowed by allegations of sexual misconduct. The centerpiece of the film is clearly James Caan, who was white-hot after his starring turn as Sonny Corleone in *The Godfather*. His career spanned several decades afterwards, working steadily until his death in 2022. And, coincidentally, he was addicted to cocaine when they shot the film.

The Gambler is by no means a great film. It doesn't have any bells and whistles; it's just straight-up long shot, medium shot, closeup. Critics were split on its artistic merits after it was released. But quality aside, it is an important film in the sense that Hollywood had never really delved into the issue of gambling as an addiction prior to this. It preferred to sell the thrill of gambling itself in films like *The Sting*. Several earlier films had hinted at addiction, including 1961's *The Hustler* with Paul Newman, and *Dark City* made in 1950 featuring Charlton "Cold-Dead-Hands" Heston. *The Gambler* certainly wasn't marketed as a film about addiction; Paramount Pictures knew better than that. *The Godfather's* graphic mob violence had turned that film into the studio's cash cow a few years earlier, so ***The Gambler's*** campaign was a classic false-flag operation. There is no mob violence in the film at all, but it was pitched to the public as if there was. The movie poster's tagline read: "*For $10,000 they break your arms. For $20,000 they break your legs. Axel Freed owes $44,000.*"

What the film certainly achieves is a sense of naturalism, thanks to Toback, who himself had a gambling addiction. He wrote the story first as a semi-autobiographical novel, and then decided to turn it into a screenplay because he urgently needed the sales proceeds to pay back his considerable gambling debts. It's reported that Toback walked into his agent's office (CAA Super-Agent Michael Ovitz) and demanded a loan against the proceeds. It was a crazy bet that paid off, and once again we see art imitating life imitating art.

Caan plays Axel Freed, a university professor during part of the day, gambling addict during the rest of the day and night. We first enter his world at an underground poker club. Things are not going well. His mental models of the future are buckling under the pressure of chance. But it's not the models that are broken; it's that something "snapped [his] rhythm." It's a simple choice of words, but it basically says it all when it comes to gambling. The idea of "rhythm" in betting is one of the keys to the gaming industry's entire business model. It's called The Gambler's Fallacy, a common cognitive bias where people believe that if the same thing happens repeatedly (say, heads in a coin flip), the next flip has a greater likelihood of being tails. Not true. The odds are always 50/50. Every single time. This simple brain fart is the author of billions of dollars in gambling losses and untold human misery.

There are other cognitive biases at work in gambling, including the Availability, Confirmation, Hindsight, and Outcome Biases—which crop up during ***The Gambler*** as well. But whatever terms you use, they are all expressions of Axel's idea of Luck—that deep sense of personal prophecy that usually helps him win, but is currently out of service. The only way to get Luck to operate properly again is to continue betting. Betting is all he thinks about. As a result, he's rather unlikeable and one-dimensional. He doesn't talk with people; he talks *at* them. It's hard to root for a guy whose only concern is his own Luck.

Then again, there is also something inherently heroic about a person who never gives up, despite all odds. We like to root for underdogs. The problem is, Axel's deep in the hole with his bookies to the tune of $44,000. His quest may be heroic, but it's also foolish and dangerous. But danger is part of the game. As mentioned above, proximity to danger is a huge part of gambling's allure. Hips, his bookie— played by go-to gangster character actor Paul Sorvino—lets Axel know that if he doesn't pay up, really bad shit will happen. But Axel shrugs the warnings off with a smirk. It's almost like he relishes the threats. When he tells his girlfriend Billie (played by gap-toothed '70s supermodel Lauren Hutton) that he owes $44,000 to the mob, he even seems proud of that fact. It's titillating. She's titillated. There's "the possibility of blood," he tells her.

Then again, the threat of violence, injury, and death forms the basis of one of gambling's co-occurring behavioral disorders: addiction to criminality.[50] There is some disagreement as to linkage. Do gambling addicts derive pleasure from criminal behavior, or do they just tend to engage in more criminal behavior like theft or borrowing from loan sharks to feed their gambling addiction? Perhaps a more direct linkage can be found between gambling and the danger inherent in criminality. Addiction to danger forms the basis of entire subcultures of adrenaline junkies like bungee jumpers and people who fly between jagged mountain cliffs in wingsuits. As danger addicts, I suppose their rock bottom is…well…a rock at the bottom of the mountain.

I got a wonderful crash course in addiction to crime and danger via a very colorful gentleman who used to attend my weekly SMART

---

[50] http://jaapl.org/content/45/4/464; https://www.psychologytoday.com/us/blog/in-excess/201809/addicted-crime

Recovery meeting. He was facing years in prison for organized criminal behavior, with a specialty in explosives used to blow up bank vaults. He explained very candidly that he was addicted to the rush of building bombs and then blowing them up. He also loved defusing bombs. He was in active withdrawal and wanted back in the game, a bit like the main character in the Oscar-winning film *The Hurt Locker*. He was also jonesing to join his bank-robber friends on their next big heist. He really missed them. I can sympathize. I felt the same way about my pub-crawl buddies after I quit drinking. I must admit, I got quite a thrill from having this guy in my meetings, so it's not a stretch to imagine Axel enjoying his camaraderie with the guys threatening to break his legs. But then again, isn't arm's-length proximity to danger one of the main reasons audiences love crime movies to begin with? Axel just happens to be one level of reality closer to the source.

We love it when the protagonist of the film isn't afraid of the bad guys. The more risk they face, the more heroic they seem. And while Axel certainly fits this mold on some levels, on others he falls short. His mother (played by the versatile Jacqueline Brookes) is a well-off doctor who has bailed him out of gambling debts before. His grandfather is a wealthy furniture store magnate. For well-off people like Axel, it's a lot easier to take careless risks when you have family to bail you out every time. Somebody who has nothing and bets everything to put her kids through college seems a lot more heroic than a guy who has everything and bets just to get high.

This is one more reason why I found it hard to care about Axel. Toback makes a few half-hearted inferential attempts to explain what led him astray. When his mother gives him the $44,000 to pay off his gambling debt, she asks him, "What did I do so wrong in raising you?" which is a classic passive-aggressive, mock-self-deprecating way of saying, "You're an idiot." And perhaps Axel believes this.

He's a lowly English professor at an inner-city community college making crap wages, while the rest of his family are successful millionaires. That's gotta sting. Maybe Axel thinks he can be one of those lucky proletariats who can out-earn his family through gambling in order to gain their respect. But his mother and grandfather make it very clear throughout the film that they love and respect him immensely regardless. Why else would they put up with all the crap his gambling addiction has put them through?

Maybe Axel is just compensating for a shortage of self-esteem. That's certainly at the core of many addictive behaviors, and gambling is no exception. It's all part of the "I use to forget that I use" circular reasoning spiral. Just like alcohol and drugs can give people a temporary blast of self-esteem, gamblers can extend their self-esteem indefinitely by either doubling down the bet or never cashing out. Because in gambling, you're not a loser until you actually lose. It's a bit like an electron that isn't really an electron until the moment it's observed. Which is why instead of paying back the $44,000 to his bookies and admitting defeat, he goes to Vegas intent on gambling so he can become an "un-loser." I bet, therefore I am.

Nuts, right? No, not at all. Luck wouldn't have it any other way. Unless Axel has bets ongoing and money at stake, Luck has nothing to do. So it resurrects itself from the ashes of Axel's previous defeats and envelops him with an exciting new cosmology of endless possibility. See, Luck comes with a handy auto-correct feature.[51] The reason it failed Axel last time wasn't its fault, it was because he was thinking too small. His bets in Vegas have to be bigger, risker. For Luck to do its job properly this time around, Axel's bets have to be so crazy they just *have* to work.

As "luck would have it," Axel wins big. He returns home with stacks of cash, his mental models a complete success. But once again,

---

51 A common auto-correct of the supernatural comes in the form of end-of-the-world predictions. When the predicted day and time comes and goes, and the faithful find themselves sitting in a cornfield in Iowa instead of the pearly gates of heaven, they simply reset their expiration date. Likely a week from Thursday, preferably a little on the later side of the morning, so everyone can get their Starbucks first.

there's nothing in play anymore, no money at risk, so Luck has nothing to do. Magical thinking is way more fun than boring old rational thinking. Axel is in withdrawal. Reality is broken. He has to get back into the game, any game. So he bets everything on some crazy basketball parlay that bombs. And it's back to square one.

He has to pay back Hips and the loan sharks the $44,000 he owes them or else they'll break his legs. His mother's out $44,000 too, but since Axel's family is Jewish, the worst that'll happen is a good guilt trip. But maybe this time he should listen to her, because the advice she gives him conveys an essential truth about gambling addiction that also applies to addiction in general: "Unless you come to terms with why you're doing this, no money's gonna get you out."

It's at the end of the film that we realize Axel doesn't ever want to get out. Even after he bribes one of his college student basketball players to throw a game and settles the debt with Hips, he can't stop. So he decides to not even bother with the avatars and tokens of gambling. He bypasses actual betting entirely, moving directly to satisfy his true addiction: real danger, real consequences, real loss, and nobody to bail him out.

He walks into a black ghetto, hires a black prostitute, then refuses to pay her. A fight ensues with her pimp, who puts a knife to Axel's face. But he's not afraid. This is what he wanted, this is where Luck has led him, and Luck is never wrong. A fight breaks out and the prostitute slashes Axel's face with the knife. As he looks at the bleeding, disfiguring gash in the mirror, he smiles. Perhaps his first genuine smile in the whole movie. The game is over; Axel can finally rest, and Luck can cash out.

Uncut Gems is a carbon copy of *The Gambler* in terms of basic storyline, but it's a far better film. In fact, in the pantheon of films about addiction, I consider it among the best. The directors, the Safdie brothers (Josh and Bennie), pack the film with just about everything you would hope for and expect in a story about gambling addiction, or any addiction for that matter. Martin Scorsese was the Executive Producer, and he rarely puts his name on a film unless he directs it or it's exceptional, like this film is. The film was financed by A24 Films, whose track record for excellence is the envy of every other independent. They've only been in business for the last 10 years and have already established themselves as up-and-coming Oscar contenders, racking up 25 Academy Award nominations—their most notable win being Best Picture for *Moonlight*.

The Safdies are the kind of directors I consider to be "the complete package" like David Fincher and Darren Aronofsky because their films check every box, from writing to editing, to camera and sound. They ally themselves with talents equal to their own. *Uncut Gems'* co-writer and editor is Ronald Bronstein, with whom they frequently collaborate, including on *Heaven Knows What*—an astonishing film about addiction which deserves its own chapter in my next book. Bronstein's script and editing on *Uncut Gems* is so anxiety-provoking, frenetic, and intense—watching it you almost feel like you're experiencing the worst withdrawals of your life and enjoying every second of it. This is not a popcorn movie; it's a Xanax movie.

I can't say enough about the film's cinematography by Iranian-born Darius Khondji, who changed the art of visual expression in film forever with *Delicatessen*, and then went on to work with masters like Fincher, Boyle, Bertolucci, Allen…the list goes on. *Uncut Gems* is a feast for the eyes. The color temperatures, graininess, camera placement, focal lengths—if you're a film geek like me you know why I'm gushing. Every image is edgy, unsettling, and beautiful. All of it is amplified by Oneohtrix Point Never (Daniel Lopatin's) music score that meshes so well with the visuals it provokes a feeling of synesthesia.

Uncut Gems won several important awards but was completely snubbed by the Oscars. I believe the reasons are two-fold. First, any film with Adam Sandler is instant Academy Award poison. He has been so typecast as a goofy lowbrow adolescent humor comedian, few people in the business realize what a truly gifted actor he is with the right material. He doesn't take serious dramatic roles very often, but when teamed up with the right director we get amazing performances like ***Punch-Drunk Love*** (Paul Thomas Anderson) and ***Uncut Gems***. Oscar consideration was also killed by the fact that A24 sold the foreign rights to Netflix, which made it into a "Netflix movie," which some purists at the Academy of Motion Picture Arts and Sciences didn't think should qualify it for any awards, nor even allow it to be considered an actual film.[52]

Uncut Gems is the story of Jewish jewelry merchant Howard Ratner (Sandler) who owes a great deal of money to a loan shark but has an elaborate plan to pay it all back and set everything right. The key part of this plan is a rare black opal that he has smuggled out of Ethiopia in the hopes of selling it at auction for over a million dollars. Sounds rather simple on the surface, but absolutely nothing seems to go as planned. There are two menacing loan collectors who threaten harm trailing him at all times. Everywhere he goes he's accosted by associates to whom he owes money. Phones ring off the hook, employees are pissed off, and his electronic security door is on the fritz. His entire world seems to be teetering on the brink of disaster. And this is just the first 10 minutes of the film.

His home life is just as chaotic. Soon-to-be-ex-wife Dinah (played by "Queen of Broadway" Idina Menzel) hates his guts because he's cheating on her with one of his employees, Julia (played by the beautiful Italian American actress/model Julia Fox). He's largely

---

52 Remember, this was the year when Steven Spielberg got his undies in a knot about Netflix, etc. https://www.indiewire.com/2019/02/steven-spielberg-vs-netflix-oscar-academy-wars-1202047846/

emotionally absent from his kids' lives, and even struggles to show up physically. His son Jonathan is barely ten years old and already a gambling-addict-in-training, and his teenage daughter, Noa, thinks her father's a putz.

"Putz" is just one of the wonderful Yiddish words that crop up in the film, along with "vig"—short for vigorish—which is the service fee a bookmaker or casino takes out of a bet. It also describes the absurdly high interest rates the loan sharks are charging Howard on the money he owes them. One of the reasons why **Uncut Gems** seems so authentic is that the directors placed Jewish culture as a centerpiece of the film's universe. The Safdie brothers' father was an actual New York Diamond District salesman. And Jewish loan sharking is a tradition that goes back several centuries. Remember, Jews in Europe were prohibited from taking most jobs because of rampant anti-Semitism, so money lending became one of the few career paths open to them.[53]

The film is also strengthened by the fact that it celebrates parts of Jewish culture and heritage. As Howard's gambling problem violently storms around him, the filmmakers take us inside his calm, close-knit Jewish family as they celebrate Passover. It's so calm, in fact, that Howard is able to enjoy the family meal with his brother-in-law Arno (Paul Bogosian), who also happens to be the loan shark who's threatening to kill him unless he pays up. Although clearly not a comedy, some of the film's funniest moments are when Jewish friends and close associates who are supposed to be "mishpachah" (family) are openly stabbing each other in the back.

The film also celebrates the history of Jews and basketball, inasmuch as the sport is another centerpiece of the story. Basketball was once referred to as a "Jewish sport" because of its mass adoption among recent Jewish immigrants at the turn of the last century. Howard even

---

[53] Sadly, the racial archetype of the avaricious Jewish money-lender fed the Elders of Zion conspiracy theories that the Jews secretly controlled the world's finances as they drank baby blood.

reminds his colleagues in the film that the first two points ever scored in the NBA were by Douglas Stark, a Jew. The Safdies and writer Ronald Bronstein leverage this history by channeling it into Howard's costly and dangerous obsession with betting on the Boston Celtics, specifically its star Kevin Garnett (playing himself).

Garnett does a wonderful acting job in the film, and he's a key character in the story. During a routine jewelry-shopping trip to Howard's store, he becomes mesmerized by the black opal Howard is about to auction off. Like Axel and Howard, Garnett has also created his own Luck cosmology to supplement his athletic prowess. Or guide it? No telling how far down the Tim Tebow rabbit hole some athletes go. Despite his misgivings about letting the opal out of his sight, Howard loans it to Garnett in exchange for holding his Celtics championship ring as collateral.

This is a pivotal point in the film. Howard claims to be nervous about giving Garnett the opal but does so quite intentionally. He knows the jewel has become his good luck charm. The magical thinking surrounding it can now be shared and amplified as part of a collective Luck mythology. Howard then pawns Garnett's ring for cash and makes a crazy parlay bet on Garnett's next game. It should make no sense, but for their Luck it makes perfect sense. Whereas Axel bribed his student to throw the game in **The Gambler**, in this film Howard is supernaturally manipulating him to win it.

And it works. The parlay nets him $600,000 and his problems should be solved— except that Arno canceled the bet with the bookie because Howard used his money to place it. Arno and his goons ambush Howard at his kid's school play, beat him up, strip him naked, and throw him in the trunk of his car. Apparently this is how family sends a message. Or at least *this* family. The situation gets even more toxic when Howard finally gets the opal back from Garnett and puts it up for auction. But the appraisal price is way less than he needs, so he begs his father-in-law Gooey (Hollywood's go-to mensch Judd

Hirsch) to bid up the price at auction, only to get stuck buying it. Adding injury to insult, Arno's goons Nico and Phil beat Howard up and dump him in a fountain outside the auction house.

Howard returns to his office a broken man. His wife won't take him back, his girlfriend cheated on him, his family hates him, his business is imploding, he owes money to just about everybody, and his pet fish is dead. If there was ever a time for Luck to rise miraculously from the ruins of Howard's life, this would be it. Instead, he cries. I mean, *really* cries. It's a rare display of vulnerability—reminding us that despite whatever crazy train they're on, addicts are still human beings. And suffering is part of the process of learning.

We now arrive at another pivotal scene in the film. It's one of those movie sequences I watch over and over, and every time I do I find more reasons to love it. Garnett visits Howard's office and buys the opal in cash. Howard can finally pay Arno back, get the goons off his back, and maybe even rebuild his reputation, his family, and his self-respect. But no. Apparently there are more lessons to be learned and more suffering to be had. He decides to bet all the cash on a three-way parlay on Garnett's playoff game that evening. Even Garnett thinks the win and the spread is unlikely, but Howard knows something nobody else does. And it's not just some simple forecast on a game; it's a prophecy. It's not a bet, it's a spiritual offering. "It's a feeling you and I both have," he tells Garnett, their Luck now magically conjoined.

I can't in good conscience give away the ending of the film. Just know that Howard's Hail Mary bet pays off, big time. The prophecy is fulfilled. Luck prevails.

But was it Luck? Or something else?

Howard didn't bet everything on the simple mechanical outcome of a card game or the spin of a roulette wheel. He bet it on a person; Garnett. And Garnett didn't put the outcome of the entire game in the hands of his lucky opal—he put it in himself, in his abilities, his positive thinking, his desire to win. Both men hoped something good would happen, and it did. Hope gave Howard the courage to trust his instincts and place that crazy bet. Hope made Garnett try just a little harder and shoot a little straighter. Maybe we don't really need Luck as much as we think we do to make our mental models pan out. Maybe Hope is a better strategy[54].

Regardless, I hope this chapter helps illustrate how gambling addiction is more than just poker chips and roulette wheels. Notions about luck, magic, faith, and hope are deeply human concerns, at times bordering on the philosophical and spiritual. And we've seen how irrational hope can either destroy, like it did in Axel's story in ***The Gambler***—or create, like it did in Howard's story in ***Uncut Gems***.

I hope you like the next chapter. I bet you will.

---

54 Brings to mind the saying, "The harder I work, the luckier I get…"

DO NOT EAT:

- apple pie
- baked beans
- bologna
- bread
- candy
- cannelloni
- cheesecake
- chocolate
- cupcakes
- danish
- doughnuts
- dumplings
- eclairs
- fettuccine
- fondue
- french fries
- gingerbread
- ice cream
- lasagna
- macaroni
- marshmallows
- muffins
- noodles
- oatmeal
- olives
- parfait
- pizza
- potatoes
- pretzels
- ravioli
- ribs
- salami
- sauces
- scraps
- spaghetti
- sund

A FILM BY ANNE BANCROFT

Fatso

Starring **DOM DeLUISE** in "FATSO"
ANNE BANCROFT · RON CAREY · CANDICE AZZARA
Written and Directed by ANNE BANCROFT   Produced by STUART CORNFELD
Associate Producer JONATHAN SANGER   Music by JOE RENZETTI
A Production of Brooksfilms Ltd.   Color by DeLuxe

PG PARENTAL GUIDANCE SUGGESTED
SOME MATERIAL MAY NOT BE SUITABLE FOR CHILDREN

READ THE BALLANTINE BOOK

© 1980 TWENTIETH CENTURY FOX

CHAPTER 12
Do I Look Too Fat in this Eating Disorder?
Fatso

Apart from sex, eating is humanity's most pleasurable yet vexing pastime. Eating can be hard work. Our ape ancestors had to dig around for roots and spend all day chewing them. That was their job, just chewing roots all day, every day, until the monotony was broken by a saber-toothed tiger that ate them. Later, hominids gathered fruits, berries, and bird eggs and other stuff that would make modern-day vegans proud, but most of the time they'd get eaten by a saber-toothed tiger too—much like some of us wish vegans today would. Eventually our ancestors learned how to throw stones and spears and hunt saber-toothed tigers and tame fire, and they got really big brains; brains big enough to have highly complex thoughts like, *Does my ass look too fat in this bearskin?*

For 95% of human history people didn't know where their next meal was coming from. Overeating (aka "feasting" or "binging") was a way to store away excess food energy in the form of fat. In other words, we're all just double-A batteries with arms and legs and the capacity to suffer from body dysmorphia. What kind of a vengeful god would visit this suffering upon us? Like the universe doesn't have enough ways to try to kill us, it had to invent obesity too? Couldn't humanity have this one thing—ONE THING! —that could be enjoyed without adverse consequences? To eat as much as we want of whatever we want whenever we want? No, apparently that's asking too much. There is *literally* no free lunch in the universe. To hell with Voltaire; we aren't living in the best of all possible worlds unless those worlds include all-you-can-eat buffets that never make you fat.

If I sound frustrated, it's because I am. Low carb? Keto caveman? Jenny Craig? I mean make up your f-in minds, people. Like billions of you, I spend way too much time worrying about what or how much I should eat. Okay, sure, from outward appearances I don't have a weight issue. I eat right and exercise. But inside, I'm a whirling cesspool of guilt and recrimination. I really enjoy food, but it really stresses me out too. To me there is no such thing as being too thin. I buy pants a size too small just to challenge myself to eventually fit into them. And once I have, I do the opposite. I laugh at it now, but anxiety about weight isn't that funny. During graduate school I exercised three times a day and only ate tuna fish. I would eventually crack, turn into a food zombie, and binge on Frosted Flakes. Then I would purge and start over.

I eventually overcame my short bout with bulimia and graduated to alcohol use disorder, but the basic thought patterns of weight-related anxiety are still with me and will probably never go away. I enjoyed a brief respite during the Covid lockdown when I decided to just "let myself go," eat whatever I wanted, and not work out. And the results were astounding. I lost weight and felt terrific. I was calmer and happier than I'd ever been in my whole life. I realized that—like addicts with their drug of choice—I had been in a dysfunctional relationship with food, just as I had been with alcohol. It had nothing to do with the food itself.

But I'm getting ahead of myself. Make no mistake; eating disorders are no laughing matter. Anorexia and bulimia are among the most lethal psychiatric disorders out there. There are several fine films on the subject for anyone who is interested. For the purposes of this book, however, I instead want to explore the touchy subjects of non-lethal addiction to overeating/poor eating, and the resulting issues of obesity and dieting, through the perspective of a feature film: **Fatso** made in 1980[55] and starring comic genius Dom DeLuise.

Fatso is not a great film; in fact it's rather disappointing. But it's one of the only films I could find with anything interesting to say about actual addiction to poor eating habits or overeating, the underlying psychology behind weight "problems," and the role of society in defining what constitutes a weight problem. Films like **Shallow Hal**, **The Nutty Professor**, and Mo'Nique's **Phat Girlz** are gratuitous eye candy, and concentrate more on the Cyrano de Bergerac angle. The theme they always return to is "it's what's inside that counts." Fine, let's take this as a given; it's the dynamics of "how much I weigh, and why does it—or *should* it—matter to me and others" that's more interesting to me, and what I want to explore here.

Hollywood studios categorically avoid the topic of obesity. You just don't bite the hand that feeds you.[56] "Serious fat" is a non-starter. But "funny fat" is totally fine. I worked at Universal to help create the international marketing campaign for **The Nutty Professor**.

---

55 Not to be confused with **Fatso**, the 2008 film by Norwegian director Arild Fröhlich which has less to do with obesity and more to do with sexual awakening.

56 Film exhibitors really only use films as a pretext to sell popcorn, M&Ms, and sugary sodas. The average tub of large butter popcorn contains 1,200 calories and a three-day supply of saturated fat.

All the marketing materials passed over to us from the domestic U.S. campaign focused on the scene of Eddie Murphy's morbidly obese family overeating. Granted, it was pretty funny. If you were an American. Given my experience growing up overseas, I felt that foreign audiences might find this scene in bad taste. I thought we should play up the Cyrano love angle between Murphy and Janet Jackson. I was laughed out of the room. And it turned out I was wrong. The film grossed more internationally than it did in the U.S. Which made me sad, because in a way we were exporting the All-American normalization of gluttony.

While the topic of obesity is a no-no, Hollywood has no problem making money off of obese actors. John Candy and Chris Farley[57] rode their physical brand of obesity-based humor to box-office stardom and then straight to the grave—just like John Belushi did with substance use-based humor. Laurel & Hardy would simply not have worked without Oliver Hardy being fat to Stan Laurel's skinny. Hardy's weight eventually killed him. Roscoe "Fatty" Arbuckle was the highest-paid actor of the silent era before his career got derailed by a Coke bottle.[58]

W.C. Fields was delightfully plump and completely drunk during his films, the first example of a coexisting disorder being mined for Tinseltown profit. Alcohol eventually killed him. Jackie Gleason made huge inroads in television in spite of, and because of, his weight. He had three different closets with clothes in three different sizes corresponding to what type of work he had at the time: filming **The Honeymooners** (bigger), doing a stand-up tour (smaller), or just

---

[57] Incidentally, at a recent addiction treatment professionals conference I attended, I hung out with Chris' brother Tom Farley, a lovely guy, who wrote a great book about his brother called **The Chris Farley Show**. He and I discussed how unfortunate it was that eating disorders weren't taken more seriously back in the day, but fortunately they are now.

[58] https://www.newyorker.com/magazine/2021/10/11/fatty-arbuckle-and-the-birth-of-the-celebrity-scandal

being himself (medium). Gleason was felled by a combination of weight-induced diabetes, related heart issues, and colon cancer—all exacerbated by his six-pack-a-day smoking "habit."

Plus sizes on TV went mainstream with John Goodman and Roseanne Barr in **Roseanne**, and society was able to more freely discuss the topic of weight. Obesity even became somewhat politicized. Largess is a key part of "American Exceptionalism." If you got an issue with Rosanne's weight, you got a problem with America, buddy. The term "Fat Acceptance" joined our popular lexicon, which was wonderful news for a movement begun all the way back in the late '60s. Kirstie Alley brought the world **Fat Actress** on Showtime in 2005, and fifteen years later the multi-talented national treasure that is Lizzo brought us **Watch Out for the Big Grrrls**. In the fashion industry, "plus-sized" models are now busier and making just as much money as their rail-thin counterparts. These are all welcome trends. It's wonderful to see stigma being smashed in eating disorders just as they are in drug and alcohol use disorders.

However, celebrating and glamorizing obesity is one thing; actually coming to terms with it is another. For most obese celebrities, being overweight is not tenable—it's a problem to be solved. And the solution usually involves amazing body transformation. Rebel Wilson, Jonah Hill, Drew Carey, Al Roker, Jack Black, Oprah, Adele, and John Goodman (to name a few) have made drastic weight loss an integral part of their brand and origin stories. Inversely, some actors like Christian Bale and Ryan Gosling add drastic weight gain to beef up their acting chops. It is only recently that obese actors have felt commercially comfortable enough to stay as they are, overweight. In some cases, they reversed course because they were missing out on work opportunities. Jonah Hill simply wasn't "as funny" thin as he was fat.

And "funny" may be the crux of the matter here. Fat people have usually been the butt of jokes (pardon the pun). As a culture, we've always thought obese people are funny. We want them to be funny. Funny feels okay; doesn't feel like we're judging them for being… you know…fat. And fat people probably played along because it got them attention, even though most were suffering inside. I know this because I was once one of those people. Fat is still funny, and several actors leverage their weight to help their comedy careers. But there is nothing funny about the people featured in shows like ***My 600-Pound Life***. Morbid obesity is a ticking time bomb with a 5% survival rate. So when does the deadly serious stop, and the funny begin?

This question seems more immediate today than it did in decades past. Obesity is a fairly recent phenomenon. We've really only been talking about it openly as a public health issue since the mid-'80s. Before that, obesity wasn't even a word most people used. People just said "overweight." And not too many people *were* overweight, not like today. In 1966 the average person's BMI was 1.5%. By 1989 that had risen to 12.3%. Now it's twice that. There are many reasons offered for why this happened so quickly. My money's on the "Blame Nixon" theory.

Okay, so as the story goes, then-President Richard Nixon wanted to distract Americans from the fact that his administration was roasting children with incendiary bombs in Vietnam. One way to do that was to lower domestic food costs. He empowered his Secretary of Agriculture, Earl "Rusty" Butz (no pun intended) of Indiana (of course) to basically end the New Deal and give farmers incentives and subsidies to vastly scale up production of corn (the most successful domesticated plant of all time).

This led to feeding more corn to cows, who got bigger and fatter (and suffered terrible indigestion), which led to cheaper meat. This led to cheaper fast food, fatter fast food marketing budgets, and dollar menus. Have some fries with that, fried in (you guessed it) corn oil. Whereas back in the day McDonald's was an occasional treat, fast food became an unbeatable value for daily meals—especially for the poor. Obesity rates skyrocketed. Insurance rates went up. Our own tax dollars were subsidizing a public health catastrophe.

But wait, there's more! Once the cows got their fill, there was still a lot of corn left over, so Japanese chemists helped U.S. manufacturers turn all the surplus into high fructose corn syrup. Whereas American kids once had only Hostess Twinkies and Ho-Hos, cheap HFCS allowed companies like Pillsbury, Kraft, and Nabisco to create hundreds of new sugary products. I grew up overseas where snack foods didn't exist. Every year on my birthday—and ONLY on my birthday—I would get a care package from my Aunt Mercedes full of Oreo cookies which I would douse in milk and eat as cereal. When I finally moved to the U.S., I realized I could do this every day like every other American kid, and of course I gained weight.

The generously subsidized economics of the food industry also affected portion sizes. When I grew up in Europe, everybody knew how much food to eat in each course (we had courses). It was considered gauche to pile too much food on a plate. It was even kind of rude to finish everything *on* your plate. There was no such thing as "leftovers." If you asked a waiter in Madrid to box everything to go, they'd never seat you in their restaurant again. In Paris, after they slapped you across the face, they'd have you deported.

You can imagine my shock and awe when I returned to the U.S. and visited a Cheesecake Factory. Overeating was now *the point* of eating out. All sense of proportionality in food had been erased, replaced by a cognitive distortion that getting more food was a better value—even though the increased price was disproportionate to the cost of actually putting more (cheap) food on the plate.

So, yes, as if the universe weren't unfair enough, we have corrupt politicians, food conglomerates, and restaurateurs to thank for making everyone obsessed about their weight. Oh, and let's not forget the chemists in their fancy laboratories who devised ingenious new ways to combine food additives and chemicals to activate the pleasure centers of our brains. Like those assholes at Purdue Pharma who peddled OxyContin®, they're well aware that their products are a highly addictive unexploded obesity ordinance. Their entire business model is predicated on it. Better life through chemistry, my ass (literally).

But is it fair to blame others—or society—for our weight issues? Heavens no. We all have free will, right? People can choose not to eat poorly or too much, just like people can choose to never drink alcohol or do drugs. But talk about the odds being stacked against us. There's a reason AA meetings aren't held in cocktail lounges, or NA meetings in pharmacies. Food is everywhere, all the time, forever, until we die. We have to eat to live. Expecting Americans to eat "healthy"[59] all the time is like expecting a poverty-stricken Appalachian child abuse survivor with anxiety disorder to never try drugs—not even once, even on a dare.

When it comes to overeating specifically, it just doesn't seem like a fair fight. Eating together is a huge part of how we socialize. Sometimes it's the only time we can or do socialize. My parents insisted on a mandatory-attendance, two-course, ask-to-be-excused sit-down family dinner every night—and in retrospect I think it did wonders in my sister's and my upbringing. Eating, eating well, and a lot, is a family's way of displaying its wealth, social prominence, and its affection for friends and family members. It's also a fundamental part of religious observances and events.

Every culture has its own feasting rituals. Italian-Americans have their Sunday pasta-paloozas. I dated a very traditional Jewish woman whose mother offered me a huge piece of bread to "help you wash down that chocolate babka."[60] Brazilian barbecues are epic; my nephew and I call it "the meatwave." Yes, we've all heard about the

---

[59] I use quotes here to highlight the fact that one of the most annoyingly common grammatical mistakes in the dieting world is to say a food is "healthy." The correct word is "healthful."

[60] I later found out that was a popular Jewish joke.

Swedish smorgasbord, but did you know there is a whole rulebook that explains what, how much, and when you should eat certain buffet items, and in what precise sequence, to guarantee you'll ingest the most amount of food without throwing up?

Feasting is not just a cultural expression; it's bound up in a country's historical memory as well. French "cuisine" isn't just calorie-rich foods, it's the basis of nationalistic pride, a way to differentiate itself from those bufoonish "sausage eater" Germans and the "rosbif"[61]-eating Brits. I spent a fair deal of time working in China, and the whole Chinese New Year thing is deadly serious stuff. The focus on food, and a lot of it, is mind-boggling. But remember, the Chinese have been dealing with deadly famines for thousands of years. The last one—from 1959-1961—the result of Mao's disastrous "Great Leap Forward" campaign, created the world's worst-ever man-made disaster and killed up to 55 million people. So, yeah, the Chinese take food very, very seriously. In fact, a common salutation in China is Chīguᵒle ma, or "Have you eaten yet?"

Besides culture, weight issues are also linked to very complicated and poorly understood genetic, psycho-social, and situational variables. While science debates the existence of a "fat gene," there is no doubt that certain body types are more predisposed to accumulate more adipose tissue (fat) more quickly or unevenly. We all know and secretly wish we could assassinate people who stay thin no matter what or how much they eat. It's genetics—the same reason I'll never build as much muscle as Mr. Olympia regardless of how much I work out. But I'd crush him at track and field or squash.

From a psychosocial perspective, eating is not just considered sustenance, it's also viewed as a reward. Key life celebrations and most holidays usually involve feasting. I sometimes bribe my nine-year-old

---

61 Roast beef. Talk to the average French person and ask them what they think of British "cuisine."

daughter, Quinn, with ice cream. We celebrate her swim team victories with pizza. One of the participants in my weekly SMART Recovery meeting calls binge-eating her "whoobie." She doesn't like it when people mess with her whoobie or try to take it away. "Stress eating" is a thing. Entire marketing campaigns target lonely unmarried or recently divorced middle-aged women and try to sell them chocolate cake as the next best thing to an actual partner.

However arrived at or with how much food, let's face it: Satiety is a simply wonderful feeling. The neurotransmitters involved are similar to those activated by hard drugs.[62] Cookies and milk before bed? Hell yes! Everything really *is* going to be okay.

And what if weight issues just boiled down to events? Past trauma perhaps. When I was eleven I was in my mom's bathroom with a few friends and hopped on her scale for fun. It read 100 pounds. My friends all laughed at me. I was taunted about it for weeks. I wasn't overweight per se. All my friends were going to hit that mark in the next few months anyway, but the fact that I was the first kid to top 100 pounds burned into my psyche; I've lived with the consequences ever since.

A kid's weight is a major factor in whether or not they will be bullied, for how long, and how aggressively. Much like a drug or alcohol addict who will use to stop feeling guilty about using, kids will turn to binge-eating to make themselves feel less horrible about being overweight. And new studies show that incidents like bullying may not even matter at all. An obese child could have his parents to blame—not for feeding them too much, but because they're alcoholics.[63] What's more, their obesity may be due to the fact that they have too much Neanderthal DNA![64]

---

62 https://pubmed.ncbi.nlm.nih.gov/2865893/

63 https://scitechdaily.com/addicted-to-food-it-could-be-your-parents-fault/

64 https://phys.org/news/2022-09-neanderthals-died-years-dna-earth.html

For a glimpse into the mind of someone with an eating disorder, I wanted to share this excerpt from a letter they wrote to me about their experiences:

> "When I wake up in the morning, I am thinking about how soon I can eat my breakfast (I make myself wait until 6). While I am eating my breakfast, I am thinking about lunch.
>
> I have found help through Overeaters Anonymous. But I still struggle with my food. Every minute of every hour of every day. It is 10am now, and my husband has a meeting at 11. We usually eat around 11. My mind is going on overdrive trying to figure out whether we will have lunch before or during the meeting."

Regardless of the causes and contexts, weight is a delicate issue that is very personal and very problematic for many people. It's one of humanity's sore spots, which is why very few films have ever been made that address it in any substantial, honest, or didactic way. In fact, I spent more time looking for suitable films for this chapter than actually writing it. And I still came up short. A good film about this subject simply has not been made yet. Perhaps it never will. So for now we have to go with what we have.

I saw **Fatso** way back in 1980 when it was theatrically released. It must not have made a good impression on me; all I can remember was feeling cheated. The marketing made it seem like it was a Mel Brooks movie because Dom DeLuise was in most Mel Brooks movies. And Mel Brooks is a comic genius of the highest order.[65] **Fatso** stars DeLuise; it was produced by Mel Brooks' company, but Mel Brooks' name is nowhere to be found in the credits. I can see why. The film is nowhere near the level of a Mel Brooks movie. But the issues **Fatso**

---

[65] I said as much to Mel Brooks in person once at the Fox Commissary. He told me to leave him alone, he was eating. It's frequently said, never meet your heroes.

brings up about weight and dieting are important, so if you'd like to just read this chapter about the film instead of spending 93 minutes of your life watching it, your secret is safe with me.

The film's writer/director was Anne Bancroft, who incidentally was Mel Brooks' inseparable wife of many years until her death in 2005. She would probably not choose to be remembered for this film, nor should she. Bancroft was one of the most versatile and gutsy actresses of the 20th century (and some of the 21st; her last appearance was on **Curb Your Enthusiasm** in 2004). She is among the few thespians to ever win the Triple Crown of Acting (Oscar, Tony, Emmy).

She won an Academy Award for Best Actress in 1962 for **Miracle Worker**, after winning a Tony for the same role on Broadway. But I will always remember her as Mrs. Robinson in **The Graduate**, the world's first-ever "cougar" in popular entertainment. Her luscious rendition of the line "*I am not trying to seduce you. Would you like me to seduce you? Is that what you're trying to tell me?*" can (also) be enjoyed at the beginning and end of George Michael's hit song "Too Funky" (Extended Version).

Perhaps **Fatso** wasn't as bad as it was half-baked. With a little development work, it probably could have achieved far more. I don't know the particulars, but it seems Dom DeLuise had a bunch of Hollywood mojo coming off **Silent Movie** and **The Muppet Movie**, and 20th Century Fox had just signed an overall production deal with Brooks Films. With fresh funds and greenlight authority, Brooks probably gave **Fatso** to Bancroft as an anniversary present and pushed the project into production at a very low budget, hoping DeLuise's "funny fat" schtick would move the needle. It didn't. It only grossed limited pickup business generated by audiences who either didn't read or care about the scathing reviews—or couldn't get in to see **American Gigolo.**

DeLuise plays Dominick, an Italian American good guy who's very Catholic and likes to eat. Nothing at the level of Monty Python's

Mr. Creosote,[66] mind you. The world would have to wait three more years to witness that brilliantly funny and disturbing scene in ***Monty Python's The Meaning of Life***. In fact, by today's ***The Biggest Loser*** standards, Dominick isn't obese at all. He's just "chubby." However, when his cousin Sal dies suddenly at the age of 39 due to his weight, Dominick realizes he has to make a change in his behavior. "No more eggplant parmesan, Sally-Boy!" proclaims a friend at the funeral.

This set up is simple enough, but keep in mind that until that point no film had ever featured a character who died as a result of their eating habits. The link between obesity and mortality was not widely known outside of the medical community at the time—and had only been hinted at as one of the causes of Elvis' death three years earlier. So thank you, Anne Bancroft, for being the first director to dramatize the fact that obesity is a contributing factor in 5 of the top 10 leading causes of death in the U.S.[67]

In the ensuing years after ***Fatso*** came out, the idea of obesity = death was further reinforced by the untimely deaths of aforementioned celebrities like John Candy, Chris Farley, and yes—Dom DeLuise himself in 2009. What I find interesting is that most of the remaining obese aforementioned celebrities like John Goodman and Drew Carey waited as long as they did to undertake their dramatic weight loss transformations. Goodman only began his journey in 2007, and largely credits his success to quitting alcohol after 30 years of problematic drinking. It took Drew Carey until 2010. James Gandolfini never undertook any dieting, and he died in 2013.

Bancroft probably didn't want to belabor the point about untimely obesity-related death, and instead puts the focus on how Dominick begins to use food as a way to cope with his and his family's grief. He's not alone. The most I've ever eaten in my life is at funeral receptions.

---

66 https://www.youtube.com/watch?v=GxRnenQYG7I

67 https://www.cdc.gov/nchs/fastats/leading-causes-of-death.htm

At the last one I went to, there were no less than six Bundt cakes for twenty guests. Feasting is both a celebration of life and success, and a commemoration of someone in death. How are people like Dominick supposed to swear off eating when it's such a huge part of their emotional processing of grief, depression, and anxiety?

The answer might be that maybe they don't. Overeating is used by some people to reduce stress—just as others use drugs, alcohol, or other analgesics. Whereas substances can cause addiction and health risks, occasional splurges during tough times don't seem that harmful by comparison, unless the binge-eating itself becomes an addiction.

To quote another friend who wrote to me to describe her eating disorder:

"For me, it's not about the food; it's about not having the coping skills to deal with frustration, upset, anger and happiness.

Eating is wound up in how I set boundaries with my family, my fear about things happening in my life, but most importantly, not having enough connections and contacts outside of my family."

This is all very messy terrain. "Binge-eating" poses health risks. But does over-treating it pose emotional ones? The term "Emotional Eating" started to be used in 2001, and the idea that people would overeat even if they weren't hungry to avoid or process negative emotions spawned dozens of research papers and an entire sub-genre in book publishing. Terms like "comfort food" and "stress eating" came into vogue and are now in common usage. So, again, by showing this on film over forty years ago, Bancroft was unintentionally prescient.

Dominick eventually "decides" to go to a doctor to treat his weight issue. I put "decides" in quotes. How much of a decision can be yours when you have the image of your deceased cousin in a casket fresh in your mind, and your hysterical sister Antoinette (played with over-the-top intensity by Bancroft herself) peer-pressuring you to lose weight? To me it's like staging a drug or alcohol intervention and forcing someone into rehab. It only works if the person wants it to work. And when Dominick sees the list of foods he cannot eat, he clearly doesn't want it to work.

In another movie first, **Fatso** dramatizes an actual diet. In fact, the idea of "following a diet" or "being on a diet" was such a novel concept at the time, the executives at Fox put the long list of prohibited foods on the movie poster as a marketing hook. *You mean he can't eat bologna? Scandalous! I MUST see this film!* However, Dominick does find some inspiration when he meets Mrs. Goodman, a neighbor who visits his greeting card shop. Funny six-degrees-of-separation story: Goodman is played by Estelle Reiner, wife of Mark Twain Prize for American Humor recipient Carl Reiner (who along with Mel Brooks wrote *The Dick Van Dyke Show*); mother of Rob Reiner, who played "meathead" on **All in the Family**, went on to direct one of my favorite films, ***This is Spinal Tap***, and who is himself a person who struggles publicly with his weight. Goodman shows off her svelte figure and claims she's easily shed 50 pounds.

How? Well, after a long list of no-go foods, she basically describes the low/no-carb "Atkins Diet." So again, Bancroft was way ahead of her time; the low-carb "new diet revolution" was still 10 years off. She hit on a dieting concept that subsequently morphed into everything from the "caveman" to the "South Beach" to the "Keto" diet and ended up being valued at zillions of dollars in associated book and program sales. Which was all a total waste of money, I might add, since a low-carb diet has been scientifically shown to be no better or worse than any other diet.

Dominick's dieting fails, and he becomes a neurotic mess. DeLuise is the perfect actor to play "neurotic mess," mind you. This was his first solo starring role; up to then he had been more of an ensemble actor or the hilarious sidekick to ground-breaking comedians like Gene Wilder and Miss Piggy. So for support, Dominick attends a "Chubby

Checkers" meeting—basically a satirical rendition of a typical mutual support meeting. Again, Bancroft was way ahead of her time. Yes, 12-Step meetings had been shown in films before (***Days of Wine and Roses***, for instance), but this was the first time they were ever satirized.

But satirized in poor taste, I'm afraid. The scene devolves into everybody in the meeting shouting "I'm fat…fat…fat!" over and over. It smacks of forced self-acceptance, one of the criticisms some people level against the Fat Acceptance movement. While a positive self-image is psychologically healthful, being inspired to trivialize or gloss over obesity's negative health consequences is not. Yes, being fat is "okay" in principle, but for most people it's not okay in practice. They want to change. It's like an alcoholic standing up in a 12-Step meeting and shouting, "I'm drunk…drunk…drunk!" What good is positive body-imaging if you're dead?[68]

It's really here that **Fatso** goes off the rails and can't decide whether it's a film about self-acceptance or a cautionary tale about obesity. Most critics pointed this out, and bemoaned the fact that Bancroft let a great problem go to waste. The result is a lumpy admixture of Borscht-belt humor and genuine human pathos.

The story does manage to take on some new life as Dominick falls in love with Lydia, a nice diabetic who works next door. Initially he thinks his weight might be a turn-off for her, but eventually gathers the self-confidence to date her. In the process, he begins to slim down without even trying. This is a very small plot point but had the potential to become the central positive theme of the film.

Much like what happened to me during Covid lockdown, Dominick adjusted (or entirely ignored) the toxic relationship with

---

[68] Some notes about the Fat Acceptance movement from my friend (quoted above) in recovery from her eating disorder: "It's not just 'we here, we're fat, let's eat!' but rather wanting to be treated fairly (doctor's office, jobs, etc.). Especially where the medical establishment is concerned, fat/obese people feel like they can't get medical care because all the doctor sees is a fat person walking in; they only want to treat the weight loss part and none of the underlying issues that got them there."

his "weight problem" and in essence solved it. We all know that not thinking about a problem doesn't magically make it go away. This isn't January 6th Denialism. But challenging what you believe about yourself, and why, is a powerful way to change those beliefs and thereby effect better outcomes. Maybe Bancroft was a fan of the Stoics and Albert Ellis. If only she had pushed this thematic envelope a little further, the film may have ended up being a classic in the Cognitive Behavioral Theory universe.

Another missed opportunity involves Dominick's weight loss program, which would have involved exercise, in addition to starvation. With Dom DeLuise's brand of physical comedy, I'm surprised Bancroft didn't put him in some hilarious workout sequence where he falls off a treadmill or dresses up in silly long socks and stumbles through (or nails!) the Jane Fonda Workout.[69] It could have been an opportunity for some barbed commentary too. Weight issues frequently involve exercise issues, and exercise can be as addictive as anything else. Again, it's all about a person's relationship to their exercise that matters. I've been trapped on the food-exercise hamster wheel my whole adult life: *I just worked out so I can eat anything I want. I need to work out because I just ate anything I wanted.* The subject of exercise addiction is a fascinating topic in and of itself. I think it's helpful that celebrities like Demi Moore and Demi Lovato have gone public with their struggles; because while exercise is generally good for your health, recovery teaches us that you can always have too much of a good thing.

Bancroft redeems herself at the emotional climax of the film, both as a storyteller and an as actress. She confronts Dominick after Lydia goes missing and he's binged three servings of Chinese takeout in order to cope. In a coming-to-Jesus moment, Dominick admits he's

---

[69] Although in fairness the whole aerobics "let's get physical" phenomenon didn't break until two years later.

always justified his overeating by making excuses. This is familiar to anyone with an alcohol, drug, or food addiction. But then he reminds her, and us, that to eat is to live. To eat is to give love and receive love. This touching scene reinforces the point that overeating can't be compared to other addictions, and it's unfair to try to do so. "I have to eat!" he proclaims, When I eat, I'm me!" Who could argue with this? Who *should* argue with this?

While a not-so-great film, **Fatso** gave voice to many of the complex issues surrounding eating disorders and was many years ahead of its time. Yes, self-esteem is important, but personal responsibility is as well. Yes, people have to eat every day, and life will always have its disappointments—but that's not a blanket authorization to self-medicate by eating too much or too badly. Yes, drinking alcohol or taking drugs is a choice. Eating is not. But that's no justification for making poor food choices.

Part of the problem when it comes to eating and weight is that society lacks the tools to truly address it coherently or consistently. When does "serious fat" end and "funny fat" begin? Does a person's BMI determine whether they need to lose weight for health reasons, or just prefer to lose weight for personal reasons? And what BMI should that be? Do people need to lose weight to improve their lives, or to conform to society's completely skewed expectations of them? Is obesity always a problem to be solved—or can it ever be an accommodation that people make to preserve their sanity, or to simply be happy?

As Dominick tells his family at his moment of truth, "You gotta love me for who I am. And so do I." Sounds great on paper. But is it ever that easy in practice?[70]

We certainly can't answer all these and countless other questions about weight issues in a book like this, but we do have storytellers like

---

70 Our father's running joke as he tried to learn how the internet worked was "Easy for you; difficult for me!"

Anne Bancroft to thank for at least trying to expand the dialogue. For so long food disorders have been much harder to talk about than other addictions. Obesity is an open sore for many people, a topic better left unbroached.

Sadly, television producers are great at exploiting the public's fascination with a good trainwreck, which is what makes shows like ***My 600-Pound Life*** and ***1,000-lb Sisters*** little more than "obesity porn" that reinforce stigmas and tired old stereotypes. The underlying reasons for food disorders are varied and complex, but certainly worth a closer, more honest look. And I think we need great fictional storytellers instead of reality TV show producers to do that. ***Fatso*** was a brave step forward in the right direction. So here's to you, Mrs. Robinson.

CHAPTER 13
Almost Nailed It! Addiction to Perfection
Black Swan
Whiplash

My introduction to the idea of Perfection with a capital "P" happened at the age of ten when I read a short story by ***The Scarlet Letter*** author Nathaniel Hawthorne called ***The Birthmark***. In it, a brilliant scientist marries a beautiful woman who is the mid-19th century equivalent of a "Perfect 10," except for a small heart-shaped birthmark on her cheek. The scientist is so obsessed with making her "perfect" that he concocts a potion to make the birthmark go away. The potion works, the birthmark fades away, but it also kills her. Oh well. Nobody ever said Perfection was easy.

And who ever said Perfection was attainable to begin with? What is Perfection anyway? It's ethereal, counterfactual. To be perfect means there are no flaws in either a material object or an idea. But this is physically impossible, objectively and (most certainly) subjectively. Physics proves that all matter is in a perpetual process of quantum flux, particle decay, and slave to the second law of thermodynamics—which states that entropy (disorder) always increases. So by that measure, the only truly perfect object in the universe is the universe itself at the moment of the Big Bang. And it was all downhill from that moment onward, save for little pockets of complexity called "humans" who struggle to stay organized. And notwithstanding Plato's Theory of Forms, ideas are completely subjective and therefore only as perfect as the imperfect people who claim that they're perfect, but aren't.

Still, human beings have no problem envisioning Perfection, longing for it, striving for it, and then getting very frustrated when they don't attain it. This sometimes leads to self-medication. We think everything is perfectible. Body. Soul. Faces. Teeth. Thoughts. Phone calls with Ukrainian leaders. We want the technical perfection of perfect bodies and spotless homes, the aesthetic perfection of a perfect hair day, the teleological perfection of complete happiness, the moral perfection earned by going to church every Sunday, the metaphysical perfection afforded by transcendental meditation. We want perfect jobs and perfect children. We all envision a "perfect life," focusing all our energies to achieve it, but forget to savor and appreciate the "normal life" that happens as we do.

We see physical examples of Perfection in real life, but they're either mirages sold to us by advertisers or bizarre coincidences. Sure, they're attainable in practice, but also at great cost. Drawing a specific royal flush at poker is physically possible, but the probability is 0.1441% (1 in 19,600 for a flop). But the cost to a gambler in terms of time, energy, and money waiting for this perfect hand to happen is incalculable. Same thing with mega-lotteries. Yes, winning hundreds of millions of dollars is a perfect outcome for one person, but it costs everyone else who didn't win. Or mountain climbers who envision the perfect summit, but it can often cost them their lives.

Not only are there perfect objects in nature, we also firmly believe in the perfectibility of human beings. Religions tell people they are irreparably broken and eternally doomed, but if they follow the rules and worship the almighty they can be perfected. Obedientiary perfection in this life means people can go to heaven in the next, which is perfect. The notion of sanctity, the sacred; that which is untarnished, unsullied by human hands—all of it implies an attainable perfection in the spiritual world. But to get there people need to practice rituals in the real world. Hence most religion's preoccupation with cleanliness and hygiene practices, rote repetition of benedictions and supplications, and the obsession with a woman's unspoiled, *perfect* virginity.

For thousands of years we have contemplated the perfectibility of society as well. Millions have fought and died working toward their unique version of it. What "it" would actually look like in real life is anybody's guess. Certainly not the "worker's paradise" envisioned by Marx. Theocracy in Iran? Socialism in Norway? Isn't politics a struggle to impose a perfect new order on society, or return to a perfect fantasy past? Many U.S. conservatives long for a return to a perfect 1950s where gas was cheap, there was prayer in schools (all of which were segregated), and the terms "woke" and "gender-preference" hadn't been invented yet. Many U.S. liberals dream of a perfect future with no guns, no god, free healthcare, and universal basic income. Democracy and the rule of law are ways to accommodate different Perfection fantasies and try to make them coexist peacefully without annihilating one another.

Yet while we obsess over Perfection, we don't realize how valuable imperfection is. Imperfections in DNA produce mutations, which produce new traits, which power evolution. A perfect crystal is theoretically possible, but totally useless. Crystallographic defects (imperfections) are what give us priceless jewelry. Representations of real or imagined things are always imperfect, and we call those rendered imperfections "art." Nature's constant battle to restore homeostasis or equilibrium in imperfect systems is the motivating force behind life itself. Want to know the ultimate purpose of life on the grandest scale? To create entropy. To burn free energy. Over the shortest amount of time. We are all literally walking, talking wastes of time and energy.

This is a bitter pill to swallow. So the quest for Perfection is humanity's way of pushing back against these laws of the universe—against entropy, against its inevitable aging, death and dissolution.[71] People's daily attempts to create some perfect order out of the chaos is one of the ways they try to stay young, relevant, and remembered. As a society people all agree "nothing is perfect," but privately they can't accept this. They delude themselves into thinking they are the one singular exception to the rule. The idea of perfectibility has almost universal buy-in, so people create mental models of perfect outcomes, alternate self-serving realities, then relentlessly pursue them until they lose all sense of perspective. They often hurt themselves and others along the way. Sometimes they die.

Which is not to say that the pursuit of Perfection, or perfectionism as it's often called, is utterly terrible. Perfectionists get a bad rap, but they also get shit done. Steve Jobs, Jeff Bezos, and Elon Musk are widely regarded as perfectionists. They accomplished great things and made some enemies along the way. Often people's perfectionism causes them to be socially isolated or ostracized. We all have varying degrees of perfectionistic tendencies. Sometimes we're the overachievers in a group, sometimes the opposite. Some people think "good is good enough." Others think "unless it's perfect, why bother?" Striking the right balance between these competing impulses at the corporate level can make the difference between a multi-billion-dollar valuation or bankruptcy. The balance also mediates how we interact with others, and especially how we parent.

---

71 Don't worry. The black hole information paradox was solved and no information about you and your amazing life can ever be fully erased from the universe.

So what does this all have to do with addiction? A lot. Addiction to Perfection can lead to anxiety when ideals of Perfection are not met. In this sense, addiction to Perfection is a meta-addiction—an addiction that causes other addictions.

Imperfections in life can lead to dissatisfaction with life, apathy, and eventual unhappiness. Add in procrastination, boredom, and social isolation, and you basically cover the key trigger points for alcohol/substance abuse and other maladaptive behaviors. But instead of self-medicating, people can choose to practice acceptance of what is, instead of an obsession with what could or should have been. If people could somehow forget that Perfection is even possible, they might stop stressing about it.

The Stoics of Ancient Greece thought deeply about these issues, and their ideas about acceptance of imperfection heavily influenced the later development of Cognitive Behavioral Theory. When applied to addiction treatment and mutual support through organizations like SMART Recovery, these ideas of acceptance became highly useful tools,[72] which I use every day in my personal life, teach my children, and share with my SMART meeting participants every week:

- Unconditional Other Acceptance (UOA) helps us deal with the fact that other people aren't just imperfect, they can often be real assholes too.
- Unconditional Self-Acceptance (USA) helps us deal with our own imperfections and not become paralyzed by them.
- Unconditional Life Acceptance (ULA) helps us step back in gratitude for what we do have in our lives instead of focusing on what we don't.

---

[72] Feel free to watch the YouTube videos where I explain these tools in person. They can all be found at SMART Recovery USA's YouTube channel.

One of the problems with the pursuit of Perfection is that it is so broadly supported in social memory and popular culture. Frustration with the inability to achieve Perfection found its ideal catharsis in society's obsession with the next best thing: Winning. Society loves winners. It "hates" losers. Winning isn't "everything—it's the *only* thing." Second place is the set of steak knives, third place is you're fired. Win or win not, there is no try. The archetypal Hero's Journey that forms the basis of most classic literature is based on the pursuit of total victory. And yes, sometimes the hero loses, and yeah it's tragic, but that just serves as a cautionary tale or inspiration for other heroes that follow. One thing a geo-politically fractured world can always agree upon is how cool it is to win gold medals at the Olympics every four years.

Hollywood mines the idea of perfectibility in every film it makes. Whether it's overcoming the system in **Mr. Smith Goes to Washington**, overcoming loneliness in every romantic comedy ever made, overcoming your physical limitations in films like **Personal Best**, or physically overcoming an adversary in a film like **Rocky**, the focus is always on overcoming—which is shorthand for winning. The more extreme the odds of winning, the better. It's always David or Goliath, life or death, sudden fame or lifelong obscurity, vast wealth or crushing poverty, galactic dominance or planetary submission. What kind of example would Hollywood be setting for humanity if they didn't glamorize winning at all costs?

Well, it turns out that the best Hollywood films on the subject of Perfection do exactly the opposite. **Black Swan** and **Whiplash** take critical aim at the relentless pursuit of Perfection in the performance of ballet and jazz drumming, respectively. **Black Swan** won a Best Actress Oscar for its star Natalie Portman, and the film finally established its director, Darren Aronofsky, as a "bankable" commodity[73] after a decade

---

73 Black Swan grossed $330 million on a $13 million budget

battling it out in the auteur cinema trenches with films like ***Requiem for a Dream*** (covered in this book) and ***The Wrestler***. ***Whiplash*** earned its star J.K. Simmons a well-deserved Best Supporting Actor Oscar, made its lead actor Miles Teller into a superstar, and established its previously unknown director Damien Chazelle as an A-List creative commodity (who would go on to direct the spectacular ***La La Land***). Although ***Black Swan*** and ***Whiplash*** have very different narrative and stylistic approaches and way different outcomes, the central theme is the same: Perfection, if attainable at all, comes at a hefty price.

Black Swan was marketed as a "psychological horror film" because horror fans are a very dedicated bunch of people, and the distributor Fox Searchlight wanted to tap into this market. But it's really more of a psychological drama, one of many classic "gaslight" yarns Hollywood has produced over the years,[74] where the lead character (usually a woman) can't tell the difference between reality and dreams. In other words, she's going insane. Or is someone else trying to make her just *think* she's going insane by "gaslighting" her?

Natalie Portman plays Nina, a waifish ballet dancer in the New York City Ballet Company. Her career seems stalled until the tyrannical artistic director Thomas Leroy (played by French actor Vincent Cassel) pushes the company's lead dancer Beth (played by Winona Ryder) into forced retirement—thus opening up the lead role in the company's upcoming rendition of Tchaikovsky's *Swan Lake*. Nina auditions for the role and performs the White Swan Odette dance "perfectly" but falters as the Black Swan Odile. Meanwhile an exciting, new free-spirited dancer, Lily (played by Mila Kunis[75]) joins the troupe, and threatens to steal the role for herself because she better embodies Odile's "dark side." Nina is obsessed with landing the part,

---

74 The first and still the best: https://en.wikipedia.org/wiki/Gaslight_(1944_film)

75 As stated previously, Kunis is the most represented actress in this book. She appears in ***Four Good Days***, ***Black Swan,*** and ***Gia***.

which means her combined performance (white and black) has to be absolutely perfect. And thus her slow descent into madness begins.

I can see why Aronofsky picked ballet to tell a story about obsession with Perfection. You'd have to be obsessed to choose ballet as a career. It's brutally competitive, incredibly exacting, and physically painful. One of my friends is a professional ballet dancer in Los Angeles and told me that compared to other disciplines he had tried—including college basketball and pro football—ballet was the most physically demanding of all. Besides pro wrestling, that is. And as it happens, Aronofsky delved into that world as well when he directed **The Wrestler** starring Mickey Rourke. Wrestling and ballet are as different as night and day, but Aronofsky reminds us that any obsession with the perfect performance is equal-opportunity crazymaking.

Ballet is lovely to look at, but behind it lies some negative and potentially harmful maladaptive behaviors too. It's established early on that Nina scratches her skin until she bleeds, often a precursor to the more serious coping strategies involving self-mutilation like cutting or burning. Portman plays Nina as a scared, little girl who could break at any second. To her overprotective mother, Erica, played by the spooky Barbara Hershey, she's an infantilized "sweet little girl"—desperate for approval, but always coming up short. To the outside world she's a commodity, judged solely on her appearance. One of the saddest moments of the film should be the happiest but isn't. Nina comes home to tell her mother she got the big part. "He picked me, Mommy…" she says tearfully, channeling a lifetime of bitter rejection, self-loathing, and derision in the process. Like any other addict, her drug of choice (Perfection) is a way to cope with the childhood trauma of having been told her whole life that she's imperfect.

But self-mutilation is just the warm-up act for self-mortification. The physical demands of ballet are so extreme that Nina, much like many other competitive athletes, has an obsessive dependence on practice/exercise. Yes, exercise is part of her training, but it's also a form of self-medication and self-mutilation. Extreme exercise can be part of the gamut of binging/purging disorders, and often self-starvation and bulimia are never far behind.

In Nina's case, all of these co-occurring disorders are in play. She practices constantly, her toes are mangled and bloodied, her bones are protruding, and she looks like she's starving. Because she is. When her mother buys her a cake to celebrate her being chosen for the big part, she struggles to eat even a small piece. Erica gets angry and threatens to dump the whole cake as retaliation, telegraphing the fact that food is a very touchy subject with her daughter. There is also a brief scene where Nina purges to relieve stress.[76]

In real life, Portman reportedly lost 20 pounds to play the role, survived on carrots and almonds to fuel eight-hour daily practice sessions, and told *Entertainment Weekly* that "there were some nights that I thought I was literally going to die." But that is the apparent cost of Perfection in ballet—and in portraying it perfectly in film. The art form itself seems to be an implicit celebration of asceticism in the extreme. Perhaps this is part of its allure. Asceticism is severe self-discipline and denial, which ballet clearly is. I think it is a very harmful impulse, but religion and spirituality have managed to shroud it in a cloak of respectability. It's considered a "noble"—even admirable—pursuit. Self-torture is a so-called path toward enlightenment and divinity, which in their own ways are paths to Perfection.

But lo, at what cost? Asceticism entails ghastly things like total celibacy, fasting (self-mortification), self-flagellation, and extreme solitude. Its practitioners would have us all believe they are reaching nirvana (another form of Perfection) by whipping themselves, having nails driven into their hands during Passion Plays, or standing up

---

[76] Perfection is a leading driver in anorexia/bulimia eating disorder. A large majority of the people who suffer from this disorder get straight A's in college, full scholarships, etc.

straight for 30 years. But really? Neurologists tell us there is little difference between the brain chemicals activated by 12 hours of silent meditation versus simply taking two tabs of Percocet.

And this kind of masochism is not just the purview of religious extremists either. Success in professional bodybuilding is based on extreme pain tolerance and privation. Check out the documentary **Bigger, Stronger, Faster** to see to what extremes some people will go to achieve freakish "Perfection." Ultra running sees people jog 100 miles a day for days on end in the sweltering heat of Death Valley. Breatharianism (aka "Inedia") is a movement embraced by thousands of people who believe the human body can survive on oxygen and sunlight alone. They become addicted to being made faint with extreme hunger and mistake that feeling for "enlightenment." How exactly are you supposed to become enlightened if you're dead?

As "noble" or as "spiritual" as many of these ascetic impulses may appear, they're pretty nuts. With the exception of bodybuilding, which has gone mainstream, most forms of extreme asceticism belong on an episode of TLC's popular show *My Strange Addiction*—which features people addicted to things like eating cat hair and having sex with cars. Anyone who tries to convince you that walking backwards for 20 years will make you spiritually perfect is gaslighting you. But it's this obsessive mindset that Nina is operating under as a ballet dancer. Yes, the art form itself requires sacrifice to attain Perfection, but in **Black Swan** Nina is being pushed to even greater extremes by the ballet company's arrogant French (of course) boss, Thomas.

Thomas is clearly very talented and knows a great ballet performance when he sees it. But like Nina, he too is obsessed with the perfect performance of Swan Lake. But it's Perfection as *he* sees it. Unlike track and field where exact objective measurements are involved, or a spelling bee competition where you either get the word right or wrong—ballet is not a sport, it's an art form, and therefore entirely subjective. Sure there are certain unbreakable conventions like posture, balance, and poses, but the perfect performance Thomas is trying to coax out of Nina only exists in his mind. And since there is no objective way to falsify or contradict his idea of Perfection, he has unchallenged and absolute power over her and her career. And "absolute power corrupts absolutely."

Thomas certainly comes off as a Svengali, the archetypal evil character who manipulates a young woman to satisfy his own lusts and thirst for power. He's rude, verbally abusive, and imperious. He pits dancers against each other to improve their performances, demeans those who don't measure up, and seems indifferent to any emotional devastation it causes. He's a male chauvinist of the highest order who would be considered a sex offender in any other context. But he's also under intense pressure from his patrons to produce an incredible ballet performance and sell tickets. Could there be a method to his madness? Is he a misunderstood but well-intentioned genius, or just an abusive asshole?

This question dovetails into what I term "The Myth of Supposed Expertise"—society's common practice of completely deferring to supposed experts. There's nothing inherently wrong with this. It's impossible for people to learn and perfect every skill they need to survive and thrive in the modern world. So we trust experts like mechanics to fix our cars, technicians to fix our internet connections, and therapists to save our marriages. But this sometimes leads to an overreliance on supposed experts without questioning their actual credentials and suffering negative consequences as a result.[77] When it comes to highly subjective skills like ballet, there is the potential for gross misrepresentation and abuse. Does Thomas truly have the requisite expertise, or is he just making it up as he goes along?

Much of the time it seems like the latter. The coaching he gives Nina is not just abusive, it's also illogical, contradictory, and confusing.

---

[77] Catholic priests, gymnast doctors, certain head coaches, etc. I highly recommend Malcolm Gladwell's ***Talking To Strangers***.

He insists she loosen up, stop trying to be so precise in her techniques, which clearly runs counter to everything ballet stands for. "Perfection is not about control; it's about letting go," he tells her. But letting go of *what* exactly? What is she holding onto? It's the Myth of Supposed Expertise at play—no need to question the experts, regardless of how baffling their advice is. And then again, this is Perfection he's talking about. The more mysterious it seems, the more desirable it becomes. These are nonsense riddles masquerading as serious pedagogy with an air of supreme authority that would make even the papacy blush.

What is certain is that Thomas has weaponized sex as a tool of control. When the powerful maestro talks, the fragile young ladies must listen. None dare speak without first being spoken to. He tells Nina her rendition of the Black Swan Odile needs to be more "authentic," but what he's really mansplaining to her is that she needs to be sexier. Only by embracing her darker (i.e. sexual) impulses can she ever hope to perform the role "perfectly." Nina's practice session performances are judged on the basis of whether the male dancers in the company would "want to fuck her." Thomas asks her if she's a virgin, suggests that she masturbate at home, and sexually assaults her during practice. But, hey, he's the expert, right?

Thomas' character is obviously sexist hyperbole, but the ballet establishment has not been immune from its share of similar criticism over the years. Harassment complaints, sextortion cases, and multi-million-dollar settlements have been reported. The architect of modern American ballet, George Balanchine, did his share of philandering, often involving the (much younger) dancers under his direction. But the deeper issue of sexism isn't just about ballet. Most performing arts have sexualized female performers to some extent. Some, like popular music, have done so to lurid extremes. It happens in sports too. The amount of skin shown by female professional athletes today leaves very little to the imagination.

Sexist or not, the abuse Thomas metes out is not inspiring Nina to improve; if anything it's causing her to mentally deteriorate. This clearly works against his goal of producing the perfect performance. But maybe his obsession with Perfection isn't just about Nina; it's really more about himself. There's the cynical old missive, "Those who can, do. Those who can't, teach." Could it be that Thomas is embittered by his own professional failures as a dancer and taking that resentment out on Nina? The toughest teachers could never themselves do what they are demanding of their students. My father, a loving perfectionist, would acknowledge as much when he taught me to ski. "Do as I say, not as I do!" he would yell. Thomas was probably never able to do anything close to what he is demanding from Nina, so he resents her for it. And punishes her for it. Because The Myth of Supposed Expertise excuses the requirement that teachers be perfect themselves. How convenient, no?

This touches on another interesting question, which is whether artistic perfection, or "genius," can even be achieved through hard work at all. A wonderful dramatization of this can be found in Tom Stoppard's **Amadeus**. Salieri is an aging, mediocre court composer whose life is totally upended when he meets the young, effortlessly talented Mozart. Why would a loving God bestow the gift of musical genius on such a buffoon? Salieri has labored his whole life but will never be as good.[78] A deadly rivalry ensues.

In **Black Swan** this question plays out as a rivalry between Nina and the new, younger, more free-spirited Lily (Mila Kunis). Lily eats anything she wants, sleeps with anyone she wants, drinks, and takes drugs—and gets away with all of it. Her black swan performance is

---

[78] One thing that's interesting about the acquisition of performance talent is how much it's like the acquisition of a language. Performance is its own language. The earlier you learn it, the more potential for perfecting it you have. If you speak a language perfectly by the age of eight, a person who tries to learn the same language starting at the age of ten will never match your linguistic skills (especially pronunciation), regardless of the work or level of language immersion involved. My father playfully demonstrated his resentment of this fact when it came to how well my sister and I spoke Spanish.

effortless, sensual, uninhibited. A work of "genius." Was she just born with Perfection? That's not fair. But who defines "fair?"

Nina, like Salieri, is jealous, resentful, afraid she'll never measure up to Lily's effortless Perfection. She imagines Lily playing off a different rule book, having sex with Thomas to steal her part. All of Perfection's odds seem to be stacking against Nina, and as the night of her big performance nears, all of her coping mechanisms activate. Scratching, starvation, purging. Paranoia turns to hallucinations, which leads to dissociation, which eventually turns into full-blown psychosis.

Desperate for a (literal) reality check, Nina visits her famous predecessor Beth (Winona Ryder) in the hospital. Once the company's ravishing lead, Beth has been reduced to broken bones and gaping scars. It's as if she's been chewed up and spit out by her own futile attempts at Perfection. Nina realizes the same fate awaits her. Perfection will be her undoing, just like it has every dancer who has come and gone before her. And that includes her own mother, whom she despises for having pushed her to achieve what she failed to in her own ballet career.

It's here where Aronofsky's mad skills as a twisted psychological storyteller really kick into high gear. By the start of the opening-night performance, Nina's hallucinations and dissociation have completely taken over. It's impossible for even us, the audience, to ascertain what's real and what's imaginary anymore. Everybody's getting gaslighted by this point, not just poor Nina. Which is what makes the climax of the film both delightfully ludicrous and oddly plausible. In her utter desperation, Nina finally takes the stage to perform as the black swan. She begins to sprout feathers, then wings, and eventually morphs into a literal black swan.

And the performance is "perfect."

Only then do we realize Thomas was right all along. He really was an expert. He didn't just coax the black swan out of Nina, he literally beat it *into* her. Now freed from the oppressive limitations of human imperfections, Nina morphs into the white swan, dances her little heart out, and dies. Literally and figuratively. And perfectly.

What does this all mean? I have no idea. Like most of Aronofsky's films, **Black Swan** leaves us with more questions than answers. Confusion is his stock in trade. It's why I'll see all his movies at least five times and still have questions. But one thing he does seem to be saying, unequivocally, is that Perfection simply cannot be taught. Despite what we've all been told, the old adage "practice makes perfect" is simply not true. And that's okay because Perfection probably doesn't exist either. So why bother chasing it? It's only going to make you go crazy, turn you into a giant black bird, and get you killed.

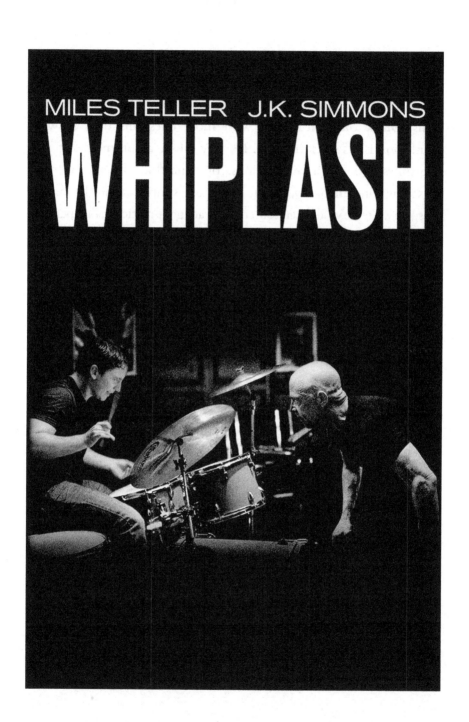

Wh*iplash* shares many elements in common with **Black Swan**; however the film is totally grounded in reality. No gaslighting or giant black birds. It's relatable, which is what makes it so powerful and difficult to watch at times. We've all had teachers or coaches who pushed us to perform, some harder than others. Some way too hard. But with **Whiplash** we see an abuse of power and betrayal of trust on a whole other level. As usual, the pursuit of Perfection exacts a very heavy toll.

Speaking about Perfection, the film's writer/director Damien Chazelle comes closer to personifying that quality than just about anyone working in the industry today. **Whiplash** premiered at the 2014 Sundance Film Festival, won the U.S. Grand Jury Prize, went on to receive five Academy Award nominations, and won the aforementioned Best Actor Oscar for J.K. Simmons. Fresh on the heels of that success, at only 32 Chazelle became the youngest-ever recipient of the Academy Award for Best Director for **La La Land**. Face it, the guy's on a roll.

Simmons plays Terrence Fletcher, a music teacher at a prestigious, competitive New York Conservatory. He's a perfectionist with a highly developed ability to detect even the tiniest imperfections in his class' jazz band performances. Which is not easy because it involves discernment of over a dozen individual instruments. Like Thomas, Fletcher is the master of a very complicated, precise craft in an extremely competitive environment populated by highly talented individuals. Accepted convention dictates that the only way to toughen up students and extract Perfection is to rant and rave and torture them.

We see this pressure-cooker dynamic portrayed in films all the time. Examples include the Navy SEAL training scenes in **G.I. Jane**, and Richard Gere getting his ass handed to him by a hyper-abusive Louis Gossett Jr. in **An Officer and a Gentleman**. Gossett won the same Academy Award for Best Supporting Actor Simmons would go on to win for his onscreen bullying in **Whiplash** thirty-two years later.

The late-great John Houseman's portrayal of a tyrannical Harvard Law Professor in ***The Paper Chase*** made me swear off ever going to law school. I worked in sales environments like those portrayed in ***Boiler Room***. Reality was way worse.

In ***Whiplash***, Simmons just seems to be following in the hallowed tradition of fully normalized abuse masquerading as "education." I'm not sure how much of the abuse is Hollywood hyperbole or actually takes place in real life. The Stanford Prison Experiment showed how easy it is for "normal" people to turn into disciplinarian psychopaths the moment you give them a position of authority over others. Maybe pedagogical abuse is just a sad and unavoidable part of human nature in some contexts. I don't see a muscle-bound basic training instructor stopping class to politely ask a scrawny new recruit how they "feel" about what they're being put through—then giving everyone in the platoon the rest of the day off to heal emotionally.

Fletcher's particular brand of abuse takes place in a special world closed off from rationality, common sense, or any oversight. The physical space where his band practices is in some sort of impenetrable basement, with no windows and a heavy door. It's a sort of musical concentration camp, where Fletcher is the head Gestapo and the students are all shivering inmates. The minute Fletcher enters the room, they all look down in fear. Because they know, just as Fletcher knows, that all it takes is playing one wrong note and their musical careers can be exterminated.

The main victim of Fletcher's semester-long musical hazing experiment is Andrew Neiman, played by Miles Teller. He's a calm, serious, ambitious young musician who happens to have chosen a very difficult path as a jazz drummer. Now, to the uninitiated, drums seem like an easy thing to play. You just bang on different drums and cymbals and extract different sounds. I did a lot of this as a John Bonham wannabe in a shitty high school band. Playing the strings, woodwinds, and brass seem way more complicated because they require precise finger placement, variable breath intensity, etc. Yet all of that complexity means zilch unless the drummer is keeping the right time with the right beat at the right tempo. Drumming has to be perfect.

Yet Perfection in jazz seems like an oxymoron. Jazz sounds like it's all over the place. Much of it is improvised. Precision is not a word that comes to mind when I think of jazz; however, those who are experts at jazz would beg to differ. So the odds of Andrew achieving Perfection are already stacked against him simply by the musical style he has chosen to perform. But that doesn't seem to deter him. He jumps at the chance to join Fletcher's band when a position is offered to him, fully aware of the Faustian bargain he's about to strike.

Because this film is more grounded in reality than **Black Swan**, Chazelle gives us neat, little glimpses into Andrew's personality and what drives him to sacrifice so much for Perfection. For starters, he sincerely likes to play the drums. When he's playing well, there's a smile on his face and a radiance we never saw with Nina as she danced. After all, performance should be a joy, otherwise why would people choose it as a career? But Andrew is also a perfectionist who is willing to over-practice to the point of bloodying his fingers, like Nina did with her toes. It becomes clear that he isn't just trying to be a good drummer; he's trying to become a living legend like Buddy Rich. That's a hell of a lot of pressure for a kid in his early 20s to put himself under.

His home life offers some explanation as to why. At a family dinner with his cousins and their parents, his achievements in music are belittled when compared to his cousins' "93-yard touchdowns"—accomplishments that adhere to more traditional societal norms of success. To counter the assertion that drumming won't pay the bills, he says, "I'd rather die drunk, broke at 34, and have people at a dinner table talk about me than live to be rich and sober at 90 and nobody remember who I was." Bloodied hands and constant abuse from your teacher seem like small prices to pay for Andrew to earn his family's respect and achieve drumming immortality.

We don't get a similar glimpse into Fletcher's family background or ambitions. All we really know about him is that he seems to live and breathe jazz music, always in pursuit of a perfect performance, but always coming up short. But unlike Thomas who is surrounded by fragile young ballerinas, Fletcher is in the company of strong, young men like Andrew. The dynamics are way different. Fletcher isn't so much a teacher as he is an Alpha male constantly trying to establish his dominance. So it comes as no surprise when he starts to get physical with Andrew, throwing furniture, and slapping him repeatedly.

The dominance Fletcher seems to seek over Andrew isn't just pedagogical; it may have an emotional component as well. There is a scene when they first meet where Fletcher basically corners Andrew, blocks him from moving by putting his hand on the wall right next to his face, and then leans in very close. Clearly, it's a dominance posture intended to intimidate. But Fletcher's dialogue as he does this is very friendly, almost affectionate. There seem to be only two possible outcomes. Either the two men are going to get into a fight or kiss each other.

A kiss wouldn't be altogether surprising nor completely out of the ordinary. Sometimes a strong (usually older) man in a position of authority over a weaker (usually younger) man will try to establish their dominance sexually. Like many Catholic priests, Greek Sophists, or Roman Senators, they may not even be homosexuals themselves. Sex is just another way to display power and exert control. Thomas used sex as a tool with Nina in **Black Swan**. Again, perhaps this all boils down to human nature. The #MeToo movement certainly laid bare the degree to which sexual assault and harassment is often a part of male-over-female power dynamics everywhere, not just in Harvey Weinstein's hotel rooms.

Notwithstanding, there are hints in the film that Fletcher may actually be gay. He isn't married nor does he have children. He gets very emotional when he tells the band members about a recent death of one of his "beautiful" former students. And he belts out one homophobic slur after another, a frequent strategy closeted gay men use to divert attention. It's quite possible that Fletcher actually hates his homosexuality because it's something totally beyond his control, so he takes his anger out on his students. At the very least he *can* control them.[79]

But these conjectures shouldn't distract from the main questions seeing themselves examined and played out in the film. With an all-important concert performance looming, we see just how much Andrew has been willing to sacrifice to attain Perfection and earn Fletcher's respect. His relationship with his father has become awkward and one-sided, and he breaks up with his girlfriend, Nicole, under the pretense that she is a distraction from his core mission. He withstands terrible abuse from Fletcher that would prompt disciplinary action and dismissal in any other context. Like Nina, he has become isolated, paranoid, and obsessed as a result. So obsessed, in fact, that what happens next borders on the surreal.

On his way to the performance his bus breaks down and he loses his drumsticks, but Fletcher will give no quarter. He has 10 minutes to show up or another drummer will take his place. Andrew's career will be over. He rents a car, speeds toward the concert hall, and suffers a terrible accident. Though severely injured and bleeding, he won't give up his chance at Perfection. But his injuries make performing physically impossible. Fletcher dismisses him from the performance, and Andrew attacks him on stage. Everything is lost. Andrew is suspended from the Conservatory and gives up his dream to follow in the footsteps of Buddy Rich.

---

[79] The internet is awash with varying theories as to Fletcher's true motives. Some people even claim Whiplash is actually a hyper-modern alternate universe retelling of ***Romeo and Juliet***.

If this were the ending of the film it would be logical, thematically consistent, and convey important messages about the ultimate futility of pursuing Perfection. It would also remind us of the terrible costs incurred along the way. But it's not the ending of the film. Chazelle has left several important interrelated questions unanswered: Is Fletcher the hero or the villain? Are his abusive methods fully warranted? Do the ends justify the means? The way Chazelle answers these questions is "perfect" as far as I'm concerned.

After testifying against Fletcher about the abuse he suffered, Fletcher is dismissed from the Conservatory. The two men are now sworn enemies, yet something still pulls them back together. No it's not romantic love or even the possibility of a casual friendship and mutual respect. It's the possibility of pulling off the perfect jazz drumming performance both men have been beating each other up to achieve throughout the film.

Fletcher invites Andrew to play at a jazz festival, and after a false start (I don't want to give away all the details), Andrew takes over conducting the performance and flawlessly renders the song *Caravan*—an incredibly difficult song to drum to. Fletcher is initially angry, but then slowly begins to realize everything he had been pushing Andrew to achieve is suddenly and magically happening, right there on stage. The two men lock eyes, Andrew cedes control to Fletcher, and as the song reaches a blazing crescendo, we finally see the deep artistic connection both men had been striving for in such different ways. The song ends. Fletcher is practically in tears. Andrew's drumming was perfect.

This is a much happier ending than **Black Swan**, but the key messages are identical. Addiction to Perfection is something we all deal with to one extent or another in our lives. Sometimes our manic pursuit makes no sense; other times it makes total sense. The costs to get there usually outweigh the benefits, but we can't know for certain unless we try.

Because that's what we human beings do. We *try*. Many of us simply refuse to be or do "good enough" and get immensely frustrated when our best laid plans to achieve Perfection fail to materialize. Often we seek to self-medicate over that frustration. That's the dangerous thing about drugs and alcohol; as far as successful self-medication goes, they *work* every time.

On the flipside, there are those who lead angst-free lives because "good enough" is literally good enough. Perfection is impossible, so why try? And yet, as age creeps up, opportunities vanish, and cynicism takes over, many may come to regret they never had the courage to at least try.

Yay, humanity! You're damned if you do, damned if you don't!

But unlike the scientist whose wife had a birthmark, that's just something we all have to accept.

CHAPTER 14
Cigarettes Are Funny and Chocolate is Satanic
Cold Turkey
Chocolat

The most ubiquitous micro-addictions of all time, tobacco, chocolate, and coffee are used (and "abused") by billions of people around the world. Some people refer to them as "social drugs." This is strange because the addictive compounds involved (nicotine, theobromine, caffeine) are usually not thought of as drugs, but they are. That's right—Marlboro, Cadbury, and Starbucks are drug companies.

The actual social dimensions of these drugs vary from culture to culture. In some parts of Europe you get together with friends and nibble on different types of chocolates. In other parts you cry yourself to sleep alone after stress eating an entire chocolate lava cake. A quarter of the population of the planet once ruled by the British

Empire sipped tea at 4pm GMT.[80] Today everybody spills their venti lattes on their laps as they drive alone to work at 7am. In Turkey and the Balkans, smoking cigarettes together is a daily social event. In the U.S. and Western Europe, smokers are social outcasts who light up in back alleys or sad little "smoking rooms" conveniently located next to noxious pet relief areas.

Like many of you I'm in a *relationship* with all three substances. I used to smoke cigarettes when I lived in Spain many years ago because literally everybody else did. Or at least that's the lame justification everybody had. I took up the habit for short periods since but am now 100% smoke-free. I remember it was incredibly addictive and tough to quit. Chocolate and I have a checkered past. I've made peace with the fact that I can't quit eating dark chocolate after dinner, so now I just moderate my consumption. When I was a kid, I had a weight problem brought upon by an Oreo cookie fetish. I drink coffee every day, along with 75% of the country (and 40% of the world). If that's a problem, please let me know and I'll totally ignore you.

We've been talking about addictions in terms of the harms they cause, but cigarettes, chocolate, and coffee inhabit a gray area of risk. Tobacco's harmful. Everyone knows the risks. But 1.1 billion people around the world assume this risk every day. Unlike with alcohol or drugs, where negative consequences play out in real-time (drunk driving accidents, heroin overdoses, etc.), smoking has no immediate consequences. They are hidden from view and culminate in an emphysema, cancer, or heart disease diagnosis in some doctor's office at some unknown future time. Or not at all. Some scientists tell us we may have an increased risk of heart attacks or stroke if we drink coffee. This mere possibility, with consequences playing out over an indeterminate length of time, amounts to no real risk at all. There are

---

80 Greenwich Mean Time (GMT) was invented so everyone around the empire could sync up their tea times. Or so the joke goes.

no adverse consequences of eating chocolate, except in excess, which can lead to weight gain and the health risks associated with obesity.

In this chapter we're going to talk about micro-addictions to cigarettes and chocolate, because there are two excellent films on the topic well worth discussing.

Unless you're over 40 years of age, you probably don't know to what extent tobacco was ingrained in society. Everybody smoked. Doctors smoked. After World War II, what was good for Phillip Morris was good for America. The first English colonies in North America would have gone bankrupt if it hadn't been for tobacco. There would have been no United States without it. Everybody in every movie smoked. It's ironic to be discussing movies about tobacco addiction when it was movies that helped get everybody addicted to tobacco in the first place. But history aside, brave scientists and lawmakers were able to overcome the criminal obfuscation of Big Tobacco and alert the world to the risks of smoking.[81] Smoking kills; no question about it. It's a terrible addiction. Nothing funny about it, right?

Well, yes and no. When we apply the universal constant of Comedy = Tragedy + Time, we arrive at the first and probably last comedy film on the subject of tobacco addiction: ***Cold Turkey***. It's absolutely hilarious and wickedly smart. It was written, produced, and directed by Norman Lear[82]—the creative force behind the transformative TV sitcoms ***All in the Family, Maude, Good Times,*** and ***The Jeffersons***. Lear was a master in the use of humor to reveal difficult societal truths. And true to form, lurking beneath Cold Turkey's slapstick satire are some important messages about addiction that are just as relevant today as they were when the film was released in 1971.

---

81 I highly recommend the film ***Thank You For Not Smoking***

82 Quick Norman Lear story: When I first came to Hollywood I did odd jobs. One was helping a friend house sit for Norman Lear. For a whole weekend I was able to see all of his Hollywood memorabilia, photo albums, scrapbooks, etc. What an amazing man, what a life lived. Keep going, Norman! 100 years young!

Here's the premise of the film: *Evil Big Tobacco wants to sell more cancer, so it hires a shady PR firm which comes up with a gimmick marketing campaign based on a $25 million challenge for everyone in a small town to quit smoking for an entire month, rallied along by a charismatic but flawed local pastor.*

The idea seems so obvious, right? It's easy to imagine what kind of hilarity will ensue. And that's what a great comedy movie premise is all about. It's a promise to deliver what the audience is expecting, as well as what it has never seen before. Hollywood delivers on these kinds of promises better than any other country, and why filmed entertainment is one of our nation's leading exports.

Cold Turkey's premise is an example of what's called the "High Concept," or as Hollywood labels it: "The Pitch." A pitch is a complex "what if" boiled down to 1-3 powerful sentences that literally anybody on the planet can understand. It's also called an "elevator pitch" because it can be articulated in less time than it takes an elevator to travel one floor. In a former life I taught students at universities around the world how to create powerful pitches that could eventually turn into sellable screenplays. You need seven key elements to make any pitch work:

a) A time and place that's interesting…
b) Where a hero with a special talent…
c) Who also has a secret weakness…
d) Trains with a mentor…
e) To fight against a nemesis…
f) To achieve some great goal or purpose…
g) And thereby change his/her world or society in general

A billion-dollar franchise like **Star Wars** boils down to this pitch: a) In a galaxy far, far away, b) Luke Skywalker is a Jedi, c) but he doesn't know it yet, d) so he meets and trains with Obi-Wan, e) to fight against Darth Vader and the Empire, f) to destroy the Death Star, g) and thereby restore peace to the galaxy.

In other words, **Cold Turkey** is the perfect pitch. a) In 1970's small-town America, b) an entire small town full of hard-working, honest Americans, c) who are also addicted to tobacco, d) rally around a local pastor, e) to fight big tobacco, f) to win the contest by quitting smoking, g) and show the world that quitting smoking is probably a good thing.

The film is a delight to watch and still spot-on funny half a century after it was released. The small town is called Eagle Rock, which is about as homespun as you can get. Bob Newhart plays the nefarious PR executive who has no intention of letting the town actually win the $25 million prize. The whole contest is a marketing stunt. Dick Van Dyke plays the local pastor who overcomes his cravings by ravaging his wife thrice daily. And then throw in a bunch of colorful local townspeople who all suffer hilarious withdrawal symptoms and employ different coping mechanisms during the 30-day challenge.

The physical comedy of everybody going nuts is fun to watch. But Lear was obviously more interested in poking fun at society and the media especially. The contest turns into a national media frenzy. If you're not a baby-boomer like me, the satire won't make too much sense. But if you are, you'll be treated to a parody of Walter Cronkite's deific reputation as "the most trusted man in America," halo over his head and everything. You may not recall the anchor team of Chet Huntley and David Brinkley, hilariously combined as David Chetley by Bob Elliot. There is also Hugh Upson (Hugh Downs), Paul Hardley (Paul Harvey), Arthur Lordly (Arthur Godfrey), etc. In this sense, **Cold Turkey** achieved a slapstick form of media criticism five years before the amazing film **Network** did the same, albeit much more cynically.

Putting comedy aside, **Cold Turkey's** real value to our overall discussion about micro-addiction is how it gives us a more lighthearted look at what early abstinence from any substance or behavior can look and feel like. It's not all gloom and doom like the majority of other films make it out to be. Yes, it's painful, it's annoying, it makes you cranky, and borderline suicidal. But it also makes you feel absurdly optimistic, energized, irrationally exuberant, and funny. It's honest, and the best humor comes from a point of honesty. Lear's funny depictions of townspeople coping with the sudden loss of their pack-a-day habit is hilarious but also very relatable. With the benefit of time, I fondly laugh at some of the crazy shit I did to stay sober right after quitting alcohol.

A lesson Lear also seems to be teaching us with this film (whether intentional or not doesn't matter) is that quitting isn't just something you suddenly do; it's something you really have to carefully map out and plan for. So many people make the decision to quit a substance or behavior with no clue as to how it is actually done. Yes, it is totally possible to beat any addiction without ever seeing a therapist, going to a mutual support meeting, taking any medication, or even telling anyone about the problem. But good luck with that. Without detailed planning and flawless execution, most attempts at abstinence will fail.

As we watch the town doctor refuse to perform life-saving surgery without smoking first, it's clear that his values and priorities in life are completely skewed by his addiction. With more careful advanced planning he could have applied, for example, SMART Recovery's Hierarchy of Values Exercise as a gut check.

Similarly, all the distressed housewives in town who turn to binge-eating to cope could have instead made a plan to volunteer together at the local church to get their minds off cigarettes. What Lear shows us with great empathy and humor is how cluelessness about abstinence plays out in the real world, from excuses to poor substitutes, to simply the shitty mood that comes from quitting.

I won't ruin the ending for anyone. Just know it's all over the place, silly and good fun. Lear managed to bury a very clear anti-smoking message within a slapstick movie confection that has withstood the test of time. I often wonder if United Artists (the studio that owns the film) will ever do a remake. Probably not. In the time since the film was released, billions more people have learned just how lethally unfunny cigarettes really are. In this sense, **Cold Turkey** was a message way ahead of its time.

From a strict moral philosophy or religious point of view, addiction can be seen as the result of weak morals, lack of restraint, and no self-control. In other words, it is the "wages of sin." The blessed are defined by what they *don't* do in life, more than what they do. Abstinence is like penitence. Sobriety is a Lent that never ends. When faith came to be viewed as a precondition for morality, strict piety, abstinence, and self-control became strict social mandates instead of personal choices. No surprise that the first temperance movements in the U.S. derived from religious organizations. Drinking was "ungodly."

But what about eating chocolate? Is that a sin?

The root of the question isn't about chocolate as a substance per se. It's about the morality of indulging in something pleasurable *like* chocolate. The word Indulgence is fitting here. Indulgences were a clever trick the Catholic Church used to grant people forgiveness for their sins in exchange for cold, hard cash. This scam was one of the reasons Martin Luther nailed his 95 Theses to a church door and helped usher in Protestantism. People were *protesting* the Catholic Church's bogus monopolistic definition, ownership, and control over morality.

But when it comes to harmful addictions, religious faith and matters of morality sometimes matter greatly. The 12-Step Higher Power concept might not be for everyone, yet it has saved millions of lives over the years. But this is because there was buy-in. It's when matters of faith and morality are imposed upon people as preconditions for successful recovery that things get dicey.

A wonderful microcosmic rendition of this metaphysical frisson between temperance and indulgence can be found in the delightful film **Chocolat**, directed by Swedish director Lasse Hallström. Hallström is the creative juggernaut behind the early ABBA videos who then took a pay cut to direct beloved classics like **What's Eating Gilbert Grape** and **The Cider House Rules**. He was nominated for an Academy Award for Best Director for **My Life as a Dog**, a fantastic film.

Addicted in Film

Chocolat is an example of the "fish out of water" drama-comedy where a hero travels to a place where they clearly don't belong. After going twelve rounds with the locals, they eventually find love/redemption/success and transform their lives and the lives of those around them. I'm partial to these kinds of films because every two years I moved from one country to the next growing up in the U.S. Foreign Service. When executed correctly, fish-out-of-water movies usually delight audiences and critics alike. I think it's because they speak to humanity's shared desire for connection and belonging.

In ***Chocolat***, the fish who's out of water is Vianne, played by the truly radiant Juliette Binoche. She wanders into a cute, little French village with her 10-year-old daughter Victoire in 1959 intent on opening a chocolaterie. She rents a run-down patisserie from Armande, played by Dame Judi Dench,[83] and transforms it into a magical place where people can come to indulge in chocolate yumminess. Problem is, this particular town is *very* set in its ways. Its highly devout Mayor Comte de Reynaud, played by a sinister Alfred Molina,[84] considers Vianne to be an existential threat to the good morals of his town. She's a single mother, doesn't go to church, dresses in colorful clothes with low necklines, and has the gall to sell chocolate during Lent. Again, it's not that she's selling chocolate—it's that she's encouraging people to indulge in something pleasurable, something *decadent*. She's a drug dealer, in other words.

And her drugs are working marvelously. A local scullery maid, Yvette, buys some chocolate "nipples," her husband Alphonse eats

---

[83] I had the pleasure of working with Dame Judi on a film I executive produced for Universal called ***Tea With Mussolini***. I was very young at the time, and she and Maggie Smith gave me so much shit about it as we partied with Cher, Joan Plowright, and Lili Tomlin. The director Franco Zeffirelli made a pass at me in the cabana. I was flattered but declined.

[84] Before he was Doctor Octopus in Spiderman, I had the pleasure of working with Molina on the film I wrote called ***Nothing Like the Holidays***. Molina is an amazingly versatile actor. He's a Brit who can play a Hispanic man, Frenchman, or Southern Gentleman at the drop of a hat.

them, and their long-dormant sex life suddenly reignites. Josephine (played by Hallström's real-life partner Lena Olin) gathers the necessary strength from eating chocolate truffles to finally leave her abusive husband. Two elderly widowers find love after consuming a couple of pralines. And thanks to chocolate cake, Armande (Dench) is able to reconcile with her uptight daughter, Caroline (played by a pre-***Matrix*** Carrie-Anne Moss) and forge a relationship with her estranged grandson, Luc.

What's wonderful about this set up is that Vianne isn't pushing anyone to take the drugs. She's not so much a force for change as she is a catalyst for people to finally surrender to their repressed desires, to give in to temptations, to live their lives guided by a desire for what's possible instead of fear of what's forbidden.

But here's the thing: While "chasing your bliss" sounds very progressive, humanistic, and romantic in theory, any substance or behavior that gives people pleasure can also lead to overindulgence, dissolution, and chaos in practice. *Addiction*, in other words. You just can't have your proverbial chocolate cake and eat it too. Seeking pleasure is a basic human right, but it can also cause misery. This is one of the central problems of human existence generally, and of addiction and recovery specifically.

There seem to be only two solutions: Outlaw pleasure-seeking and punish the pleasure-seekers—or give people the freedom to seek whatever pleasure they want, make mistakes, then help them to not repeat those mistakes. In ***Chocolat***, Director Hallström has these competing worldviews duke it out for supremacy in the idyllic French countryside, with chocolate as their only ordinance. On one side he puts Mayor Comte de Reynaud (Molina)—an uptight prude who uses the bully pulpit of religion to force sensual abstinence on everyone, even as he himself swoons at the mere sight of a croissant. And on the other he puts Armande (Dench), Josephine (Olin), and all the other townspeople whose honest and humble pursuit of self-gratification at

Vianne's chocolaterie has opened their hearts to the humanistic values of love and reconciliation.

Is the Mayor wrong for trying to dissuade people from pursuing their baser instincts and possibly harming themselves and others? Is Vianne just an agent provocateur who's too naive and idealistic to admit humans can be their own worst enemies? Must there be only one winner here? Is there a middle way?

Well goddamn it, this is Hollywood after all, and in the case of **Chocolat** the answer is a resounding YES! The Mayor finally surrenders to his own pent-up desires, devours a ton of chocolate, and goes into a sugar coma. It's the confectionary equivalent of an overdose. He wakes up covered in chocolate and forges a peace treaty with Vianne, finally owning up to the fact that people in glass houses shouldn't throw stones.

The townspeople all come together in a mirthful party in the town square where all the hatchets are buried and new friendships are forged. Everybody's drinking, but nobody's getting drunk (this is France, after all). There's plenty of chocolate to go around, but nobody's stuffing their face. People are dancing, but they're not twerking. In other words, they have found happiness in moderation. Sure, it's a little Hollywood, but I'll take that ending any day of the week. With a little whipped cream on top too, thanks.

PART III: RECOVERY
They Tried to Make Me Go To Rehab:
Fantasy vs. Reality In and Out of Treatment

CHAPTER 15
Seriously, I Can Stop Any Time I Want
Clean and Sober

No analysis of the on-screen rehab experience would be complete without a look at 1988's ***Clean and Sober***, a film written by Tod Carroll and directed by Glenn Gordon Caron. It was really Hollywood's first commercial tent pole foray into the drug and alcohol rehab world, warts and all.

It must have been quite a gamble for just about everybody involved. The director, Caron, had no big feature film credits to his name. But he had managed to get Hollywood's attention with his series ***Moonlighting***, which introduced the world to a former bartender named Bruce Willis. Imagine Entertainment, the production company run by Ron Howard and Brian Grazer (whom I had the privilege of working with on ***Apollo 13***), that produced the film, was flying high after becoming one of the first indie production companies to go public in 1986. But by the time they had finished producing **Clean and Sober**, Wall Street had somewhat soured on the company, and its biggest hits were still a few years off.

Clean and Sober represented an even bigger stretch for its lead actor Michael Keaton—a comedian best known for playing offbeat characters in films like **Beetlejuice**, released just five months earlier. Were audiences ready for Keaton to play it straight as Daryl, a commercial real estate salesman turned coke fiend embezzler and accessory to a fatal drug overdose? Probably not. While his performance pleased the critics and earned him a National Society of Film Critics Award for Best Actor, the film had a tepid opening and topped out at $9 million in the U.S. box office. Warner Bros didn't even bother releasing it overseas. Said Keaton in response to this: "*I'm Batman.*"[85]

Like many films about addiction and recovery, **Clean and Sober** is a classic redemption tale. Guy gets addicted. Guy ruins his life. Guy goes to rehab. Guy recovers. Guy builds his life back. So in this sense the story is timeless, but the film is also very much a product of its time. Tod Carroll wrote the script at the height of the Reagan-era "War on Drugs" mass hysteria spin cycle, and in some respects the movie is part public-service announcement about the dangers of cocaine addiction. But it is also much more. While the national narrative at the time was dominated by images of poverty-stricken inner-city blacks addicted to crack cocaine, **Clean and Sober** highlighted how

---

[85] Here is where Hollywood screenwriting legend William Goldman's famous quote, "In Hollywood, no one knows anything," is proven true once again. Who knew Keaton would go on to play Batman in the first two blockbusters of the franchise, then languish in movie jail for the next two decades, only to have his career be resurrected—Phoenix-like—with a career-turning role in 2014's Best Picture Oscar winner **Birdman**? And how ironic that in reprising his role as an addict in the TV Series **Dopesick** (also featured in this book), he would end up winning an Emmy, a Golden Globe, a Critics' Choice, and a Screen Actors Guild Awards for Outstanding Performance in a TV series?

successful, privileged whites could fuck up their lives just as effectively with powder cocaine. Then-President Ronald Reagan watched the film at Camp David. It apparently had no effect on his world-view because he continued signing mandatory minimum sentencing laws for even minor drug possession (disproportionately targeting blacks), all while Daryl (Keaton) gets off scot-free after stealing $92,000 and overdosing a young woman with cocaine.[86]

The film opens with a powerful close-up of Hollywood character actor M. Emmet Walsh giving testimony at an AA meeting. Walsh is the kind of character actor you can't afford to take your eyes off, even for a minute. Beneath his everyman nice-guy appeal lurks simmering emotional possibilities. Like a poor-man's Wilford Brimley, you just never know when he might go to the Dark Side. But in **Clean and Sober** Walsh plays the moral anchor of the story and Daryl's eventual 12-Step sponsor. His opening scene monologue is simple on the surface, but conveys a powerful truth about substance addiction: *"You never lose interest…"*

As our story begins, Daryl (Keaton) wakes up from a coke bender with a naked woman passed out on his bed, and a frantic call from his business partner about a missing $92,000. So he does what most cocaine aficionados do: takes a bump and lights a cigarette. Or, as it's called in the cocaine addiction world: Monday. And his bender would continue were it not for the inconvenience of the naked woman having overdosed. Keaton plays the unfolding scenes with a maddening degree of callous indifference. He has nosy police detectives and paramedics in his home, and the only thing that seems to register is how the girl's overdose has killed his buzz.

If the filmmakers had stuck to a typical 3-Act story structure, they could have gotten away with a lot more addiction eye candy in the 1st act. Scenes of Keaton taking drugs, spiraling downward, hitting rock

---

[86] For more on the sad story of drug criminalization and its blatantly racial pretexts, I recommend you read **Chasing the Scream** by Johann Hari.

bottom, etc. As we've discussed previously, this tactic seems to be the modus operandi of many reality TV shows about addiction. While this imagery might be alluring to those with a fondness for schadenfreude, it's really not helpful to the overall conversation about addiction. It just leads to stigmatizing addicts instead of helping them. We avoid all that crap when Daryl checks himself into rehab a merciful 12 minutes into the film.

But like so many people in rehab, it immediately becomes obvious that Daryl's there because he *has* to be, not because he *wants* to be. Why not hide out from the police, his boss, and the angry creditors he stole from? Rehab is a kind of warm and cushy purgatory, a temporal offset to the hell he's made of his life. Daryl obsesses over how long his detox will take (48 hours), desperate to check that box and move on. And this is really the crux of the movie, and why it's such an important film to digest. The hero's journey he is about to take in this story is not just to check a few boxes and end his addiction—it's to truly understand and acknowledge that he has one to begin with.

Enter Morgan Freeman as Craig, the rehab facility's no-nonsense director. For a performer with the acting chops and gravitas to play God so convincingly, it's funny to see an earlier iteration of him—younger, yes, but no less authoritative or compelling. He's like Darth Vader playing Mother Teresa. The stentorian voice, every single consonant coming out of his mouth so crisply articulated…it's almost like he was born in character. The funny thing is, he's not even acting. I met with him once to talk about a movie role back in the late '90s, and he was just as deific in real life as he is on screen.

Craig immediately goes head-to-head against Daryl's addiction denialism. It's a wonder to behold, anchored around Freeman's gentle but powerful performance. You just know that a guy with his job has literally heard it all. Mostly lies, confabulations, patients' earnest claims of victimization. Nothing is *their* fault.

I've spoken with some rehab facility directors and they've told me that 20% of the job is cheerleading and 80% of the job is bullshit detection. In a fit of rage over not being able to use the house phone (to call his dealer), Daryl belittles Craig for his meager monthly salary. While played for drama, the scene highlights the difficulties real rehab employees face in their day-to-day efforts to help people recover successfully. As far as I'm concerned, they are the true unsung heroes in the fight against addiction. In a perfect world their starting salaries should be in the six-figures. Sadly, this is not the case, and why there are such disruptively high staff turnover rates in the inpatient/outpatient recovery industry.

Whereas the popular rehab film **28 Days** (released 12 years later) would go on to show a highly sanitized, almost Disneyesque version of a treatment facility—full of lovable and quirky characters—the **Clean and Sober** set designers created something probably closer to real life: a dirty, smoky, uncomfortable dungeon with stained carpets, stale coffee, and a shitty TV. The cast of characters in this rehab are a semi-representative cross-section of real life: an upper-middle-class yuppie binge drinker who's only there to please his family, a (sadly stereotypical) "angry black man" addicted to crack, and two women, Charlie and Iris. Charlie is in a codependent relationship with another addict, and Iris is your garden variety party girl.

While Charlie goes on to be a focal point of an ensuing romantic relationship with Daryl, Iris is jettisoned from the program early for attending group meetings when she's high. Interesting trivia point about the intersection of art and life: The actress who plays Iris, Claudia Christian, would go on to have a real alcohol problem after she appeared in the film. She eventually addressed her problem using the Sinclair Method,[87] a technique originally developed by U.S.

---

[87] The Sinclair Method is controversial. It involves taking Naltrexone, an opioid antagonist, right before you drink alcohol. That's right, people using this method can continue to drink as long as they take a Naltrexone pill one hour beforehand. In fact, it is recommended that they drink as part of the treatment. Naltrexone is basically a buzz-kill. It takes the fun and euphoria out of drinking. The idea is that over time, your brain becomes less interested in drinking alcohol because it doesn't derive any pleasure from it. Drinking days become fewer, drinks per sitting become

neuroscientist Dr. John Sinclair and adopted by the Finnish Ministry of Health (where Sinclair conducted the bulk of his research). Christian gave a Ted Talk about how it saved her life, and crowd-funded and starred in a documentary film about it called **One Little Pill**. Worth a look.

The group eventually goes to their first AA meeting. This was arguably the first time a large general audience had ever seen an actual meeting depicted in a mainstream film. The filmmakers decided to shoot it at a lovely church with stained glass windows and pack the audience with chain smokers. But that's not anomalous. The smoking is a well-established inside joke. And AA does have a religious foundation, and many would argue that the Higher Power is just shorthand for God. But so what if it is? Whatever works, right?

As rates of self-proclaimed secularity rise in America, more and more people have sought out secular alternatives to 12-Step recovery programs like SMART Recovery, Refuge Recovery, etc. The filmmakers seemed to have anticipated this trend; and the religiosity of AA is kept neatly nestled in the background throughout the film. Words like "Higher Power" and "God" are avoided entirely. That decision probably also has its roots in the best practices of Hollywood studio marketing departments at the time. Before **The Last Temptation of Christ**, matters of faith were marketing kryptonite. My boss at Universal Studios, the legendary Nadia Bronson, told me she received death threats as the studio was preparing to release the film. I co-produced a film[88] with Willem Dafoe, and he told me that years later he still watches his back.

---

fewer, and some people lose interest in drinking entirely. Important caveat: People using this method can never drink alcohol without first taking the pill, because it screws up or reverses the neurological conditioning. Some clinicians call bullshit; others think it's a miracle pill. It depends on a myriad of factors we don't have time to get into here.

88 **Snowflower and the Secret Fan.** And FYI, Dafoe usually plays crazy characters in films, but in real-life he is actually a very gentle, sweet, kind and generous person.

Like many who attend their first meeting, Daryl feels totally out of place. Let's face it, it's hard admitting—much less publicly declaring—that you're an alcoholic and/or addict in a room full of strangers. The mass refrain "*Hello, Daryl*"—while presumably intended to be a warm group welcome—comes off rather cultish. That, and the Higher Power element, are some topline reasons many people don't choose to continue with the program.

But in Daryl's case, he finds an upside: trying to pick up girls. Even though this is intended as a simple plot point to highlight Daryl's lack of seriousness about recovery, it's not entirely divorced from a real-life problem. Many women are reluctant to attend AA meetings because an uncomfortable majority of attendees are men. It is not uncommon for bad actors to try to seize on a woman's vulnerability to further their romantic goals. A film was even made about it called ***The 13th Step***. The producers' Facebook page describes the film as "about the criminal and sexually predatory behavior that occurs systematically in Alcoholics Anonymous." I'm sure this has happened from time to time, but it's the exception not the rule. AA meetings are generally safe, supportive environments.

Luckily Richard, played by M. Emmett Walsh, swoops in at the last minute like an Obi-Wan Kenobi of the recovery universe. He gives Daryl his telephone number and offers to be his sponsor. And with this simple yet profound gesture, the story really takes off. The student was ready; the master appeared. Whether Daryl knows it or not, he now has a recovery plan. And someone to help him follow it. Say what you will about AA (good or bad), but the sponsor system is pure genius. Sponsors are society's loyal foot soldiers in the fight against addiction. The kindness and empathy I experienced from my own AA sponsor back when I attended meetings is something I will never forget.

But we all know how addicted people can be their own worst enemies—even when things are going in the right direction. Daryl gets furloughed from the treatment facility and must now face life unsupervised. Therein lies the rub, and why I think this film is required viewing for the newly sober. While a stint in rehab can be a vital piece of the recovery puzzle,[89] if patients transition too quickly back to "real life," the odds of long-term success are low. "Real life" is often the problem to begin with: same setting, same people, same temptations, same triggers. So it's wonderful to see how the filmmakers structured the film in a way to accurately show how the hard journey of Daryl's recovery doesn't end with detox and discharge—it literally begins.

Left to his own devices back home, Daryl tries to score some blow. He ransacks his office searching for an overlooked stash. Keaton's acting is superb here. He deftly channels the mounting frustration and rage caused by his inability to score. In one of the saddest moments of the film, Daryl tries to convince his mother to take out a second mortgage on her home. Why not liquidate his inheritance now instead of waiting for her to die? The scene grazes the surface of a much bigger story about the tremendous collateral damage addiction can inflict on friends and family members of those affected. We covered some of these issues in Chapters 9 and 10.

Luckily, a silly mistake ends up (probably) saving his life. Instead of reaching his dealer, Daryl accidentally dials Richard. They meet at a diner where Richard urges Daryl to write out all his wrongs (Step 8 of the 12 steps) as a precedent to making amends (Step 9). He then helps de-triggerize Daryl's apartment. All the booze gets poured down the toilet. Each dresser drawer gets cleaned with a hand vacuum. This seems simple enough, but zillions of best-laid plans have been derailed by someone who finds a half bottle of vodka underneath their couch, or a vial of coke nestled between the cushions. People with alcohol use disorders specifically like to stash emergency reserves but then get too

---

89 Rehab definitely works; however, about 75% of people get over alcohol all on their own without AA, SMART Recovery, therapy, or anything but getting tired of the consequences. George Bush is an example.

drunk to remember where they put them. One's own home can be a ticking relapse time bomb.

And then comes the worst part of Daryl's recovery: time. For many addicts, alcohol or substance use is their primary way of filling time, and they have to retrain themselves to fill that time with healthier pursuits. It's wonderful to see how the filmmakers portrayed this challenge cinematically with a collage of Daryl slowly watching the walls close in, underscored by haunting monotonous music. What's tripped up so many people new to sobriety is how tantalizingly easy it would be to get immediate and guaranteed relief from this monotony. Unless you live in the wilds of Montana, liquor is usually sold within one walkable mile of 95% of the U.S. population (probably less in Utah). Home delivery is a click away, usually within an hour, for literally ANY liquid or substance one might desire. One of the main drivers for addiction relapse is simply easy access.

To pass the time, Daryl decides to pursue a relationship with his rehab friend Charlie (played by Kathy Baker), despite her having a boyfriend. Because along with having to fill the time, he realizes how lonely and socially isolated his addiction has caused him to be. Johann Harari (whose book I mentioned above) famously stated at a TED Talk, *"The opposite of addiction is not sobriety, it's human connection."* But this is only partially true. People with alcohol use disorders have rich social lives built around drinking. One of the downsides of sobriety is the risk of alienating or eliminating an entire social network.

But we can't argue the benefits of reconstructing a new and better social network free of drugs and alcohol either. As Daryl (or indeed anyone in recovery) soon learns, the process is both awkward and painful. The simple act of taking Charlie to a matinee movie—a thing that "normal" couples might do—turns into a dumpster fire. Then he invites himself to dinner with Charlie and her boyfriend Lenny, played with sinister intensity by Luca Bercovici. Another dumpster fire. For so many new to sobriety, normal life seems like you're a square peg being forced into a round hole.

Part of the problem is that people in the cozy purgatory of rehab envision a new life on the outside full of rainbows and unicorns. But the minute they get out, they find the opposite is true. Often it's a shared delusion. It's very common for couples to fall in love in rehab based solely around a strong shared interest in sobriety. Once outside, they realize they have nothing in common *except* sobriety.

And this is the trap Daryl falls into with Charlie. He pressures her to leave Lenny, begs her to move in with him—narcissistically positioning himself as her savior. But his impulses, while well-intentioned, are really just ways for him to delay or avoid the heavy lifting required to save himself. Sometimes for recovery to succeed, people need to experience loneliness—truly experience it, free of the usual numbing agents—because it refocuses their energy inward. That's where the most powerful recovery happens. My father always told me that the greatest life skill a person should develop is the ability to withstand loneliness.

There's no "Hollywood ending" in **Clean and Sober**, at least not in the typical sappy sense. And this is important because it's true of recovery in real life. Yes, there's always a silver lining, but it's usually only in the long term. You don't die. In the short term, regardless of all the suffering and determination people like Daryl have invested in their recovery, they can still lose their jobs, all their money, court cases, the girl or guy, and all their family and friends. Life doesn't magically solve itself because of sobriety, but it most certainly makes whatever life is left more manageable. Acceptance of this fact is difficult, and a reason why many people eventually relapse. The typical defeatist thought process is probably very familiar to many of you: "My life is just as fucked up now as it was when I was using; fuck it, I might as well go back to using."

Daryl does manage to dodge the embezzlement charge by agreeing to pay back his commercial real estate employers. But they also fire him, and he is faced with the prospect of finding a job with much less pay. He doesn't get the girl in the end either. Recovery may have brought Daryl and Charlie together in rehab, but it's hardly the foundation of living happily ever after in the real world. Daryl learns the hard way that only Charlie can do Charlie. None of his imagined sober superpowers can change that. In the dramatic climax of the film, Richard says it best: "Somebody who thinks that they control somebody else's addiction needs to know how overblown his thinking is…"

When Daryl accepts this difficult but fundamental truth about recovery, he is finally freed up to focus inward and realize he has a problem that only *he* can solve. His heroic quest throughout the film wasn't merely to kick the habit, but to be truly honest with himself about…himself. It's a journey as old as time. The Delphic maxim to "*know thyself*" is said to have been inscribed on the Greek Temple of Apollo, followed by…and this is truly remarkable given what we're discussing here…"*nothing to excess.*" Think about that: Over forty centuries ago the Greeks foresaw that addiction would be one of the central problems of human existence.

And this makes Daryl's AA meeting speech at the end of the film all the more satisfying, and early proof that Keaton is one of the greatest actors of his generation. Despite everything he's lost and as shitty as his life may seem in the short term, he literally glows with infinite possibility. Sure, there will be very hard work to follow, and countless urges to overcome, but for now he's on the path toward the metaphorical "better angels" of his nature. And I don't mean that in any religious context, I mean he's becoming the best version of himself. And that's why **Clean and Sober** is an important contribution to the pantheon of films about addiction and recovery. It shows us that there are no guaranteed happy endings, just steady human progress, life examined, life lived.

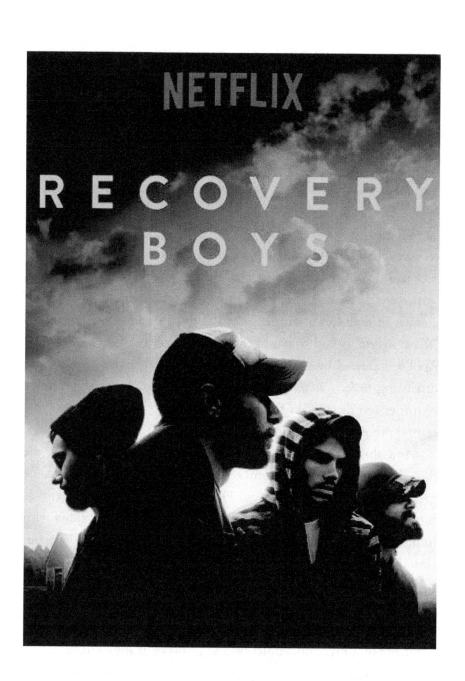

CHAPTER 16
Nailed Rehab; Now What?
Recovery Boys

Let's take a momentary detour from narrative feature films and series about addiction and recovery over to a television…documentary on the subject. Witnessing other people's micro-addictions and macro-addictions consumes sizable chunks of our time spent watching television, which itself is a habit. Series like **Hoarders** and **My Strange Addiction** are great eye candy because they concentrate on the extremes of addictive behaviors. It's all about watching the trainwreck, not what to do about the trainwreck or how to avoid the trainwreck. But such is life, and I'm not above watching a good train wreck.

Celebrity Rehab With Doctor Drew is a creature unto itself; nobody has enough time in their life nor the mental energy to examine what that show's immense popularity says about our culture at large.

The show ***Intervention*** has many fans and has helped dozens of addicted individuals kick their habits and lead happy, healthy lives. Personally, I have watched every episode at least twice. But the show does have its share of detractors. Is it ethical to trick alcohol and drug users into thinking they're the subject of a documentary when in reality they're being set up for an intervention? And does intervention guarantee successful recovery?

This brings up the broader issue of intervention as a practice. There are licensed "interventionists" who work with families to help push their loved ones into treatment. But is "intervention" even the right word? Perhaps better words are "coercion" or "ultimatum." The stark choice usually presented to the user looks like this: either go to rehab or lose your family's support. And lose your family too. And the free place to live. And the money to buy the alcohol and/or drugs you need to avoid hideously painful withdrawal symptoms and potentially deadly grand mal seizures.

Is intervention ethical? I don't know the answer to this question. Nobody does. Anybody who sides against it has probably never experienced the desperation of their 15-year-old daughter selling her body to truck drivers in the back of a gas station for $20 so she can score a hit of China White. Society leans in the direction of coercion under the premise that the addicted individual is mentally unqualified to assess the risks their behavior poses to their life. An intervention can be seen as the mini-me version of what's known as "Involuntary Commitment"—a legal recourse currently available in 37 States. Google it.

When it comes to TV shows or documentaries about addiction and recovery, sadly there are very few that focus on the recovery portion of the topic. The clear majority of shows go the use-and-abuse route. Graphic depiction of intravenous drug use is the norm, especially on TV. Actually, it's the requirement. And that disclaimer at the beginning: "Warning, what you are about to see…"? The producers aren't legally obligated to do that. They do it to stop you from changing the channel or flipping over to Hulu. They know *exactly* what you want to see. Another trainwreck.

Does that make *you* part of the problem? Well, let's see…

To make these kinds of shows, producers with questionable morals entreat addicted individuals to use drugs on camera. The producers need to have these individuals sign legal release forms before they can be filmed. Often those releases come with cash consideration. I know this because I produce videos in one of my businesses. Just not videos like these. And I would venture a guess that most times you watch a person in a TV show using drugs, they have been paid money to be on camera. And what do most users do with the money they earn? Buy more drugs, of course.

So please indulge me as I do some "morality math" here. You pay a monthly fee to a streaming service. The streaming service knows (thanks to big data) that audiences like to see programs that feature addicted individuals using drugs on camera. They pay license fees to producers to produce documentaries that feature people using drugs on camera. The producers pay money for the clearance rights to film these people using drugs on camera. These people use this money to buy more drugs. Conclusion? Never mind, this is giving me a headache. Let's move on.

A notable oasis of positivity, hope, and simple human decency in the addiction and recovery story is **Recovery Boys**, a wonderful documentary on Netflix. It tracks the recovery of four young men in West Virginia over the course of 18 months at a facility called Jacob's Ladder.

The facility is billed as "Farm-Based Residential Rehab" funded by the older-brother-we-all-wish-we-had-in-real-life, Dr. Kevin Blankenship. Blankenship made his fortune in urgent care facilities and now gives back. He also experienced heroin addiction firsthand through his son, who was three years sober at the time of filming.

Make no mistake. Blankenship is a hero, just like a first responder, Covid ward nurse, or a soldier who rescues hostages. We need more of these kinds of people in the world.

All four young men, Adam, Rush, Jeff, and Ryan—are in their mid-to-late 20s and facing legal trouble. They have been given various choices, including going to Jacob's Ladder rehab, going back to prison, or—in Jeff's case—losing custody of his two children forever. Are these fair choices? Are they ultimatums? In this instance, who cares? These poor guys all live near Huntington, West Virginia, the once-dubbed "overdose capital of America." I'm just happy they got help.

Jacob's Ladder's approach to rehab is complete isolation from the outside world in an idyllic natural setting. The facility also mandates that the guys do farm work. Really, really hard farm work. Bales of hay. Cow shit. Castrating bulls. But it seems like a small price to pay for state-subsidized rehab and a get-out-of-jail-free card. And it works. The guys kick their habits. At least at the beginning of the film.

As we've seen in other films and in some recovery programs in the real world, there is this prevailing notion that hard, back-breaking, often demeaning physical labor is a great way to find sobriety. Some people think it's the only way to find sobriety. This fallacy no doubt derives from the Christian idea of penance and subservience. This also involves a fair degree of prostration, which menial jobs like cleaning floors, toilets, and gutters entail. The late-great antitheist Christopher Hitchens had some choice things to say about this concept in his book ***The Missionary Position: Mother Teresa in Theory and Practice.*** Who knew Mother Teresa was such a Debbie Downer?

One wonders why some religious people think debasement and hard labor are pathways to sobriety. The reality is probably the opposite. This paradigm logically assumes non-sobriety is a sin. But tell that to any Christian and they'll laugh you out of the room as they drink their sacramental wine. Devout Muslims get a free pass on this one.

There is also the other prevailing notion that communing with nature is the path to sobriety. I'm not saying it's not. I think many people-problems can be reframed, mitigated, or even solved by a nice, long walk in the park. The central idea of nature-as-solution draws from many areas of human thought, including the literature of the English Romantics in the 18th century. Writers like Lord Byron and Mary Shelley sought to reconcile with nature through poetry, summers at Lake Geneva, and a few opium-fueled orgies.

The nature idea increased its street cred with the American transcendentalist movement around the same time, led by Henry David Thoreau. His book **Walden** is a meditation on the graceful pleasures of both living in nature and respecting it. His work presaged modern-day concerns like ecology and environmentalism by more than a century. French artist Paul Gauguin bailed on France in the late 1800s and moved "back to nature" in French Polynesia where he produced some of his most notable works. Nature has been a source of inspiration and healing for millennia, across many intellectual traditions and media.

The "back to nature" idea in relation to sobriety took literal form in Germany's Lebensreform ("life reform") movement of the early 20th century. It forbade alcohol (and drugs of course; although who had them?) and tobacco and consigned its victims to a strict vegetarian diet. Some of Lebensreform's head honchos found their way to sunny California and were tangentially responsible for the creation of what we now know as "hippies."

Why does nature help people with addictive behaviors? Here is a theory I've been playing with: Most scientists agree our brains were perfectly adapted for a small-group, hunter-gatherer, tribal existence. Agriculture brought with it the mixed blessing of stable food sources (grains, etc.) and surpluses (which makes overindulgence possible). Agriculture also caused the creation of larger tribes, and eventually large societies. Our hunter-gatherer brains were great when it came to the social connections and checks and balances enforced within small groups of no more than 150 people (the processing limit of the human brain, according to anthropologists).

When society scaled up above 150 people, our brains started to stress out. Some brains reacted with apathy and resignation (hence many kinds of non-chemical depression and general ennui). Others reacted with anger (hence internet trolls). Others reacted with anxiety and found ways to quell that anxiety through addictive substances and/or behaviors. Returning to nature where there are very few people around like, say, a farm, may be an antidote to that anxiety.

Regardless of the backstory, in **Recovery Boys** the return to nature seems to have paid very healthy dividends. The guys whistle while they work, take time to really listen to the birds sing, go swimming in a lake, take a hayride, and—last but not least—don't inject heroin into their veins. However, the film does a wonderful job of reminding us of that ever-present danger when the guys take a field trip into town for an Overdose Awareness Day event. The city gives out $3,600 worth of Naloxone auto injector kits (an opiate inhibitor used in emergencies) and holds a touching moment of silence for the fallen. Welcome to West Virginia. Although this could be any of a number of states. Or actually all of them.

The filmmakers do a great job of gently introducing us to the guys through casual conversations, 12-Step meetings, phone calls with family and friends, and a few one-on-one interviews. It's hard not to sympathize with these guys, even though some of the things they have done to themselves and others are deplorable.

Jeff has two young kids, but barely looks old enough to drive. He struggles every day with the guilt of knowing his poor decision making led to one of his daughters being sexually molested in foster care.

Rush seems a bit more mature and seasoned for his age, perhaps because he's survived fourteen overdoses. Even contracting Hepatitis

C didn't deter his addiction. He struggles to meditate. Yoga is probably not going to happen either. Even sitting still is agony for him.

Adam is your run-of-the-mill country boy who struggles with the guilt of having stolen all of his 86-year-old grandmother's money to buy drugs. She's forced to sell her meager belongings to Goodwill to pay her heating bill. And yet, she forgives him.

Ryan is a late entry to the program and gets dropped off at the farm literally right off the street after his arrest. Very little is known or discovered about him except that he wants to get off heroin and return to a real life. Jittery, exasperated, and broken—his recovery seems like a long shot.

All four guys have various reasons for being there. Primary among them? Location, location, location. Apart from shooting heroin, "there's just nothing else to do here (in their West Virginia town)," says Adam. And that may seem true to many. Work is scarce (especially if you're a convicted felon, like some of these guys are), and outside entertainment options are limited to bars, strip clubs, or loitering outside a corner liquor store.

Another factor working against them is not just where they are, but who they are with. Jeff doesn't know a single sober person back home. Everyone in his family uses drugs. So do all his friends. Addiction is a problem handed down from one generation to the next. Adam's grandparents probably drank moonshine during prohibition, his parents probably did weed and crack (his mother is recovering), and he does heroin because it's cheaper than anything else on the market. Also keep in mind that many beers are cheaper than bottled water.

The effects of this intra-generational addiction is also manifested in childhood trauma. Rush tells us he was raped when he was six. Adam's references to his father seem to indicate abuse was a factor in his parents' divorce, both to his mother and to him. The amount of trauma millions of people have suffered because of their parents' drug and alcohol use is probably only matched by the pain and suffering they now inflict upon themselves with the same substances as a result.

Is drug addiction always the direct result? People can make choices, right? True, but the more time we spend with these guys, and see where they live, the more we realize that the space within which they can make better choices is small and slowly collapsing in on itself. All the coal has been mined. Work is drying up. Non-alcohol-related recreation is limited or non-existent. Public assistance is running out. Non-addicts are leaving or are already long gone.

Sure, one could tell these guys to "buck up." To pull themselves up by their "bootstraps." But for many of them, the question ultimately becomes Why bother? Jeff expresses this simply when he says, "What's this life for…?"

All this being said, the filmmakers do instill powerful glimmers of hope along the journey. The guys all go to a local barn dance, nervous about what the locals will think of the "junkies" who live out on the farm. There's also concern about the fact that alcohol will be served. But all the guys seem to flourish in this environment and dance the night away with little blue-haired old ladies.

Other scenes telegraph the promise of an eventual happy ending to the film. Ryan gets visited by some of his friends from the "outside world" and we realize how sobriety has fundamentally changed his attitude toward them. It's opened a path for him to value people for who they are—not what they can give him, or do to help him score drugs. As a result, he will have the social support he needs when he leaves rehab and returns home.

The various "graduation ceremonies" in the film are earnest and heartfelt. Jeff vows in a tearful speech to never go back to using. Adam declares himself healed. Adam's mother is so proud of him for completing the program she decides to go ahead and buy another television without the fear that Adam will sell it for drugs. Again. And like Ryan, Adam's sobriety has opened up a path for her to give and receive genuine affection from her son, where before there was only distrust.

But now with the treatment program over, reality sets in. The guys are forced to return to the "real world." The world that created them and is partially to blame for their behaviors to begin with. And this sudden transition between worlds is abrupt, to say the least. Properly supported "re-entry" into the real world after rehab is often overlooked for the sake of expediency. This leads to recycling where individuals without proper support mechanisms in place relapse immediately after their discharge, and immediately return to the same facility they just left.

Luckily the rehab's owner and everyone's big-brother Dr. Blankenship eases this transition by moving them into a sober living home under construction. In return for their labor to help build the house, the guys get to live there for free. And they can get real jobs and start to live real lives again. And that's where the trouble begins.

There's a very telling scene in the documentary which speaks volumes about what these guys are up against. As they drive Rush to work at a coal mine at 4:30 AM, a gangster rap song blasts on the car stereo glorifying drug dealers and drug addicts, and denigrating law enforcement and women. They drive by one liquor store, brewery, and bar after another, each festooned with bright neon signs. If this documentary were filmed today, there would be huge legal cannabis dispensary billboards along every highway. Jeff's new boss smokes weed in front of him. Many of Rush's co-workers shoot up during their lunchbreaks.

Ryan, the guy who at the beginning didn't seem like he would make it, skips sober living and gets his own apartment with the help of a state-provided Recovery Coordinator. He gets a dog, a turtle, and a yoga mat. But the only job he can get is washing dishes at a local brewpub. He is literally surrounded by liquor bottles, taps, and people drinking booze 12 hours a day.

Addicted in Film

Is this even a fair fight?

In the end, the fight seems to be lost, at least for Adam, Rush, and Jeff. Blankenship discovers the guys have all been drinking alcohol on the down low. He's forced to kick everybody out for violating the terms of their stay in sober living. Adam goes to another sober living house in Minnesota. Rush chooses to go back to Jacob's Ladder and start all over again. Jeff gets odd jobs and decides to live with his family.

Nobody can fault Blankenship for casting these guys out back into the real world. Like any therapist trained to help family and friends of addicts will tell you, a line must eventually be drawn somewhere. But he knows what will likely result from this decision. He predicts that Jeff, now enmeshed in the intra-generational dynamic of his family's addictions, will likely shoot up within the next 24 hours, and be dead within a week. The only thing that might stop this is the threat of Jeff losing custody of his daughters forever. But given Jeff's instability, that is probably the ideal outcome anyway.

Jeff actually ends up getting temporary custody of his children, and this generates one of the funniest yet most unsettling scenes of the film. He's washing dishes while his girls destroy everything in their path, and cry at the top of their lungs. He spirals. I get it. I have two young children myself. But in Jeff's case, the bitter irony is that the thing he most wants—custody of his girls—is the thing that causes him the most anxiety. "I thought more about getting high today than I ever did at Jacob's Ladder," he tells the camera.

Adam comes back from Minnesota and fails a drug test at his new job. He moves in with his mother, who now regrets buying the new TV her son will undoubtedly sell for money to buy heroin. He bails on detox after only two days. "He had it all three weeks ago," his beleaguered mother tells us, as she scrapes together enough money to buy Adam some suboxone to ease his withdrawal symptoms.

Meanwhile, Rush starts taking Zoloft for depression and tries another sober living situation. Odds are he'll make it. Ryan ends up becoming a Certified Recovery Coach. He seems to have made it. Jeff tries to get a job, fails, relapses, gets arrested a third time, loses custody of his kids, and disappears. He probably won't make it.

Much like narrative films like **Leaving Las Vegas** and **Days of Wine and Roses**, this excellent documentary shows us again that successful recovery is never guaranteed. It's often the exception to the rule.

What also struck me about this film is the fact that it's raw and honest and underproduced. No clever editing or motion graphics. No addicts being paid to shoot up for the cameras. The reality of the situation speaks for itself. Expectations are created. Hopes are dashed. And like recovery itself, the ending can't be predicted.

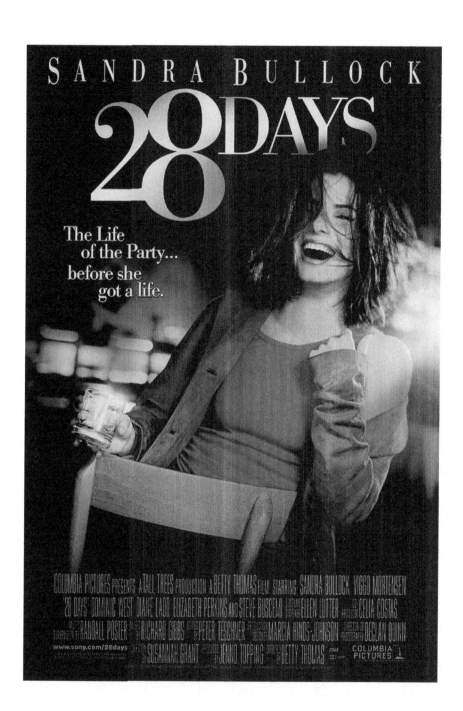

CHAPTER 17
Rehab as a Luxury Staycation
28 Days

If you ask people in who have overcome addiction what their favorite movie about recovery is, a lot will say it's **28 Days** starring Sandra Bullock. And if you ask people who haven't been addicted whether they've seen the film, they'll probably say yes, and that they loved it. **28 Days** is one of those rare films included in this book that managed to accomplish two things: 1) raise awareness about alcohol use disorder and treatment, and 2) sell a lot of movie tickets. So congratulations to Sony Pictures for opening the film at number 2 at the U.S. box office when it was released in April of 2000.

The success of the film must have come as a delightful surprise to the studio given the subject matter. It had been twelve years since **Clean and Sober** was released, and its box-office results were tepid.

The producers also took a bit of a gamble on director Betty Thomas, who was better-known as a cast member on **Hill Street Blues**. She had broken out of TV jail by directing low-brow feature comedies like ***The Brady Bunch Movie***, ***Private Parts***, and ***Dr. Dolittle***. But she amply showed that her films could make money, and **28 Days** continued her hot streak. Sandra Bullock was more of a question mark because of her waning star power in Hollywood at the time (how do you top the success of ***Speed***?).

Many critics and recovery bloggers loved the film because it seemed very true to its subject matter. I would go a step further and posit that **28 Days** also had a profound and positive impact on public perception about recovery and the rehab industry as a whole. I've been involved in treatment center marketing, and all my clients tell me **28 Days** was extremely helpful in the public's perception of their important work. The facility featured in the film, "Serenity Glen" (not a real place), actually becomes one of the stars of the film. The food looks great. The people are happy. Everyone watches soap operas together every night, cuddled together under blankets. The facility seems so pleasant and transformative it makes recovery seem almost…*fun*.

But let's start with Sandra Bullock's wonderfully authentic performance as Gwen Cummings, a rather run-of-the-mill party animal who likes to drink a lot. She has the ideal wing man in the form of her boyfriend, Jasper, played by British actor Dominick West (of ***The Wire*** fame), in one of his more devilish performances. We meet the couple out at a club drinking and dancing the night away with friends, filmed in a grainy, low-quality video format, akin to watching granny's old VHS tapes. It was a wonderful choice by director Thomas because grainy and low-quality is precisely what memories seem like after a night of heavy drinking.

Gwen awakens after her night of partying and doesn't even realize what day it is. The scene is played for laughs in the film, but for most people with alcohol use disorders this is usually cause for terror. At least it was for me. At any rate, it's Saturday morning and Gwen and Jasper must get dressed and out the door quickly to attend her sister's wedding. Getting dressed quickly is stressful, apparently, so they start drinking all over again.

The couple make it to the ceremony (barely) and we're introduced to Gwen's sister, Lily, played by the always-amazing Elizabeth Perkins (no relation, but I wish). In a short scene in the dressing room right before the nuptials, Lily's frosty demeanor toward her sister wonderfully telegraphs the number of years she's had to tolerate Gwen's antics. It's summed up perfectly in Lily's line: "You make it impossible to love you."

Cut to the wedding reception where Gwen and Jasper, clearly hammered out of their minds, try to dance. Every bride's worst nightmare comes true as Gwen loses her balance and crashes into the wedding cake. How else was it supposed to go, really? She then has the brilliant idea to steal a limo and drive drunk to find a cake shop. Instead, she crashes into a house. Thankfully there are no injuries. It could have been so much worse. And in reality, it usually is.

Now, given the severity of what she's done, and the fact that she's such an unsympathetic character up to that point, I would have expected her to go to prison. But this being a movie, and Gwen probably having great insurance, she gets a 28-day stay in cushy rehab instead. Makes you wonder what happens to most people who don't have great insurance, or any insurance, or money to pay for highly motivated private attorneys instead of beleaguered, overworked public defenders.

This brings up another dicey topic. An ongoing debate in the addiction and recovery space centers on the question of whether "Fate and the State" (drug and alcohol arrests leading to state-mandated jail time) pays better long-term dividends than state-supported (or subsidized) treatment programs aka "Harm Reduction." A similar conundrum is familiar to anyone who has children: Do you discipline your kids with punishment, or with other less "harmful" ways? We discussed some of these issues in Chapter 8.

Countries like Portugal, the Netherlands, and Switzerland have completely decriminalized drugs (and alcohol-related arrests) and moved all the money they would have spent on correctional facilities that punish people over to rehab facilities that help them, as well as job creation programs. Does it work? United Nations commissions seem to think so. So do most rational people. But for some reason most countries, including and especially the U.S., are reluctant to tread into these waters.

At any rate, Gwen shows up to rehab and is as unenthusiastic as one might expect. Director Betty Thomas and her production designer Marcia Hinds do a marvelous job of imbuing the facility with a character all its own—complete with creepy group-hug kumbaya moments outside, group singing, and hilarious public address system announcements like: "Tonight's Lecture: What's Wrong with Celebrating Sobriety by Getting Drunk?"

Needless to say, Gwen is not down with the program. She makes it very clear that she "does not belong there," that she is not like "those people." Well listen, Gwen, I got news for you: There are people who have been going to support meetings and stayed sober for the better part of half a century and still don't think they're like "those people." Any program has its share of denialists. Apparently some countries do too.

Gwen is also put off balance by the ritualistic nature of the program she is now forced to participate in. Perhaps so too were audiences who had never been inside an actual rehab facility or attended a 12-Step meeting. Let's face it: They can come off as a little "cultish." There are those who even accuse it of being an actual cult. Most movies default to 12-Step programs in their depiction of recovery, even though there are many other programs available (like SMART Recovery or LifeRing), which seem decidedly less cultish because they are science- and evidence-based. So congratulations to the film's exceptionally talented screenwriter Susannah Grant (writer of **Erin Brockovich**), who seems to have anticipated the cult issue and done her homework. Words like "disease" are used less than they normally would in such a context, as are the words "God" and "Higher Power." At one point the facility director Cornell (played with unusual seriousness by usually over-the-top-weird actor Steve Buscemi) does throw out the time-tested "God doesn't dump more on you than you can handle" bromide, but it's meant more as a metaphor than actual therapeutic advice.[90]

In keeping with the typical 3-Act structure of all successful screenplays, Gwen spends all of the second act transforming from a cynical "here but not here" forced participant into a fully engaged "I get it now" joiner. She loses her shit in a support meeting, which in 12-Step programs represents a major breakthrough. She's forced to clean toilets, in keeping with apostolic and monastic traditions of salvation through menial labor. And she does some equine therapy and rock climbing. Any clinician will tell you, there are multiple pathways to recovery.

Along the way we learn through flashbacks that Gwen's mother had a drinking problem and perished as a result. There was no father in the picture either. These sad realities do create a sense of empathy for Gwen. However—I wish there was a softer way to say it—tragic backstories can only go so far to justify continued self-abuse. Part of the reason Gwen is in rehab to begin with is not just to *have* those flashbacks, but to *do something* about the feelings they provoke without self-medicating.

28 Days succeeds at being earnest, but it is also really funny. Gwen's journey to redemption and sobriety is helped along by a hysterical

---

[90] For anyone who is interested, this phrase can be scrutinized from the point of view of Theodicy, or why God allows bad shit to happen to us to begin with. A wonderful book I highly recommend is **The Courtier and the Heretic: Leibniz, Spinoza, and the Fate of God in the Modern World** by Matthew Stewart.

ensemble cast that transforms the typically somber affair of rehab into something more like a cool-kids summer camp. And screenwriter Grant confects characters that cover the gamut of addictions and personality types:

There's Azura Skye playing Gwen's fragile heroin-addicted teenage roommate; English actress Marianne Jean-Baptiste affecting an Inner-City welfare-mom accent as gossip-queen pill-popper Roshanda; Mike O'Malley as Oliver, a wisecracking recovering cocaine user who sleeps with every woman (minus Bullock, although not for lack of trying); the legendary Diane Ladd as moonshine aficionado Bobbie Jean, representing the "elderly" recovery demographic (which is surprisingly large); Reni Santoni as a curmudgeonly Doctor Daniel (yes, doctors get addicted a lot); and lastly Alan Tudyk as Gerhardt, the German who can't stop crying. Ask anyone who has seen it: Gerhardt singlehandedly steals the movie. Tudyk steals any movie he's in.

Casts can only take you so far. All successful Hollywood movies need a bad guy and a love interest. I would argue that the "bad guy" in this film is actually Addiction itself. It is brought to life in the character of Gwen's boyfriend, Jasper. He so perfectly embodies what Addiction would actually say that you forget he's a living, breathing character. On his first visit, Jasper slips Gwen some Vicodin. After all, Addictions need to convince their hosts to feed them.[91] On the next visit, he tries to convince Gwen she doesn't have a problem. Everybody else does. When that doesn't work, Addiction tries other word salad gems like (not quoted verbatim): "The whole point of life is to care less…people aren't happy unless they drink…the point of life is to minimize the pain of existence; that's where I come in…" and my personal all-time mind-fuck favorite: "Your life is so incredibly screwed up—you might as well screw it up even more!"

Thanks, Addictions! You're so thoughtful! Always got my back!

---

91 And misery loves company…

Jasper eventually proposes to Gwen out of desperation. After all, Addictions will promise you anything not to leave them. And apparently they're quite jealous too. Like when Jasper gets into a fight with Gwen's in-rehab "love interest" Eddie, played by **The Lord of The Rings** hall-of-famer Viggo Mortensen.

It is with the character of Eddie, a dual-diagnosis alcohol/sex-addicted pro baseball player, that the film hits a bit of a speedbump. The rules of a typical Hollywood movie would see Gwen and Eddie falling in love during rehab and then living happily and abstemiously ever after. But apparently the film's producers got the memo: The point of rehab isn't to find love, it's to find yourself. So as a result, Eddie doesn't have much of a role to play in the film except as a chisel-jawed sounding board for Gwen. That and the hypotenuse of a love triangle with Gwen and Jasper that never quite materializes. But Eddie does tell Gwen she should steer clear of Jasper. And that's probably the best professional or non-professional advice anyone could give her.

The scene of Gwen's eventual reconciliation with her sister, Lily, is brief but satisfying. And this is no small task, given the complexity of family dynamics as they pertain to a loved one struggling with addiction. Lily has obviously been to war and back with Gwen's problem. And, if this were the real world, Lily would be long gone. But thankfully this isn't the real world. The film shows us that forgiveness is always possible, regardless of how bad the circumstances. It also reminds us how crucial relationships are for successful recovery.

Kudos to the filmmakers for also staying true to the depressing statistics about relapse. Just a few short scenes after the curmudgeonly Dr. Daniel is discharged, he returns with a black eye and no recollection of how he got it. He embodies just one of the seven-out-of-ten people who will fail at long-term recovery and end up recycling through treatment centers.

Will Gwen be one of the seven who fail, or the three who make it? Director Betty Thomas certainly teases the possibility of failure when Gwen returns home to New York City. Declan Quinn, a superb cinematographer, infuses each shot with bright neon liquor store and bar signs. Alcohol seems to be everywhere. As it is in real life.

But this is a Hollywood movie after all, so the story ends on a positive note. Gwen ends her relationship with Jasper, and seems to be in the clear, recovery-wise. But for a person like Gwen in real life, the end is really just the beginning. Quitting is the easy part. Now the real work begins. And we hope Gwen does it, because anyone's recovery success—in film or in real life—is cause for celebration.

28 Days has a well-deserved place in most everybody's list of Top 10 movies about addiction and recovery, and it was a pleasure to include it here. The filmmakers don't sugar-coat rehab, but don't expose its sordid underbelly either. The film proves that difficult messaging about challenging topics can be accomplished with levity and honesty and a great deal of humor.

CHAPTER 18
Star-Studded Sexual Sobriety
Thanks for Sharing

The films we've discussed reflect the in-patient rehab experience and its immediate aftermath. But there is so much more to the drug and/or alcohol macro-addiction recovery story. Rehab is the easy part. It's the "rest of your life" part that screws many people up. And to me, no film captures the depth, the nuances, the humor, and the "sober" realities of life after rehab quite as effectively as ***Thanks for Sharing***.

The film is the perfect Hollywood vehicle: Big "bankable" movie stars like Gwyneth Paltrow and Mark Ruffalo. Big "indie cred" actors like Tim Robbins. Great "up-and-coming" talent like Josh Gad (pre-Olaf). And a complete show-stealing "cross-platform" co-starring appearance by music demigoddess Pink. The marketing of the film was straight down-the-line Tinseltown: A movie about SEX! Er, uh, sex addiction, rather. But not the yucky kind!

Appearances deceive. This film is a great example of what I call the "Fortune Cookie Effect," where filmmakers have to cleverly hide ideas inside confections so audiences don't gag. Nobody likes preachy. The outside of this cookie is shiny and new and appealing. As it should be. Movie stars get paid millions of dollars to emote. And getting butts into theater seats costs millions more. But inside this cookie one discovers several profound, challenging, and difficult topics and themes about a person's real-deal post-rehab recovery experience, and the recovery community in general.

And don't let the "sex addiction" thing fool you. Sex may be more marketable than drugs or alcohol, but **Thanks for Sharing** is really about recovery from any macro-addiction, especially drugs and alcohol. In fact, many times during the movie, it's easy to forget it's about sex addiction at all.

Also, I have categorized this as a "Post-Rehab Recovery Film" instead of a "Sex Addiction Film." A full discussion about films involving sex addiction happened a while back. If you missed it, I won't tell you the page number, because you'll probably blow off this chapter and go right back to the sex. Don't do that. This chapter is really cool.

Thanks For Sharing tells the recovery story from the point of view of Alcoholics Anonymous and the 12 Steps (although the entity itself isn't mentioned explicitly in the film because AA won't allow it). This includes adherence to the "Disease Model" of addiction, the submission to a Higher Power and the frequent use of several other phrases and terms that are proprietary to that program. 12-Step is a widely recognized and highly regarded pathway toward recovery. I enjoyed all the meetings I ever attended.

However, today there are other proven pathways to recovery, and I personally use SMART Recovery. I like that it's science and evidence-based. SMART doesn't tell me that I am "powerless"; it gives me tools to make myself, and help others, become more powerful. And I don't have to outsource my recovery to a "Higher Power." While that may work for some, atheists and agnostics like me have trouble doing that. And like my intellectual hero Christopher Hitchens, I will not accept Pascal's wager now or on my deathbed.

In the film, the 12-Step meeting experience is only used as a structural device and is not the thematic centerpiece. Oscar-nominated writer-director Stuart Blumberg uses it as a way to explore a host of very complex themes and powerful teachable moments told in three commingled storylines featuring Ruffalo, Robbins, and Gad. To successfully achieve this and also make a film that's accessible, funny, and entertaining is no easy feat but Blumberg pulls it off masterfully.

Mark Ruffalo plays Adam, a recovering sex addict who has been "sober" for five years. No orgasms, through whatever means, period. (No, this is not a science fiction movie). He decides it's finally time to enter the dating pool, fortified with a hard-earned respect for (What? Monogamy? Missionary Position? No toys? It's never made clear.) He goes to a party and meets Phoebe, played by Gwyneth Paltrow. No doubt he'll fall in love with her. Despite her recent notoriety, and an actual "Goop"-like product placement moment in the film, I think she remains one of the sultriest actresses of all time. My God, that voice.

But theirs is an odd coupling, really. Physically, Ruffalo doesn't seem to be playing in the same league as Paltrow. The filmmakers don't even try to cheat the fact that he's much shorter than she is, and less physically imposing—which is ironic given that he now plays ***The Hulk***. But what Ruffalo lacks in stature he makes up for with brilliant acting, and the wonderful "everyman" quality he shares in common with actors like Tom Hanks.

Next we meet Josh Gad who plays Neil, an emergency room doctor and (ironically) an addict who specializes in treating addicts who come to the hospital as overdose victims. He attends 12-Step meetings so he can check a box, and it's clear that when it comes to the actual work of recovery, he's phoning it in. If sex addiction was on a spectrum (and it is), Neil would be inching down toward the paraphiliac end of it, with frottage and voyeurism being his drugs of choice. For the first 20 minutes of the film Gad basically plays a pervert, and I'm still scratching my head as to how a reputation-conscious entity like Disney felt comfortable enough to cast him as the lead snowman in **Frozen**.

Rounding out the three storylines we have Tim Robbins playing the role of Mike, a 12-Step veteran who is at the top of his local meeting hierarchy, and Ruffalo's AA Sponsor (who, similar to multi-level marketing, is by extension Gad's sponsor). But when his macro-addict son Danny crashes the tiny New York condo he shares with his on-screen wife Katie (played with wonderful grace by Joely Richardson), we soon realize that Mike is also a domineering, sanctimonious "dry-drunk"[92] with a checkered past.

The film opens with an absolutely brilliant juxtaposition of ontologies. Fade into a medium shot of Adam (Ruffalo) on his knees, bedside, praying to his Higher Power, safely cocooned in his private oasis of innocence. Cut to him walking down the temptation-soaked streets of sin-city Manhattan. Bus signs smeared with bikini-clad models. Billboards oozing with sexually suggestive ads. Every single woman he lays eyes on is a short-skirted, bra-less Perfect 10. Poor guy. Kind of.

But luckily he has the 12 Steps for support. At a meeting he sits down with his fellow defensive linemen in their precarious formation against drugs, alcohol, and hyper-sexualized human existence. They're all doing okay, but it's only a matter of time before someone in the line misses a tackle. Because, according to statistics, with alcohol

---

92 I personally hate this term, but it is used widely.

specifically, only 1 in 10 of them will successfully recover in the long-term without going to the dark side at least once; some twice, most multiple times. Some will die homeless, alone, and penniless in a gutter. And yet there these people are, drinking shitty day-old coffee, pushing back the offense, day in and day out against these ridiculous odds.

With a combination of sly humor and evocative visuals, writer-director Blumberg manages to frame the never-ending battle against the "moral weakness" of addiction in subtle, day-to-day human terms. It's impossible not to root for these guys. And I don't say this just because I used to be one of them. I challenge anyone—with or without an addiction, to *anything*—to go to a meeting (*any* type of meeting) in a dingy church basement or stuffy community center, own up to being a liar, admit that life is unmanageable, and beg total strangers for help.

But having said this, some people are more dedicated to their recovery than others. Unless you have round-the-clock supervision, an on-call sobriety coach, and/or daily/hourly drug and breathalyzer tests (some people do have the money to pay for this), sobriety pretty much relies on the honor system. And it doesn't always work. I know this from personal experience. Some people meet at bars after their support meetings to celebrate a week of sobriety. Some people indulge in their cocktail, substance, or behavior of choice every day *except* their meeting day and call themselves success stories. And other people, especially Josh Gad's character Neil, seem to gravitate to sex-addict meetings hoping to meet fellow sex addicts. For sex. (As previously mentioned, in AA parlance, this strategy is called **The 13th Step**.)

Gad is hysterical in this role, and it's easy to see how he became a big star. He's always offering implausible excuses to Adam, his sponsor, for why his 12-Step homework isn't done on time. The classic "dog ate my 3rd Step" defense. He accepts abstinence chips, but obviously hasn't earned them. And then we see why. Neil's always at home, alone, in a tiny apartment, jerking off to online porn and scarfing down donuts.

And the reasons for his co-occurring disorders? Take your pick. He's an on-call doctor with no time to meet people outside of work. He's overweight, and probably has trouble getting women to sleep with him. Not because he's overweight per se, but because he's bought into the whole "dopey but lovable fat guy" routine. And despite the popular notion that addictions have deep, complex, multi-faceted origins in childhood traumas and PTSD, this scene shows us how addiction sometimes just boils down to boredom.

Meanwhile, Adam meets Phoebe (Paltrow) at a party. Their flirty repartee seems fairly innocuous on the surface. But given what we know about Adam's sex addiction, and what Phoebe *doesn't* know about his sex addiction, the scene plays out like a merciless game of cat and mouse—where he's the mouse, and she's the cat. A cat who likes to play with her food. In any normal context, she'd be considered a bit of a tease. In the context of this film, and Adam's secret vulnerability, she's a sexual predator.

The story then delves into Mike's (Tim Robbins) strained relationship with his son Danny, played by **Almost Famous** alum Patrick Fugit. Strained, because Danny is an on-again off-again addict who's lied and stolen money from his parents to support his drug habit. But the real problem between them isn't just Danny's addiction; it's Danny's strategy (or lack thereof) for overcoming it. Mike is old-school. To him, like many other die-hard 12-Steppers, getting "in the rooms" is the ONLY way to overcome addiction.

This is one of the reasons some people get turned off by AA. It's not that meetings are such a huge inconvenience ("90 meetings in 90 days" certainly can be), it's that AA tells you that *they* are the only true path to successful sobriety. Here is a quote from one of my SMART Recovery meeting participants about why they were hesitant about AA meetings:

I didn't like the idea that I would never recover on my own; I needed to go to their meetings for the rest of my life. Everyone was telling me that I would never achieve full recovery in my lifetime, only day-by-day sobriety. Without the meetings I would relapse. Guaranteed. It's like I had taken The Red Pill and there was no going back.

This kind of messaging is difficult for your average millennial with a normal social life who just got their first DUI and has to attend 12-Step meetings as a condition of their parole. It's such an overwhelming message that many people new to the program end up relapsing or quitting meetings as a result. And that's unfortunate, because even though many of these first DUI offenders don't have an alcohol use disorder per se (at that time), many will go on to develop one over time and not seek help from any mutual support group, not just AA.

Perhaps for these or other reasons, Danny tells his father he would rather continue his recovery on his own. No meetings. He'll make it this time. Things are different. But Mike's been to this rodeo one too many times and thinks Danny is lying. Once again. As he always has. Because that's what addicts do.

Is Danny lying?

When it comes to addiction, the answer isn't always a simple yes/no. When someone asks an addict if they're sober *now*, the answer is either the truth or a lie—depending on whether they are sober or not. But when someone asks an addict if they'll be sober tomorrow, ten years from now, or in ten minutes, there is no fully honest answer. How can they know? The honest answer only exists as a spooky quantum-like superposition of possibilities, with literally billions of variables in play. Addicts are only 100% honest at the moment a measurement is taken of their sobriety. The future is completely indeterminate. Think of it like Schrödinger's Addict.[93]

---

[93] Michael Werner, past President of the American Humanist Association, and author of the upcoming book **Quit Your Addiction Now,** disagrees with me as

Regardless, Danny's mother Katie is an optimist. She loves her son and wants him to be safe. Like any parent, and over Mike's "better judgment," she makes the gut-wrenching decision to let Danny stay, try one more time, and give him one last shot. Anyone who has struggled to save a friend or loved one who is slowly killing themselves in front of their very eyes knows how hard this decision is to make. (We covered many of these dynamics in our chapter on **Beautiful Boy** and **Four Good Days**).

Meanwhile across town, Adam builds up the nerve to ask Phoebe out on a date, his first in *five years*. No pressure. They meet in Central Park, and predictably the sparks fly. We already know what Adam's issues are. And Phoebe wastes no time telling him hers: she's a breast cancer survivor, her ex was an alcoholic, she won't date addicts, hates everyone but Adam, and just ran a 10K and didn't break a sweat. Afraid she'll run another 10K in the opposite direction, Adam decides to keep his sex addiction a secret.

From a story structure point of view, this is the proverbial "Deal with the Devil" (another form of a Faustian bargain) the lead actor always makes in the First Act of a movie, usually on or around page 30 of a script. The Romantic Comedy Rulebook states that the lead character must either lie about themselves or disguise themselves in order to win over the love interest. But the union is based on a big lie. As time goes on, the lie and/or disguise starts to unravel, the tension builds, and eventually the big lie comes back to bite the liar in the ass in Acts 2 & 3. It's a bit like people hiding their drug and alcohol use in real life. It eventually catches up with them.

Because the focus is on Adam's sex addiction in this movie, it's easy to overlook Phoebe's glaringly obvious micro-addictions too. This first date scene shows she's got some dicey feedback loops running in

follows: "Sure we can't predict the future completely. But all the studies show the number one factor for long-term sobriety is a permanent commitment to sobriety. A commitment doesn't say you are perfect but that this is their long-term course of action no matter what. People can predict the future by making it."

that beautiful head of hers. Her claim that she "hates everyone except" Adam? Sure, on one level, this could make a guy feel really special. On another, it begs the question: Why would you *ever* join a club that would only admit you as a member? Total Red Flag. Exercise freak: Yellow flag. But, hey, love is blind, right?

And then they kiss. And it makes you wish you actually *were* blind. Because it's one of the worst movie kisses in the history of people kissing in movies. Phoebe (Paltrow), the consummate pro, is in it to win it with full labial activation. She is fluent in French and Spanish, after all. Meanwhile, Neil (Ruffalo) channels Captain Kirk's 1970's pursed lip stratagem, a favorite of the boys over at NBC's Standards & Practices. The kiss is just another example of the physical mismatch between the two actors. But this time even great acting can't save the scene.

That said, I do have an enormous amount of sympathy for poor Mark (we're on a first-name basis in this paragraph, just FYI). You see, like Mark, I too have taken part in a screen kiss gone horribly wrong…

The setting is Cartagena, Colombia, in 2018. I was co-starring as the "husband" of a local actress in an indie production directed by one of my former screenwriting students. The script read something like: "Maria awakens from her year-long coma, sees her husband, and the couple kiss in celebration." So I'm thinking, *Hey, my movie wife's in a coma, probably groggy, doesn't know where the hell she is, just a simple peck on the lips, and it's a wrap.* But no. It seems Maria was catching up for a year of lost time. The director yelled "¡Acción!" What happened next is still a blur, but I'm pretty sure the actress playing Maria raped my face.

It was awesome, but troubling as well. Even though it's all about the craft, I was married at the time. And this wasn't Vegas, so what happened in Colombia wasn't staying in Colombia unless I took drastic measures, like never telling *anyone* the actual name of the film. Don't

Addicted in Film

bother trying to Google it. I bought all the relevant SEO Keywords and buried them in my neighbor's backyard. To this day I break out in cold sweats when Netflix premieres foreign films *En Español*.

Anyway, back to my happy place: Crippling Addiction and Uncertain Recovery.

So, about 30 minutes into the film, the mood of **Thanks for Sharing** begins to deviate away from Hollywood fantasy into real-world serious. We start to see real consequences. Neil (Gad) goes first. He loses his job for trying to take secret videos up his (female) boss' skirt. Total pervert stuff. But what follows is one of the most powerful scenes in the film. In his 12 Step meeting right after his termination, instead of taking another sobriety chip he hasn't earned, he shares. He admits he's been lying about his sobriety the whole time. He adds, tearfully, "I'm out of control. I'm scared."

For anyone who has experienced a similar come-to-Jesus moment in a 12-Step meeting (even as a spectator), you know how powerful and transformational they can be. For some people, this is the most important moment in their lives. A moment that might *save* their lives. And that is why at this precise instant of what amounts to a confession, AA provides you a solution: Surrender to your Higher Power. Steps 1-3. Ask any Evangelical Christian who has "seen the light" about their conversion experience. They're almost identical to what people often experience in a 12-Step meetings. This is pretty powerful stuff.

Even though I'm agnostic, I'm glad Neil's "conversion" moment happened in the way it did. Hollywood has a tendency to make light of mutual support meetings, or even turn them into the butt of jokes. Remember **Fight Club** where Tyler Durden and Marla Singer argue over which support meetings they want the other to avoid? "*Sickle Cell Awareness Group*" and "*Tuberculosis Wednesday Night Confessional.*"

Even **Finding Nemo** features a scene where Bruce the shark and his support buddies all get together for their "Fish Eaters Anonymous" meeting. Don't get me wrong. The ***Nemo*** scene is absolutely hilarious. And as I've always said, you need a good sense of humor to succeed at the whole recovery thing. So it was refreshing to see the power of the "conversion" moment conveyed respectfully and honestly in this scene with Neil (Gad), instead of being played for laughs.

After his powerful share, it's also nice to see the power of the AA fellowship in action. All the members of the group embrace him, support him, and offer help. Even Adam, who has every right to be mad at his sponsee for lying to him the whole time, embraces this as an opportunity to deepen his own resolve. People often forget that what happens outside of meetings is just as important as the meeting itself. The 12-Step Fellowship generates a wonderful multiplier effect. To be "of service" is tantamount to serving yourself. And it's one of the reasons I facilitate my own weekly SMART Recovery support meetings.

But we must remember that this is still a Hollywood movie, so Neil's 12-Step meeting moment needs to lead somewhere. In this case, it crashes headlong into Dede (Pink), a fellow sex addict, who he befriends. Maybe because she's Pink, and her whole M.O. is "I don't give a fuck what you think," she's arguably got the best lines of the whole movie. There's nothing cosmetic about her in-group shares. They're blunt and honest, a bit titillating, and also strangely hilarious. "I ruined my relationship with my best friend by fucking her old man." Maybe it's her deadpan delivery that makes a screw-up like this seem funny. Regardless, when the laughter stops, a harsh reality also sets in when she says, "There has to be another way or I'm going to fucking *kill myself*."

This line reminds us that, all laughter aside, there are serious lurking consequences here. It's perhaps also why movie critics felt the film's tone was all over the place (it is) and didn't quite know whether it was a comedy or a drama. I would argue that it's both, and everything else in between, for that matter. It's the reason the film is so important and effective at what it does. It packs so much into a mere 1 hour and 52 minutes. And for me, it totally works.

By contrast, Adam has had a relatively easy time during the whole movie. He and Phoebe hook up and decide to go steady. They make love, but since it's consensual and monogamous, it doesn't constitute a relapse. She does a wonderful striptease performance for him, and he barely raises an eyebrow, even after five years on the lam. Just what is his "problem?" Whatever "sex addiction" he has is the cute and cuddly kind and doesn't seem to have negatively affected him or anyone else.

But, unfortunately, his Faustian bargain eventually comes due and Adam's forced to come clean to Phoebe. And this is where the "sex addiction" that's been a whimsical narrative pretext throughout the film suddenly takes on a more ominous dimension. Neil confesses to compulsive masturbation, rampant womanizing, and hiring prostitutes. The latter is the bitterest pill to swallow for most women in a committed relationship, not just Phoebe. Any boyfriend can cheat on you at any time with anyone and give you a nasty sexually transmitted disease. Unless you're celibate, it's the cost of doing business. But imagine the calculus when your boyfriend is an admitted sex addict who may still have the escort service's number on speed dial?

What's poor Phoebe to do? Well, like everyone else who loves an addict, she has to trust. And that's an even more bitter pill to swallow sometimes. There is a telling scene where she breaks into tears in front of Katie (Joely Richardson). Katie also loves an addict, her husband Mike. She always worries that he could relapse at any time. This is something Phoebe will have to learn to also accept if she wants to be in a relationship with Adam. There are never 100% guarantees. Any promise that Mike or Adam will be sober only exists as an indefinite possibility, not a fact. Imagine for a moment what this is like for people like Katie (and now Phoebe). They are basing their entire emotional life around people who can destroy everything they try to build together in one single moment of stupidity.

The scene is perfunctory, and could easily have ended up on the cutting room floor and not changed the outcome of the story either way. But writer-director Blumberg chose to keep it because it's beautiful and sincere, and allows Katie to tell Phoebe (and the audience) something critically important to the friends and family and loved ones of addicted individuals. The best way for them to live with the constant uncertainty, the ever-present possibility of a loved-one's relapse, is to focus on self-care. To work on themselves. To get stronger. They cannot stop living their lives just because everything could end at any moment. And they can't live their life thinking that it will end at any moment. So they trust, but verify. And wait. And hope. And live.

Sadly, when Phoebe does try to verify whether Adam is telling the truth, it kills their relationship. It's a simple set-up, and happens in relationships all the time. One partner overhears a suspicious conversation, usually late at night. The partner hangs up when the other enters the room. In this case, Phoebe asks Adam who he was speaking to so late at night. Adam's tepid answer is unconvincing. So Phoebe does something you can and *should* do with a confessed addict like Adam: Trust but verify. She asks to see his phone so she can see who he was actually talking to. Adam says no. He refuses to let Phoebe invade his privacy. She grabs the phone, and realizes he was telling the truth. But the damage is done. They part ways.

This scene is pivotal, well-written, and well-acted. But it also highlights an aspect of the family and friends of addicts story that takes on added significance if you've actually lived it. And I have, with my ex-wife, many times. It is common—and in many respects healthy—for someone with an addiction to want to "move on" with their lives. But in the same way that substances like alcohol distort your thinking, sobriety does as well. The result is what I call "Sobriety Sanctimony." Desperate to put the past behind them, an addict becomes angry when a loved one pushes back on a verification. Just like Adam does in this scene.

I can't tell you how many times this happened to me. My wife would look at me, squint, and ask, *"Have you been drinking?"* I would get angry and say, *"Of course not. Are you crazy?!"* I would literally expect her to trust me. I would sometimes demand it—even though she had no reason to trust me. She would push back and say, *"Trust you? Dude, you've been sober a week!"* And yeah, she shouldn't have trusted me. *I* wouldn't even have trusted me. I'm glad she verified. It is a frustrating feature of recovery, but it's also a necessary maxim: An addict's relapse rate will always be non-zero. And you're only as good as your last breath test.

This dynamic plays itself out in a similar but more complex way in Mike's home. He and Katie discover that a bottle of pain pills has gone missing. They automatically assume Danny took them and has relapsed. And why wouldn't they? They have every reason to. So they confront Danny, who denies stealing anything. An argument begins. And in the ensuing five minutes, writer-director Blumberg uses the conflict to channel some very powerful and deep insights about addiction and recovery.

As they argue, it becomes clear just how deep Mike's own "Sobriety Sanctimony" goes. If he says Danny took the pills, Danny took the pills. End of story. Danny should have gone to meetings. End of story. Mike's way is the *only* way. The *right* way. After years of sobriety, he thinks he's "earned" the right to be right. But he hasn't earned anything.

What's more, in the argument it comes out that when Mike was drinking, he used to come home drunk and beat Danny. Mike's sanctimony gets ratcheted up even higher. How dare Danny bring that up?! Why isn't he *over* that? The past is the past! We're talking about *right now*!

Danny fires back, calling his father out for never, *ever* apologizing.

"Dad, say you're sorry!" says Danny.

"I'm not saying I'm sorry to you!" his father answers, utterly tone deaf to what's happening around him. And indeed, why should he apologize? Because let's face it, sober sanctimonious people are always right. Why would they ever need to apologize?

And here is where the film takes the recovery conversation to its zenith. I have watched this scene over and over. Not because I understood Mike with all his flaws, but because I had been Mike with all his flaws. Even though my alcohol problem never led to my wife suffering any physical abuse, there's always the emotional kind. The worry of not knowing if I'd get home okay. The anxiety caused by my mood swings. For years I had demanded that my wife forgive me. I had apologized in the best ways I knew how. So I expected her to forgive me. On my timeline, not hers. Because I had done the work. Because I was sober now. Because this time was "different."

"Don't you get it?" I would ask her.

Turns out I was the one who wasn't getting it, because I was too busy trying to be right. So I totally understand why Mike wants to move on from the past. Because for any addict, the past kind of sucks. Bringing it up generates a lot of guilt. Guilt causes anxiety. Anxiety exacerbates urges. And urges lead to relapses.

There are two opposing forces at work here. There's Mike's desire to put his past behind him, lessen the guilt, and lower his risk of possible relapse. And then there's Danny's need for his father to truly atone for his sins, apologize, and seek forgiveness. It's really the only way father and son can both move on with their lives. But, as in my own experience—and that of millions of others grappling with the same rival impulses—you simply cannot expect people to forgive your behavior on your timeline just so *you* can move on. They need to move on first.

Here the film takes a dark turn. But it's important that we see it because it reflects what happens in real life for real people in real recovery. After his blowout with Phoebe, Adam relapses. And we finally see how what started as Adam's Cute and Cuddly Sex Addiction is really Adam's Kinky and Weird Sex Addiction. He masturbates, hires a prostitute, and hooks up with one of his old S&M slaves. Basically most of the sex-related sins of the bible, minus incest. But by the morbid look on Adam's face as he pleasures himself, I'm not sure we should rule that out either.

Similarly, Mike's blowout with Danny also causes him to act out. It's almost an autonomic response. The mental dialogue—which I'm sure many of you reading this know quite well—is usually: *"Well fuck that, fuck you, fuck everyone, fuck my life, I'm going to get plastered to show everyone that I won't be bossed around anymore!"*

There is a name for this relapse technique: "The Fuck-its." And yes, of course it's a childish temper tantrum, but it has caused more relapses than anyone cares to mention.

And this is exactly what happens to Mike as he visits a neighborhood convenience store after the fight with Danny. Fuck it. After hemming and hawing for a few seconds, he asks the clerk for a bottle of Jameson Whisky. Tim Robbins' expression is priceless. It so precisely conveys the absolute confusion, madness, and banality of that moment. I've been through it dozens of times, and all I can say is that it's as close as you can come to having an out-of-body experience. You're literally watching yourself fuck up your own life and doing nothing to stop it. And it's all so banal, so simple. You buy a fifth of whiskey. It's usually cheaper than bottled water. You drink it. And then…utter chaos.

The scene also deftly captures how a simple trigger can derail even the most die-hard, longest-running teetotalers like Mike. Pride and reputation and achievement count for *nothing* at that moment in the liquor store. I know people who have had 30 years sober, gone to a thousand meetings, become leaders in the recovery community, and then go on to order a glass of wine at dinner for no particular reason and wind up living in a park addicted to meth six months later. We always think of relapses as catastrophic, and they are, but only as they relate to eventual consequences. The *act* of relapse itself usually takes less than a minute. T.S. Eliot said it best: The world "ends not with a bang, but a whimper."

But luckily at this whimpering moment Mike gets a phone call from Katie that Danny has been in a bad automobile accident. He rushes to the hospital to find that, luckily, Danny is alive, albeit roughed up, and handcuffed to the hospital bed because he relapsed and totaled his car. Turns out that Mike was right after all. Danny couldn't do it alone. But will Mike's Sobriety Sanctimony kick in? If it did, we could also add Sobriety Hypocrite to his nametag. But luckily Mike's paternal instincts prevail, and he hugs Danny instead of judging him. And this is how it usually goes down in a lot of these situations. Against the mind's better judgment, the heart chooses to forgive. And to forgive is to move forward, albeit always into indeterminism and uncertainty. Because that *is* recovery.

A similar rapprochement happens between Adam and Phoebe. With the benefit of time, distance, and a little water under the bridge, they meet in Central Park and are reminded of how the other person made them feel, versus the problems that forced each to overthink their relationship. Phoebe had every reason to mistrust Adam, but she also admits she has her own issues to address, like perfectionism.[94] Sobriety Sanctimony sometimes cuts both ways, and it's too easy for the non-addict in the relationship to lord this over their loved one. We are reminded that "those who live in glass houses shouldn't throw stones."

Rounding out the three storylines we end on Josh Gad's character, Neil. His arc during the film has been entirely the reverse of Adam's and Mike's. He faced his demons at the beginning of the story, and by the end—thanks to Pink's help—he is a 12-Step warrior ninja. His full acceptance of the program, his patient implementation of the steps, and his dedication to his own recovery journey shows that the 12 Steps can work "if you work it."

And Neil does, by buying a bike, avoiding subways (and associated frottage temptations), and talking it all out with his mother and

---

[94] Covered in a previous chapter.

(maybe?) his new love interest, Dede. It is also important to note that Neil was an atheist at the beginning and remained one at the end. This demonstrates something important about recovery programs in general. In the words of AA: "Take what you need, and leave the rest." And Neil clearly does.

In summary, ***Thanks for Sharing*** is an enjoyable, funny, precise, and honest film that reveals great truths about addiction and recovery. It's the perfect "Fortune Cookie Movie" for me. It shows us the nice parts and the not-so-nice parts of recovery. Because, hey, everybody knows that long-term, successful recovery isn't all rainbows and unicorns. This wonderful film shows that, regardless of what program you follow (or don't follow), there is life after rehab, and recovery really works "if you work it."

PART IV:
Final Thoughts

As we've seen, the subjects of addiction and recovery can inspire powerful stories of triumph, tragedy, and redemption. Filmed entertainment is a wonderful way to capture these stories and convey them to millions of people around the world. Even though they are fictions, movies are excellent chroniclers of human foibles and human potential—mirrors to our deepest truths.

Richly drawn but deeply flawed characters like Bad Blake in ***Crazy Heart*** and Ben Sanderson in ***Leaving Las Vegas*** deserve the world's attention because they embody a struggle that touches everyone's life in one way or another, sometimes very negatively. While not everyone will identify with these characters, there are bits and pieces of them in all of us. Bad found the courage to step back from the abyss of addiction and completely transform his life. Ben made a choice to quit fighting and give up. Life demands courage. Success is never guaranteed. For people to change, they must want to change, and try to unconditionally accept life as it is, instead of as they hoped it would be.

Film is the perfect medium to show this change in action. Stripped to their essence, movies are just dramatizations of how reluctant heroes fight adversity in order to change themselves and the world around them. Change implies transformation, and transformation implies a belief in the perfectibility of human beings. That's why films like **Clean and Sober** and **28 Days** are so compelling and necessary. The filmmakers were able to show dramatic transformations, demystify the world of addiction treatment, and render it more accessible to anyone who may someday find themselves in need of that kind of help. That's not just entertainment—that's a public service that could save lives.

But film's biggest superpower is its ability to dramatize conflict. The heroes of the films we've discussed didn't just coast along to their quaint Hollywood endings. They fought against each other, themselves, and the world to get sober, to help others get sober, and to heal. Sometimes these conflicts are scrappy and mean, but the tougher the battles, the more meaningful the victories. Forget about what Vince Lombardi said. Winning is pointless if nothing can be learned from the struggle. The films **Four Good Days** and **When a Man Loves a Woman** show how the best teachable moments can come from our lowest points of parenting and marriage, when even love doesn't seem to be enough to heal what's broken.

Film is entertainment, but I've also tried to show how it's a medium that can examine the philosophical dimensions of addiction as they relate to questions of free will, meaning, moral responsibility, and even existentialism. **Another Round**, a clever Danish comedy dramatizes a riddle that has vexed philosophers for millenia: "How much is too much?" Isn't self-indulgence a key part of what the Greeks called *eudaimonia,* or a life well lived? Some crazy Scotsmen in **Trainspotting** showed us how heroin is a well-reasoned antidote to a reality that's broken, a life that's lost all meaning. Existence is hard, but we are reminded that it's better to accept reality than trying to soften it or erase it with addictive substances or behaviors.

Film is fantasy too, full of countless crazy stories, just like the ones that people tell themselves. Humanity is blessed and plagued by magical thinking and beautiful delusions. The supremely talented Darren Aronofsky shows us in **Requiem for a Dream** how the substances we use aren't nearly as dangerous as the lies we tell ourselves about ourselves. Our mental models help us survive, but they also allow us to create harmful, self-serving mythologies. We convince ourselves that we are somehow special and can defy the rules of chance, and bend causality to our own liking through sheer will alone.

It's unpleasant to talk about certain addictions, either because we don't understand them or because we are silently suffering their consequences. Films let us deconstruct our natural impulses to always be better, to win at all costs every time, to always look and feel and perform perfectly, to convince ourselves and others that we are happy because we *must* be happy. These are all burdens we place on ourselves to various degrees and at various times in our lives. Is it any wonder we search for ways to hop off that hamster wheel from time to time?

When I taught screenwriting, I always told my students that the key to a great film is heroism. Nobody will pay good money to sit in a crowded theater and watch a movie star complain for two hours. They have to *do something*, something that tests their physical and emotional limits and fundamentally changes who they are in the process.

What they do can be something as big as saving the world from alien invasion, or as seemingly small as changing a lightbulb so an Afghan girl can learn to read. But whatever it is, doing it, *really* doing it, requires courage, resolve, commitment—and an honest desire to change.

Successful recovery from addiction requires all these things and more.

Recovery is an act of heroism. I'm surprised there aren't more movies made about it. For now, I'm pleased to have shared some of the ones that were.

If you would like to keep the conversation going, join the Addicted in Film Movie Club. It's free.

Just go to www.addictedinfilm.com and sign up for our monthly newsletter. You will receive invitations to our free bi-monthly Addicted in Film Movie Night Watch Parties on Amazon Prime Video followed by open discussion via Zoom.

If you enjoyed this book please also leave a review on Amazon.

Go to the product detail page under "Your Orders." Click on "Write a Customer Review" in the "Customer Reviews" section, and tell us what you thought.

Positive reviews help get the book in front of more potential readers and help them on their recovery journey.

You never know; your review may help save a career, a family, or a life.

That's the main reason I wrote the book.

—Ted Perkins

Index

Symbols

1,000-lb Sisters (TV Series) 231
9½ Weeks 167, 169
10 (Film) 138
12-Step 92, 101, 120, 145, 146, 157, 175, 177, 182, 228, 265, 273, 276, 288, 298, 299, 306, 307, 308, 309, 311, 314, 315, 321, 322
13th Step, The 277, 309
20th Century Fox Studios 79, 224
28 Days 4, 177, 275, 295, 296, 299, 302, 324
50 Shades of Grey 168, 169, 186
95 Theses 265
#MeToo 141, 252

A

A24 Films 206
ABBA 265
Abstinence Pledges 166
Academy Awards 4, 5, 12, 23, 29, 31, 58, 87, 122, 139, 206, 207, 224, 249, 265
Ace Ventura: Pet Detective 139
Addict Porn 64
Adele 217
AIDS 72, 73
Al-Anon 137, 156, 157
Alcoholics Anonymous (AA) 17, 18, 21, 22, 130, 137, 145, 146, 177, 220, 273, 276, 277, 278, 281, 306, 308, 309, 310, 311, 314, 315, 322
Alcohol Use Disorder 7, 11, 137, 145, 172, 214, 295, 311
Alexander, Libby 112
Alien (Film) 64
Alley, Kirstie 217
All in the Family (TV Series) 227, 259
Almost Famous (Film) 122, 310
Amadeus (Play) 245
Amazon 93, 326
American Exceptionalism 78, 217
American Gigolo (Film) 224
American Medical Association 45
Anderson, Ian 164
Anderson, Paul Thomas 207
Andrews, Julie 138
Anorexia 215, 241

Another Round (Film) 31, 32, 34, 37, 324
Anslinger, Harry 44, 45, 46, 47
Apartment, The (Film) 139
Apocalypse Now (Film) 145
Apollo 13 (Film) 271
Arbuckle, Fatty 166, 216
Archilochus 163
Aristophanes 163
Aronofsky, Darren 40, 57, 58, 59, 60, 61, 63, 64, 206, 238, 240, 246, 247, 325
Arthur (Film) 138
Artisan Entertainment 57
Asceticism 241, 242
Atkins Diet 227
Attack of the Killer Tomatoes (Film) 42

B

Bad Lieutenant (Film) 167
BAFTA Awards 130
Baker, Kathy 279
Balanchine, George 244
Bale, Christian 217
Bancroft, Anne 224, 225, 226, 227, 228, 229, 231
Barr, Roseanne 217
Basic Instinct (Film) 167
Bass, Ron 154
Batman (Film) 272
Beautiful Boy: A Father's Journey Through His Son's Addiction (Book) 122
Beautiful Boy (Film) 107, 111, 122, 123, 130, 146, 312
Beetlejuice (Film) 272
Beharie, Nicole 187
Belle de Jour (Film) 167
Belushi, John 216
Bercovici, Luca 279
Bezos, Jeff 93, 236
Bickford, Charles 142
Bigger, Stronger, Faster (Documentary) 242
Biggest Loser, The (TV Series) 225
Binoche, Juliette 266
Birdman (Film) 272
Birthmark, The (Book) 233
Black, Jack 217
Black Swan (Film) 233, 238, 239, 242, 244, 245, 247, 249, 251, 252, 254
Blair, Selma 172

Blair Witch Project (Film) 57
Blankenship, Dr. Kevin 285
Blue Velvet (Film) 167
Blumberg, Stuart 307
B-movies 47, 167
Body Mass Index (BMI) 218, 230
Bogosian, Paul 208
Boiler Room (Film) 250
Bonham, John 250
Bowie, David 51
Boy Erased (Film) 160, 177, 179, 180, 183
Boyle, Danny 39, 50
Bracco, Lorraine 173
Brackett, Charles 18
Brady Bunch Movie, The (Film) 296
Breakfast at Tiffany's (Film) 137
Breaking Bad (TV Series) 48
Breatharianism 242
Bridges, Jeff 79, 80
Brimley, Wilford 273
Brinkley, David 261
British Film Institute 50
Broken Circle Breakdown, The (Film) 122
Bronson, Nadia 276
Bronstein, Ronald 206, 209
Brookes, Jacqueline 202
Brooks, Mel 223, 224, 227
Bugsy (Film) 199
Bulimia 214, 215, 241
Bullock, Sandra 4, 295, 296
Bunyan, Paul 172
Burke, Edmund 103
Burning Bed, The 144
Burstyn, Ellen 58, 59, 62
Buscemi, Steve 299
Butz, Earl "Rusty" 218

C

Caan, James 190, 199, 200
Cage, Nicolas 4, 21, 22, 23, 24, 29
Caligula 165
Call Me by Your Name (Film) 122
Camus, Albert 28

Candy: A Novel of Love and Addiction (Book) 122
Candy, John 216, 225
Cannes Film Festival 2, 12, 22, 50, 172
Canterbury Tales, The (Book) 164
Carangi, Gia 4, 51, 67, 68, 69, 70, 71, 72, 73, 74, 88, 239
Carangi, Kathleen 70
Carangi, Louis 70
Caravan (Song) 254
Carell, Steve 122
Carey, Drew 217, 225
Carlyle, Robert 54
Caron, Glenn Gordon 271
Carrey, Jim 139
Carroll, Tod 271, 272
Casino Royale (Film) 33
Cassel, Vincent 239
Cazès, Lila 22, 26, 29
Celebrity Rehab With Doctor Drew (TV Series) 283
Center Will Not Hold, The (Documentary) 87
Chalamet, Timothée 122
Chasing the Scream (Book) 46, 273
Chaucer, Geoffrey 164
Chazelle, Damien 239, 249
Cheesecake Factory 219
Cherry (Film) 6
China Film Group 168
Chinese New Year 221
Chocolat (Film) 257, 265, 266, 267, 268
Chris Farley Show, The (Book) 216
Christian, Claudia 275
Christianity 98, 113, 163, 164, 177, 179, 217, 275, 276, 286, 314
Christie, Agatha 100
Churchill, Winston 34
Cider House Rules, The (Film) 265
Civil War 44
Clean and Sober (Film) 177, 271, 272, 273, 275, 280, 281, 295, 324
Close, Glenn 111, 123
Coal Miner's Daughter (Film) 88
Cobain, Kurt 88
Cobb, Thomas 79, 85
Cocaine 5, 60, 71, 91, 199, 272, 273, 300
Codependency 12, 109, 114, 115
Codependent No More: How to Stop Controlling Others and Start Caring for

Yourself (Book) 114
Cognitive Behavioral Theory 229, 237
Cognitive Dissonance 112, 118, 150
Cold Turkey (Film) 257, 259, 260, 261, 263
Collateral (Film) 175
Collins, Jackie 186
Comprehensive Crime Control Act of 1984 47
Confirmation Bias 143
Conley, Garrard 177
Connelly, Jennifer 58, 59
Consumer Product Safety Commission 41
Cooper, Bradley 3, 79, 87, 88
Cooper, Scott 79
Cooper, Wilhelmina 69
Cosmology 196, 203, 209
Country Music Television 79
Courtier and the Heretic, The: Leibniz, Spinoza, and the Fate of God in the Modern World (Book) 299
Crazy Heart (Film) 77, 78, 79, 85, 87, 88, 89, 91, 93, 94, 323
Crime of the Century, The (Documentary) 98
Critics' Choice Award 130, 272
Cronkite, Walter 261
Crowe, Russell 122, 178
Cuarón, Alfonso 149
Curb Your Enthusiasm (TV Series) 224
Cyborg 2 (Film) 68
Cyrano de Bergerac 215

D

Dafoe, Willem 276
Dangerous Liaisons (Film) 186
Dark City (Film) 199
Dark Matter 195
Darth Vader 261, 274
Da Silva, Howard 14
Davies, Luke 122
Dawkins, Richard 161
Dawson, Rosario 100
Days of Wine and Roses (Film) 133, 137, 138, 144, 146, 150, 152, 228, 293
Deauville American Film Festival 68, 84
Debbie Does Dallas (Film) 186
Deep Throat (Film) 167
DeGeneres, Ellen 71

Delicatessen (Film) 206
Delirium Tremens 145
Del Toro, Guillermo 149
DeLuise, Dom 215, 223, 224, 225, 227, 229
Dench, Judi 266
DeNiro, Robert 197
Dever, Kaitlyn 98
Diagnostic and Statistical Manual of Mental Disorders (DSM) 114, 118
Dick, Philip K. 178
Dick Van Dyke Show, The (TV Series) 227
Didion, Joan 87
Dirty Shame, A (Film) 160, 171, 175
Disease Model 306
Divine (Actress) 171
DNA 161, 179, 222, 235
Dogme (Film) 32
Don Jon (Film) 169
Dopesick (TV Series) 97, 98, 99, 101, 102, 103, 104, 272
Double Indemnity (Film) 18
Douglas, Michael 93
Downs, Hugh 261
Dr. Dolittle (Film) 296
Dry-Drunk 308
Dunaway, Faye 69
DuPont 45
Duvall, Robert 84

E

Ebert, Roger 154
Edgerton, Joel 178
Edwards, Blake 137
Ed Wood (Film) 40
Ehrlichman, John 47
Einstein, Albert 54
Elders of Zion (Book) 208
Eliot, T.S. 321
Elliot, Bob 261
Elliott, Sam 91
Ellis, Albert 229
Emmy Award 98, 224, 272
Empire of Pain: The Secret History of the Sackler Dynasty (Book) 98
Engels, Friedrich 197
Entertainment Weekly 241

Entropy 81, 234, 236
Epigenetics 179, 192
Epstein, Jeffrey 172
Equine Therapy 299
Erin Brockovich (Film) 100, 299
ER (TV Series) 122
Esper, Dwain 40
Ethanol 26
Everything Must Go (Film) 25

F

Fall of Valor, The (Book) 13
Falsifiability 196
Falwell, Jerry 167
Farley, Chris 216, 225
Farley, Tom 216
Farrell, Colin 82
Fassbender, Michael 169, 185
Fast Times at Ridgemont High (Film) 167
Fat Acceptance 217, 228
Fat Actress (TV Series) 217
Fatal Attraction (Film) 167
Fate and the State 297
Fatso (Film) 213, 215, 223, 224, 225, 227, 228, 230, 231
Faustian Bargain 16, 26, 90, 251, 312, 316
Fawcett, Farrah 144
Federal Bureau of Narcotics 44
Female Trouble (Film) 171
Fen-Phen 61
Fentanyl 110, 114
Ferrell, Will 25
Fields, W.C. 23, 216
Figgis, Mike 21, 23, 29, 32
Fight Club (Film) 314
Fincher, David 206
Finding Nemo (Film) 314
Finnish Ministry of Health 276
Finnix, Samuel 98
Flight (Film) 6
Fonda, Jane 229
Food and Drug Administration (FDA) 98, 99, 100, 102
Fortune Cookie Effect 262, 306
Four Good Days (Film) 107, 111, 119, 122, 123, 239, 312, 324

Fox, Julia 207
Fox Searchlight Pictures 79, 188, 239
Franken, Al 154
Frankl, Viktor 28
Freeman, Morgan 274
French Lieutenant's Woman, The (Film) 199
Freudian 180
Fröhlich, Arild 215
Frozen (Film) 308
Fuckland (Film) 32

G

Gad, Josh 305, 307, 308, 309, 314, 315, 321
Gambler's Fallacy, The 200
Gambler, The (Film) 190, 199, 200, 206, 209, 211
Gandolfini, James 225
Garcia, Andy 149
Garcia, Rodrigo 111
Garnett, Kevin 209
Gaslight (Film) 239
Gasnier, Louis J. 40
Gauguin, Paul 287
Gay Conversion Therapy 180, 183
Gere, Richard 23, 249
Gia (Film) 4, 51, 67, 68, 69, 70, 71, 72, 73, 74, 88, 239
G.I. Jane (Film) 249
Gladwell, Malcolm 243
Gleason, Jackie 216, 217
Godfather, The (Film) 149, 199
Godfrey, Arthur 261
Golden Globe Award 98, 272
Goldman, William 4, 272
Golino, Valeria 24
González Iñárritu, Alejandro 149
Goodfellas (Film) 173
Goodman, John 217, 225
Good Times (TV Series) 259
Google 161
Gordon Caron, Glenn 271
Gosling, Ryan 217
Gossett Jr., Louis 249
Graduate, The (Film) 224
Grant, Susannah 299

Grazer, Brian 271
Great Leap Forward 221
Greek Temple of Apollo 281
Gyllenhaal, Maggie 81

H

Hairspray (Film) 171
Hallström, Lasse 265
Hanks, Tom 307
Hank Williams Syndrome 78, 84
Hardy, Oliver 216
Hari, Johann 46, 273
Harm Reduction 297
Harrison Narcotics Tax Act of 1914 44
Harvey, Paul 261
Hawthorne, Nathaniel 233
Hays Code, The 166, 167
Hays, Will H. 166
HBO Films 67, 98, 111
Hearst, Patty 175
Hearst, William Randolph 44
Heaven Knows What (Film) 206
Hedges, Lucas 178
Hemingway, Ernest 67, 98, 111
Herman, Paul 82
Heroin 5, 39, 40, 44, 46, 50, 51, 52, 53, 54, 55, 58, 59, 60, 61, 62, 63, 64, 67, 68, 69, 70, 72, 73, 108, 109, 110, 111, 112, 113, 115, 116, 119, 120, 127, 154, 181, 258, 285, 288, 289, 292, 300, 325
Hero's Journey 238
Hershey, Barbara 240
Heston, Charlton 199
Higher Power 146, 265, 276, 277, 299, 306, 307, 308, 314
High Fructose Corn Syrup (HFCS) 219
High Times Magazine 42
Hill, Jonah 217
Hill Street Blues (TV Series) 296
Hinds, Marcia 298
Hirsch, Judd 209
Hitchens, Christopher 286, 307
Hitler, Adolph 34
Hoarders (TV Series) 283
Hoffman, Philip Seymour 154
Holiday, Billie 46

Homosexuality 13, 179, 181, 253
Honeymooners, The (TV Series) 216
Hoogenakker, John 100
Hopper, Dennis 145
Hostess Ho-Hos 219
Hostess Twinkies 219
Hot Shots! Part One & Deux (Films) 24
Houseman, John 250
Howard, Ron 271
How to Undress in Front of Your Husband (Film) 40
Hudson, Rock 72
Hulk, The (Character) 307
Hulu 97, 112, 285
Huntley, Chet 261
Hurt Locker, The (Film) 202
Hustler Magazine 167
Hustler, The (Film) 199
Hutton, Lauren 201

I

Idiots, The (Film) 32
Imagine Entertainment 271
Impens, Ruben 123
Imposter Syndrome 90, 91
Iñárritu, Alejandro González 149
Indecent Proposal (Film) 167
Intelligent Design 177
Internal Affairs (Film) 23
International Creative Management (ICM) 79
Intervention (TV Series) 64, 284
In the Realm of Hungry Ghosts (Book) 116
In the Rooms 310
In Treatment (TV Series) 111
Isaak, Chris 171

J

Jackson, Charles 13, 18
Jackson, Janet 216
Jacob's Ladder Treatment Facility 285, 286, 292
James Bond (Movie Franchise) 33, 51, 186
Jaws (Film) 64
Jean-Baptiste, Marianne 300
Jeffersons, The (TV Series) 259

Jennings, Waylon 78
Jenny Craig 214
Jerry Maguire (Film) 122
Jesus 126, 178, 181, 229, 314
Jethro Tull 164
Johansson, Scarlett 169
Johns Hopkins University 78
Jolie, Angelina 4, 67, 73
Julien Donkey-Boy (Film) 32
Just Say No Campaign 64

K

Kama Sutra (Book) 163
Keaton, Michael 98, 101, 272, 273, 278, 281
Kelvin Scale 172
Khondji, Darius 206
Kidman, Nicole 178
Kirk, Capt. James T. 313
Klugman, Jack 145
Knoxville, Johnny 172
Kraft 219
Kristofferson, Kris 87, 88, 95
Kronos Quartet 58
Kryptonite 72, 169, 276
Kunis, Mila 70, 111, 112, 239, 245
Kurt Cobain: Montage of Heck (Film) 88

L

Ladd, Diane 300
Lady Gaga 79, 87, 91
La La Land (Film) 239, 249
Landau, Martin 40, 41
Last Tango in Paris (Film) 167, 169
Last Temptation of Christ, The (Film) 276
Laudanum 44
Laurel, Stan 216
Law of Attraction 52
Law of Unintended Consequences 40, 42, 64, 78
Learning Channel, The (TLC) 242
Lear, Norman 259
Leaving Las Vegas (Film) 4, 21, 22, 23, 28, 29, 293, 323
Lebensreform 287
Lembke, Anna 48

Lemmon, Jack 137, 138, 139, 140, 145
Lennon, John 54, 123
Lesbian 71, 173, 181
Less Than Zero (Film) 6
Leto, Jared 58, 59
Lewis, Marc 48
Libatique, Matthew 61
Licata, Victor 45
Liese, Bruce 48
LifeRing 298
Lindholm, Tobias 33
Lionsgate Films 57
Lolita (Film) 167
Lopatin, Daniel 206
Lord Byron 287
Lord of the Rings, The (Movie Franchise) 42, 301
Los Ricos También Lloran (TV Series) 94
Lost (TV Series) 71
Lost Weekend, The (Film) 11, 12, 17, 18, 19, 25, 28, 35, 53, 137, 145, 177
Lovato, Demi 88, 229
Luther, Martin 265
Lysistrata (Play) 163

M

Mad Max (Movie Franchise) 186
Mad Men (TV Series) 140
Mandoki, Luis 149
Man on Fire (Film) 175
Mansell, Clint 58
Man's Search for Meaning (Book) 28
Mao Zedong 221
Marijuana 39, 40, 41, 42, 45, 46
Marijuana Tax Act of 1937 45
Marquis de Sade 165
Marvel Comics 97, 169
Marx Brothers 1, 7
Marx, Karl 1, 7, 197, 235
Maté, Gabor 48, 116
Matrix (Film) 183, 267
Maude (TV Series) 259
McCarthy, Joe 14
McDonald's 218
McDowell, Malcolm 41

McGregor, Ewan 50, 51
McQueen, Steve 185, 186, 187, 188, 189
Medically-Assisted Treatment (MAT) 109
Mellon, Andrew 45
Ménage à Trois 133
Men's Journal 135
Menzel, Idina 207
Merchant-Ivory 27
Mercury, Freddie 73
Methadone 53, 72, 102, 109
Methamphetamine 5, 60, 91, 118, 122, 123, 124, 125, 127, 129, 130, 146, 320
Michael, George 224
Midnight Movies 42, 64, 171
Mikkelsen, Mads 33
Milland, Ray 12, 145
Miller, JP 146
Mink Stole (Actress) 171
Miracle Worker (Film and Play) 224
Miramax Films 51
Missionary Position, The: Mother Teresa in Theory and Practice (Book) 286
Miss Piggy 227
Mitchell, Elizabeth 71
Molina, Alfred 266
Mo'Nique 215
Monty Python's Life of Brian (Film) 167
Monty Python's The Meaning of Life (Film) 225
Moonlight (Film) 206
Moonlighting (TV Series) 271
Moore, Demi 229
Moore, Dudley 138
Moral Weakness 309
Morphine 44
Mortensen, Viggo 301
Moss, Carrie-Anne 267
Mother Teresa 274, 286
Mountcastle, Richard 100
MPAA 175
Mr. Olympia 221
Mr. Smith Goes to Washington (Film) 238
MTV 67
Mullan, Peter 53
Mulligan, Carey 187
Munchausen Syndrome by Proxy 117

Muppet Movie, The (Film) 224
Murphy, Eddie 216
Musk, Elon 81, 236
My 600-Pound Life (TV Series) 218, 231
My Life as a Dog (Film) 265
My Strange Addiction (TV Series) 242, 283
Myth of Sisyphus, The (Essay) 28
Myth of Supposed Expertise 243, 245

N

Nabisco 219
Nabokov, Vladimir 167
Nader, Ralph 41
Narcotics Anonymous (NA) 59, 72, 101, 112, 177, 220
National Institute of Health (NIH) 125
National Organization for the Reform of Marijuana Laws (NORML) 41
National Public Radio (NPR) 180
National Society of Film Critics 272
Navy SEAL 249
NBC's Standards & Practices 313
NC-17 Rating 175, 188
Nembutal 71, 73
Netflix 87, 177, 207, 285, 314
Network (Film) 261
Newhart, Bob 261
New Line Cinema 42
Newman, Paul 199
Nickelodeon 3
Nielsen Ratings 46
Night Porter, The (Film) 167
Nixon, Richard 43, 46, 218
No Exit (Play) 107
Northwestern University 78
Nothing Like the Holidays (Film) 266
Nutty Professor, The (Film) 215
Nymphomaniac (Film) 169

O

Obesity Porn 231
Obi-Wan Kenobi 50, 277
O'Brien, John 28
Oedipus (Play) 163
Office Space (Film) 119

Office, The (TV Series) 122
Officer and a Gentleman (Film), An 249
Olin, Lena 267
O'Malley, Mike 300
One Flew Over the Cuckoo's Nest (Film) 15
One Little Pill (Film) 276
Opiates 44, 52
Opioid 44, 97, 101, 104, 111, 275
Oreo Cookies 219
Orwellian Thoughtcrime 178
OxyContin® 5, 97, 98, 99, 100, 101, 102, 103, 104, 220
Oxytocin 124

P

Paltrow, Gwyneth 169, 305, 307
Pamplona (Running with the Bulls) 197
Paper Chase, The (Film) 250
Paramount Pictures 12, 122, 199
Paraphilia 174
Pascal's Wager 307
Pasteur, Louis 82
Past Life Regression 114
Peele, Stanton 48, 124
Pentobarbital 71
Percocet 242
Perfect Day (Song) 51
Perkins, Elizabeth 297
Perkins, John 127
Perkins, Quinn 124, 222
Permanent Midnight 6
Personal Best (Film) 238
PG-13 Rating 168
Phat Girlz (Film) 215
Phillip Morris Company 259
Pi (Film) 57
Pill-Mills 103
Pillsbury 219
Pink Flamingos (Film) 171
Pink Panther (Film) 137
Pink (Singer) 305, 315, 321
Plato 234
Playboy Magazine 162
Pop, Iggy 51

Porky's (Film) 167
Pornhub 162
Pornography 164, 166, 186
Portman, Natalie 238, 239
Poulter, Will 99
Pray Away (Documentary) 177
Precrime Unit 178
Presley, Elvis 225
Priapeia (Poems) 163
Priapism 163
Private Parts (Film) 296
Prozac 168, 175
Punch-Drunk Love (Film) 207
Purdue Pharma 97, 98, 99, 100, 101, 220

Q

Quantum Physics 234, 311
Quinn, Declan 302
Quit Your Addiction Now (Book) 311

R

Rabinowitz, Jay 59
Radden Keefe, Patrick 98
Rain Man (Film) 24, 154
Ramseyer, Randy 100
Raw (Film) 123
Ray, Darrel 188
Ray (Film) 68
Reagan, Nancy 64
Reagan, Ronald 13, 47, 114, 167, 272, 273
Recovered Memory Movement 114
Recovery Boys (Documentary) 152, 283, 285, 288
Recovery Coach 293
Recycling 291, 301
Reed, Lou 51, 185
Reefer Madness (Film) 39, 40, 41, 42, 43, 47, 48, 64, 65, 145
Reiner, Carl 227
Reiner, Estelle 227
Reiner, Rob 227
Reisz, Karel 199
Remick, Lee 137, 139, 140
Requiem for a Dream (Film) 39, 40, 57, 60, 63, 64, 115, 239, 325
Richardson, Joely 308, 316

Rich, Buddy 251, 253
Risky Business (Film) 167
Robbins, Tim 305, 308, 310, 320
Rocky (Film) 42, 238
Rocky Horror Picture Show, The (Film) 42
Roker, Al 217
Romeo and Juliet (Play) 253
Roosevelt, Franklin D. 34
Roseanne (TV Series) 217
Rourke, Mickey 240
Royo, Andre 130
Rózsa, Miklós 18
R Rating 168
Ruehl, Mercedes 70
Ruffalo, Mark 169, 305, 307
Ryan, Amy 129
Ryan, Meg 137, 149
Ryder, Winona 239, 246

S

Sackler, Richard 99, 100, 104
Safdie, Bennie 206, 208
Safdie, Josh 206, 208
Sandler, Adam 190, 207
Sands, Julian 27
Santoni, Reni 300
Sappho of Lesbos 163
Sarsgaard, Peter 100
Sartre, Jean-Paul 107
Saslow, Eli 111
Satan 113, 165
Saturday Evening Post 137
Savage, John 41
Scarlet Letter, The (Book) 233
Schadenfreude 94, 177, 274
Schindler's List (Film) 139
Schrödinger's Addict 311
Scorsese, Martin 206
Screen Actors Guild Awards 130, 272
Searchlight Pictures 79, 188
Second Law of Thermodynamics 81, 234
Secretary (Film) 45, 168, 218
Seitz, John F. 18

Self-Mortification 240, 241
Sex Addicts Anonymous 175
Sex and the City (TV Series) 174
Sex & God: How Religion Distorts Sexuality (Book) 188
Sex Maniac (Film) 40
Shakespeare, William 14
Shallow Hal (Film) 215
Shame (Film) 117, 160, 169, 171, 174, 175, 185
Shaye, Robert 41
Sheen, Charlie 93
Sheen, Martin 145
Sheff, David 122
Sheff, Nic 122
Shelley, Mary 287
Shelton, Blake 78
Shepherd, Suzanne 173
Shue, Elizabeth 22, 26
Silent Movie (Film) 224
Silver Linings Playbook (Film) 197
Simmons, J.K. 239, 249
Sinclair, Dr. John 276
Sinclair Method 275
Skarsgård, Stellan 169
Skye, Azura 300
Sleepless in Seattle (Film) 149
Slumdog Millionaire (Film) 50
S & M 167, 168, 320
SMART Recovery 7, 91, 110, 202, 222, 237, 262, 276, 278, 298, 306, 310, 315
Smid, John 178
Snowflower and the Secret Fan (Film) 79, 276
Some Like it Hot (Film) 139
Sony Pictures 295
Sophocles 163
Sorvino, Paul 201
South Park (TV Series) 161
Special Relativity 54
Speed (Film) 296
Spielberg, Steven 207
Sploshing 174
Stanford Prison Experiment, The 250
Star is Born, A (Film) 3, 68, 77, 78, 79, 87, 88, 90, 92, 93, 94
Stark, Douglas 209
Star Wars (Film) 260

Stevenson, Robert Louis 17
Sting, The (Film) 199
Stoics, The 229, 237
Stoppard, Tom 245
Stormy Monday (Film) 23
Strange Case of Dr. Jekyll and Mr. Hyde, The (Book) 17
Straton of Sardis 163
Streisand, Barbra 87
Strong, Danny 98
Studio 54 67, 71
Stuhlbarg, Michael 99
Suboxone 109, 292
Sudden Infant Death Syndrome (SIDS) 53
Suicide 16, 27, 28, 29, 73, 74, 77, 90, 92, 93, 115, 138, 169, 177, 188
Sundance Film Festival 112, 249
Sunk Cost Fallacy 115
Sunset Boulevard (Film) 18
Super-16mm film 23
SuperLotto 74
Superposition 311
Svengali 243
Symbionese Liberation Army 175
Szalavitz, Maia 48

T

Talking To Strangers (Book) 243
Tchaikovsky, Pyotr Ilyich 239
Tea With Mussolini (Film) 266
Tebow, Tim 209
TEDTalks 101
Teller, Miles 239, 250
Terry, Phillip 13
Thanks for Sharing (Film) 169, 305, 306, 314, 322
Thank You For Not Smoking (Film) 259
Theory of Forms 234
There's a Tear in My Beer (Song) 78
This is Spinal Tap (Film) 227
Thomas, Betty 296, 298, 301
Thoreau, Henry David 287
Tierney, Maura 122
Tiger Woods Defense 161
Time Dilation 54
Titane (Film) 123

Toback, James 199
Tom, Lauren 151
Tony Award 224
Touchstone Pictures 149
Trainspotting (Film) 3, 39, 50, 51, 55, 64, 325
Transgressive Cult Films 171
Triumph of the Will (Film) 64
Tudyk, Alan 300
Twain, Mark 7, 227
Tweak: Growing Up on Methamphetamines (Book) 122
Twilight Zone, The (TV Series) 15
Twin Peaks (TV Series) 171
Tyler, Steven 88

U

Ullman, Tracey 171
Uncut Gems (Film) 190, 199, 206, 207, 208, 211
Universal Studios 276
University of Michigan 135
University of Southern California (USC) 69
Urkel 51
U.S. Foreign Service 266

V

Van Dyke, Dick 227, 261
Van Groeningen, Felix 122
Vicodin 4, 300
Vinterberg, Ida 32
Vinterberg, Thomas 31, 32, 33, 34, 35, 36, 37
Vivitrol 111, 115, 119
Voight, Jon 68, 84
Voltaire 214
von Trier, Lars 31, 169
Voyeurism 308

W

Wahlberg, Mark 122, 199
Walden (Book) 287
Walk Hard: The Dewey Cox Story (Film) 88
Walk the Line (Film) 68, 88
Wall Street (Film) 93, 272
Walsh, M. Emmet 273

Walt Disney Studios 3, 149, 308
Warner Bros. Studios 2, 139, 272
War on Drugs 43, 44, 45, 46, 47, 272
Washington Post 111
Watch Out for the Big Grrrls (TV Series) 217
Waters, John 42, 171, 174, 175, 180, 188
Wayans, Marlon 59
Weinstein, Harvey 51, 252
Wendler, Amanda 112
Werner, Michael 311
What's Eating Gilbert Grape (Fillm) 265
When a Man Loves a Woman (Film) 133, 137, 149, 157, 324
When Harry Met Sally (Film) 149
Where Truth Lies (Film) 41
Whiplash (Film) 233, 238, 239, 249, 250, 253
Whitley, Keith 78, 80
Whitman, Mae 152
Who's Afraid of Virginia Woolf? (Film) 136
Wilder, Billy 11, 12, 18, 35, 139
Wilder, Gene 227
Williams, Hank 78, 84
Willis, Bruce 2, 271
Wilson, Bill 137
Wilson, Rebel 217
Winehouse, Amy 88
Winfrey, Oprah 217
Wire, The (TV Series) 48, 296
Wood, Ed 40
Woods, Tiger 161
World War I 44
World War II 167, 259
Wrestler, The (Film) 239, 240
Wright, Curtis 102
Wyman, Jane 13

Y

YouTube 7, 18, 50, 98, 225, 237

Z

Zoloft 292

Made in the USA
Middletown, DE
26 October 2022

13520491R00199